Practical jQuery

Mukund Chaudhary

Ankur Kumar

Apress®

Practical jQuery

ISBN-13 (pbk): 978-1-4842-0788-8

ISBN-13 (electronic): 978-1-4842-0787-1

Managing Director: Welmoed Spahr
Lead Editor: Louise Corrigan
Technical Reviewer: Jose Dieguez Castro
Editorial Board: Steve Anglin, Mark Beckner, Gary Cornell, Louise Corrigan, Jim DeWolf,
    Jonathan Gennick, Robert Hutchinson, Michelle Lowman, James Markham, Susan McDermott,
    Matthew Moodie, Jeffrey Pepper, Douglas Pundick, Ben Renow-Clarke, Gwenan Spearing,
    Matt Wade, Steve Weiss
Coordinating Editor: Jill Balzano
Copy Editor: Michael G. Laraque
Compositor: Spi Global
Indexer: SPi Global
Artist: SPi Global
Cover Designer: Anna Ishchenko

Distributed to the book trade worldwide by Springer Science+Business Media New York, 233 Spring Street, 6th Floor, New York, NY 10013. Phone 1-800-SPRINGER, fax (201) 348-4505, e-mail orders-ny@springer-sbm.com, or visit www.springeronline.com. Apress Media, LLC is a California LLC and the sole member (owner) is Springer Science + Business Media Finance Inc (SSBM Finance Inc). SSBM Finance Inc is a Delaware corporation.

For information on translations, please e-mail rights@apress.com, or visit www.apress.com.

Apress and friends of ED books may be purchased in bulk for academic, corporate, or promotional use. eBook versions and licenses are also available for most titles. For more information, reference our Special Bulk Sales–eBook Licensing web page at www.apress.com/bulk-sales.

Any source code or other supplementary material referenced by the author in this text is available to readers at www.apress.com. For detailed information about how to locate your book's source code, go to www.apress.com/source-code/.

*We would like to dedicate this book to all those
who believe in honesty and hard work.*

Contents at a Glance

Contents

About the Authors

Mukund Chaudhary is enamored of technology and keeps himself up-to-date through avid reading. In his leisure time, he can be found reading articles on current affairs and technologies alike. A perfectionist, he is a product manager by profession and is quite strict when it comes to delivery deadlines. He feels that 24 hours in a day are sufficient, provided a person has plans that are correct and clear.

Ankur Kumar is a software engineer by profession and an adventurer by nature. He is a person who reads people's faces by instinct. He believes that being honest and true to oneself works wonders. He also believes that knowledge is relative in this world, and that it is no big deal to accept that learning never stops as long as a person is alive. Ankur has worked on open source web technologies for a major part of his professional career. He offers thanks to the Almighty "for making us what we are and showing us the way ahead!".

About the Technical Reviewer

Jose Dieguez Castro is a senior system administrator, working currently as a freelance consultant, who has worked in a wide range of projects—from small to large infrastructures, in the private and public sectors. When asked about his specialty, he answers: "Get the job done." He also likes to think of himself as a developer, who cares too much about software libre. Photography, sports, music, and reading are his preferred ways of freeing his mind from work. He can be reached at jose@jdcastro.eu.

Acknowledgments

I take this opportunity to express my gratitude to everyone who supported me at all times. I am thankful to the editors for their aspiring guidance, invaluably constructive criticism, and friendly advice.

I sincerely thank everyone, including my parents, my better half, friends, and teammates, who gave their suggestions for improving this book. Special thanks to my grandfather, the late Kameshwar Chaudhary, who always inspired me to write.

—Mukund Chaudhary

I take this opportunity to thank the Almighty, as well as the extremely careful support staff at Apress, which was there at all times to guide us in the right direction. I particularly acknowledge the editors, who took great pains to understand my intent, and the way they managed the activities pertaining to giving this book its current form. Although thousands of miles away, I always received abundant assistance from them.

I also received enormous support from my parents all the while I was writing. Special thanks to my wife, Neha, who was patient enough to let me focus on providing quality content for this book.

—Ankur Kumar

Introduction

This book aims to provide information to developers who have worked on JavaScript and wish to gain hands-on experience with jQuery. It starts by reviewing some JavaScript concepts and forges ahead to establish the need for a standard framework. This need is addressed by this book, which explores jQuery as a JavaScript framework and covers further developments, with the aim of helping readers to become familiar with the way problems are solved using jQuery.

Practical demonstrations are offered throughout the book, and the same examples are used across multiple demonstrations to ensure that readers receive a multidimensional view of the subject matter. The book concludes by providing information on how to test applications written in jQuery or JavaScript.

CHAPTER 1

■ ■ ■

Evolution of jQuery

The first and foremost question that web developers about to start working on jQuery face is, Are JavaScript and jQuery related, or are they two completely different entities altogether? Although we could simply reply, yes, they are related, and move on, we will attempt in this chapter to introduce jQuery and its evolution from JavaScript. By the end of this chapter, we hope to have explained the following:

- How JavaScript is used to solve common web development problems
- The most common challenges that web developers face
- Changing times and, hence, technology
- The mastermind behind jQuery
- Why jQuery is an important component of web development

Traditional JavaScript Basics

The evolution of web technology saw a transition from Web 1.0 to Web 2.0. The impact of this change was expected to alter the way web-based applications—essentially web sites—would replace desktop-based applications, both in terms of the functionality they provided, as well as their look and feel. By this time, and due to this objective in their development plans, web developers were strongly feeling the need to add dynamic behavior to their static web pages. JavaScript was the only savior, according to the old school of web development. For each and every dynamic behavior to be performed on a web page, JavaScript code had to be written. The job of the web developer was facilitated by JavaScript, because the code worked fine.

A JavaScript developer now had the freedom to use some default objects that became available. These objects made possible some methods and operations that improved the dynamic behavior of web pages. In most cases, the code would roam about using the basic program constructs of JavaScript. A walk through some of the objects and associated methods and properties (or attributes) available by default with JavaScript will help you understand the basic functionality that the library could provide. This will make you understand how JavaScript contributed to solving common web development problems (and helps even today). The most basic validations were easily achieved by these components provided by JavaScript.

The Window Object

There is a mother object—window—that contains everything in it a developer might need. A window object represents an open window in a browser and provides a number of methods pertaining to an open window. This object, just like a normal class object, encapsulates a number of member functions or methods, properties, and a number of child objects as well. The child objects, which we discuss in the next section, in turn encapsulate some other functionality and ensure keeping JavaScript code readable and maintainable

1

(as in the case of all other languages following the object-oriented programming [OOP] philosophy or paradigm). Before turning to the child objects, however, let's consider some common window object methods and attributes.

Methods

Some extremely common methods, accompanied by a brief description, in addition to the common problems they solve, are stated in the succeeding text.

> **alert()**: The common problem that this alert method is used to solve is to display some message upon some validation error, let's say, or some happening of interest to the end user currently viewing the web page you have created. You could pass on some string—simple or composite—to the alert method, and the method would treat all such valid strings alike.

> **setTimeout()**: This method is used to delay the start of some method. Using the setTimeout method, you could add some delay to the response that was to be conveyed to the end user viewing your web page. This is particularly useful in those cases in which you know beforehand the expected time that a certain method will take to execute, so you could queue the next method after a specified time interval.

> **clearTimeout()**: This method is used to cancel the alarm you might have set using the setTimeout method in such a way that the delayed execution will not take place anymore.

> **setInterval()**: The setInterval method is used to execute a task repeatedly at certain timed intervals. It would be quite natural for you to ask why the regular for / while / do-while loop is not considered a candidate for the repeated task. To this, we would answer that for / while / do-while loops keep the execution thread busy, and this could even result in freezing the user interface! This method is commonly used to achieve some animation effect inside a web page or even to have some data synchronization logic run at regular timed intervals. The animation effects, for example, are achieved using this method, by adding timed delays to the object to be animated, to give a perception to the human user that the movement is being delayed/slowed down. So, a heavy-looking object could be made to move slowly by adding a larger time interval, and the light-looking object could be made to move faster by adding a smaller time interval.

> **clearInterval()**: Similar to clearTimeout, this method is used to clear any repetition that you might have specified, using the setInterval method.

> **focus()**: This method, when called, attracts the input focus to the currently selected window. This solves the common problem of making a new window (a pop-up window, for example) visible to the end user after its creation/generation programmatically.

■ **Note** It is important to note that a method with the same signature but called under a different context (HTMLElementObject) is used to shift focus to some HTML node, such as an input box, defined inside a window.

Attributes

In addition to the methods, some of the common attributes provided by the window object are

> **innerHeight**: This attribute denotes the available and usable content area in a window. This ignores the width of the window interface elements, such as toolbars. This attribute can be used in mathematical calculations to find out, for example, the available height for an element on a web page, as follows:

```
var availableHeight = window.innerHeight / 2;
```

> To find out the maximum possible height for an element on a web page, you could implement the following code:

```
var possibleHeight = window.innerHeight * 4;
```

> **outerHeight**: This attribute is similar to the innerHeight attribute, except that it considers the elements provided in the window interface.

> **innerWidth**: This attribute is similar to innerHeight, because it returns the available width of the window, except for the width of the interface elements available with the window.

> **outerWidth**: This attribute provided by the window object gives the total width of the window, along with the width of the interface elements, such as toolbars.

Child Objects

The window object encapsulates some child objects as well. Because everything you see is seen inside the browser window, these child objects exist to represent the entity and the associated functionality. In walking you through the window object, it is imperative that we discuss child objects as well. Therefore, descriptions of some of the key child objects that exist inside the window object follow.

The Document Object

HTTP was designed to link documents available over geographically distributed regions. So, essentially, whenever a web page is loaded into the web browser, it becomes a document for the window, hence the name of the object: document. Because this object represents a web page loaded into the web browser, the document object acts as the only agent to access all of the properties and facilities provided by and for the web page. Speaking in terms of class and real-world entities, the document object represents the root node of the HTML document. Visualizing the document object in the form of a tree, all other nodes in the HTML document, such as the element nodes (the document object model [DOM] elements such as div, span, section, etc.), text nodes (the text contained in the DOM elements), attribute nodes (the attributes of the DOM elements, such as CSS attribute style, etc.), and comment nodes (the HTML comments) lie under the document node only.

Figure 1-1 provides a rough tree-like representation of the document object and its most common child nodes, where N1 through N9 represent the nodes and ROOT represents the document object.

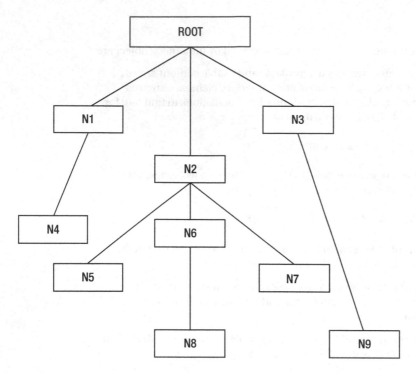

Figure 1-1. *A drawing of the document object tree*

The document object, like all other objects, encapsulates a number of methods and classes, some of the commonly used methods and attributes are described in the following list. The methods encapsulated under the document object represent actions that can be taken on the HTML elements rendered in the browser, for example, adding, deleting, and making changes to the DOM tree.

> **document.createElement()**: This method is quite handy for all those cases in which you want to create a new HTML element in an existing document. The method is quite useful in situations in which you want to modify a document by adding more nodes to it. So, if there is a need to create a new div element to fulfill some business requirement(s), the following method is used:

> ```
> var div = document.createElement('div');
> ```

> **document.getElementById()**: Most web developers look upon this method as a close friend. It is used to access any node in the document for which an identifier has been specified. It returns an object of the type HTML<Element Name>Element, which represents the element identified by the identifier mentioned. So, for example, in case some element color attribute has to be changed, you could use this method. The use of this method is as shown by the following code snippet:

> ```
> var div = document.getElementById("some-div-id");
> div.style.color = 'red';
> ```

So, the value contained in the div variable is an object of the class HTMLDivElement. Similarly, if span is selected, the name of the object would be HTMLSpanElement, and so on.

document.getElementsByClassName(): This method is used to obtain from the rendered web page a list of HTML elements that have a specified CSS class name as their attribute. The method returns an object representing the NodeList class. The NodeList object can be looped through to get all of the HTML elements available, with some specified CSS class. The use of this method is as follows:

```
var classElements = document.getElementsByClassName("some-css-class");
classElements[0].style.color = 'red' ; //This changes the text color to red
```

document.getElementsByTagName(): Similar to getElementsByClassName, this method provides a list of HTML elements in the rendered web page that have a specified tag name. Tag name is the name of the HTML tag that is present on the nodes in the DOM tree. So, to make all the text color inside all divs across the rendered web page red, you would have to do something like the following:

```
var tagElements = document.getElementsByTagName("div");
tagElements[0].style.color = 'red';
```

document.getElementsByName(): The HTML input tag and select have a name attribute, which acts as the index to the data that is passed from one page to another via the HTTP request methods such as GET or POST. Thus, the document object allows this method, document.getElementsByName, to access any such element having the name attribute as some specified value. To change the text inside all elements having the name attribute as username to the color red, you could use the following code snippet:

```
var nameElement = document.getElementsByName("username");
nameElement.style.color = "red" ;
```

document.write(): The write method provided by the document object allows you to write a string or a number of strings to the output stream, which happens to be the web browser itself. You can pass a single string as an argument to this method or a sequence of strings to this method. The strings will be output to the stream in the order they have been passed on as arguments. You can output HTML tags as well, using this method. Thus, if you are required to write some HTML to the web browser, you could use the following code snippet:

```
document.write("What is JavaScript?");
document.write("<p><br/>How to work with JavaScript?", "<br/>What is jQuery?</p>");
document.write("<div>Hello Madhav</div>");
```

Having had a look into the commonly used methods encapsulated by the document object, we would like to draw your attention to an important child attribute of the document object that is worth mentioning here: the readyState. The document object allows this readyState (used as document.readyState) attribute to obtain the current status of the web page (the document) that is being loaded into the web browser. Upon call, this property (or attribute) returns one of the following values, which also happens to be the state of the document being loaded. The values are: *uninitialized, loading, interactive, complete*. So, when a document has not begun being loaded into the browser, the value is *uninitialized*. While being loaded, the status becomes *loading*. When the document has loaded sufficiently for the user to be able to interact with it, the status is *interactive*. Upon the completion of loading, the status becomes *complete*.

■ **Tip** For a refresher, more information on the document object can be obtained from the Mozilla Developer Network located at `https://developer.mozilla.org/en-US/docs/Web/API/document`.

The History Object

The `window` object provides a `history` object as well. This (child) object takes care of the URLs that you would have visited while being inside the same window. It provides methods to go back to the last URL you had visited, or even some other URL from the list of URLs you would have visited. Thus, the methods provided by this (child) object are

> **go**: This method provides a means to go back to any random URL in the list of URLs opened for a particular window. The go method accepts a number that could be positive or negative. The positive number provides the forward URL, and the negative number provides the previous URL visited. The use of the method is as follows:
>
> ```
> history.go(-3); // Would go back 3 urls visited before the current
> url from the session list
> history.go(2); // Would go ahead 2 urls visited after the current
> url from the session list
> ```
>
> **back**: Quite similar to go, back provides a mechanism to visit the last visited URL from the window session list. The use of this method is as simple as writing
>
> ```
> history.back();
> ```
>
> **forward**: The `forward` method available in the `history` object provides a way to go forward one URL ahead of the current URL from the window session list. The use of `forward` is as simple as writing
>
> ```
> history.forward();
> ```

As with the other objects outlined in the discussion to this point, there are attributes or properties exhibited by the `history` object. So, there is a `length` attribute encapsulated by the `history` object. This attribute represents the number of URLs that you have visited inside a particular window. The use of this attribute is as simple as

```
var numberOfUrls = history.length;
```

which would lead to the variable `numberOfUrls`, containing the number of URLs that you had visited in the current window.

The Location Object

The Web is an interlinked network—the interlinking done on various locations where information is stored. So, it is quite natural to have some business requirement related to these locations, and, hence, JavaScript makes a provision for that as well. The window object exhibits a location object for that eventuality. In sync with the name of the object, it contains the information about the URL that is currently being viewed in a window. The location object allows certain operations on the current location (which is used interchangeably for the URL). These operations are available in the form of methods, just as they would have been in the case of any other programming language following the OOP paradigm. We provide a very brief description about these methods, in addition to the common web development problems that are solved using these methods programmatically.

assign: This method loads a new document (a web page) into the window. The URL of the web page to be opened is passed as an argument to this method. So, if, for example, you wish to load the home page of Apress Media, you would have to write

```
location.assign('www.apress.com');
```

reload: This method is used to reload the current web page. You can either reload the document from the browser cache or reload it from the server itself. To reload the document from the browser cache, you have to write location.reload(), whereas if you had to reload the browser from the server, you would write

```
location.reload(true);
```

replace: This method is used to replace the web page displayed currently in the browser window with some other web page, in the same window. This method is similar to the assign method, except that this method removes the replaced URL from the history, such that you cannot go back to that URL anymore. So, if you wish to load apress.com so that the previous URL is forgotten, you have to write

```
location.replace("www.apress.com");
```

There are a number of properties exhibited by the location object that pertain to the common properties of a location (the URL, necessarily). Here, we take the opportunity to cover the utility of such properties. Look at the following properties and the common problems that they can solve:

href: This attribute represents the full URL of the current page being viewed. However, it can set the href property of a web page as well, so that the browser is redirected to the new location. You have to assign a valid URL to this property to make it work. The usage is as follows:

```
var currentUrl = location.href; // Get the current url
location.href = "http://www.apress.com"; //Set the current url to apress home page
```

hostname: This attribute represents the domain name of the web site page that is being currently viewed.

pathname: This attribute represents the path name of the resource or the web page currently being viewed in the browser window.

The Navigator Object

The user agent plays an important part in the way a web page gets rendered. Thus, the `window` object provides a (child) object with the name `navigator`, which represents the browser as a whole. So, this (child) object can be used to determine a good deal of information about the browser, such as the name of the browser (`navigator.appName`), the language of the browser (`navigator.language`), the platform on which the browser is intended to be run (`navigator.platform`), the rendering engine of the browser (`navigator.product`), or the user-agent header the browser would send to the HTTP server (`navigator.userAgent`). You could also check if the browser being used is Java-enabled or not. That way, this method checks whether or not Java content, such as applets, can be executed on the browser. The method returns a value of type `Boolean`, and the value is `true` when Java is enabled and `false` otherwise. So, if you write

```
document.write(navigator.javaEnabled);
```

it would output `true`, if the browser on which you are executing the script is Java enabled, and `false` otherwise.

The Screen Object

A major part of web development runs around writing code for the web browser. There are situations/scenarios/business requirements for which you will be required to have information about the screen on which the HTML is to be rendered. To fulfill this purpose, the `window` object owns another (child) object, called `screen`. This (child) object exhibits properties that pertain to the screen of the end user who is viewing a web page. With the help of this (child) object, a number of attributes can be obtained, such as

> **`screen.availHeight`**: This denotes the available height in the user's screen, i.e., the height of the user's screen without the mandatory elements provided by the operating system, such as the taskbar. Thus, if the screen resolution of the user's screen is 1366 × 768 pixels and the height of the taskbar is 25 pixels, this property will return 768 - 25 = 743 pixels.

> **`screen.availWidth`**: Just as with `availHeight`, this property returns the available width in the user's screen. Thus, as in the previous case, this property will contain a value of 1366 pixels if there are no vertical interface elements provided by the underlying operating system.

> **`screen.height`**: This property denotes the actual height of the user's screen. The value would be 768 in the aforementioned case.

> **`screen.width`**: This property denotes the actual width of the user's screen. The value would be 1366 in the aforementioned case.

Old School Challenges

Having had familiarity with JavaScript, most of web developers felt at ease, owing to the large number of methods and properties available with the native JavaScript library. This ease, however, came at a cost. The cost involved was to overcome the challenges that appeared while using the same JavaScript method across different browser environments. Some of the attributes and properties were not standard, and, hence, there was no standard implementation for those attributes and properties. Every browser implemented its own version of the property, and, therefore, discrepancies started appearing.

Some of the challenges are worth mentioning. The developers had to overcome these challenges by adding extra checks and balances in their codes. While this served to solve the problem in most instances, it led to a new problem: even web developers started growing unsure of their code across various platforms. In the section that follows, we make a concerted attempt to list some of the challenges that were faced.

Challenges Pertaining to the Window Object

The window object appears as the mother object, representing almost every action possible or every attribute available for a browser window, yet it presents some challenges to the web developer. Let us proceed in this direction and discover the challenges potentially obstructing the path of the web developer.

The innerHeight property works fine on Firefox and Chrome, as expected. Internet Explorer adds exceptions for this property. Versions older than 8 in IE display errors while trying to access this property. Thus,

```
window.alert(window.innerHeight);
```

would give an alert box with the value undefined under IE8. The same goes for innerWidth, outerHeight, and outerWidth. All the properties, when accessed, return "undefined" to the calling procedure. Thus, on writing any of the following, there would be an alert showing the message "undefined" to the cited web browser:

```
window.alert(window.innerWidth);
```

```
window.alert(window.outerHeight);
```

```
window.alert(window.outerWidth);
```

The question that looms large now is how to obtain this particular property when it is unknown by the known feature. The answer lies in the particular browser's JavaScript implementation. Internet Explorer has some implementation to access the same property for the window, albeit in a different way, as compared to the other browsers under our radar, Firefox and Chrome. Internet Explorer 8 and older browsers have a different hierarchy, and the effective height is provided by a clientHeight property defined by the documentElement object of the document object. Thus, under Internet Explorer, you would have to write

```
alert(document.documentElement.clientHeight);
```

if you wished to alert the effective height of the browser window.

Similarly, each of the following two lines would alert the same result under a non-IE web browser:

```
alert(document.documentElement.clientWidth);
```

```
alert(window.innerHeight);
```

■ **Note**   IE8 and older versions do not have the outerWidth and outerHeight properties.

Challenges Pertaining to the Document Object

In the document object as well, there are similar challenges to the web developer. For certain elements, the method getElementsByName ceases to work under IE8 or older browsers. So, if you have some HTML such as

```
<div name="apress">This is a practical in jquery</div>
```

and if you write

```
document.getElementsByName("apress")[0].innerHTML);
```

it will alert "This is a practical in jquery" on non-IE browsers and "undefined" on IE8 and older browsers.

What could be the workaround? For all those HTML elements for which the name attribute is not caught by this document method, you can try adding "some-id" as the id attribute, to make the document.getElementById("some-id") work.

Another method that exhibits inconsistent behavior is the getElementsByClassName provided by the document object. When accessed on non-IE browsers such as Chrome or Firefox, the method works properly. But on IE8 and older browsers, it shows errors in the browser console. To demonstrate the difference, let's say the HTML is

```
<div class="madhav">This is to test some challenge.</div>.
```

So, if you were to write

```
alert(document.getElementsByClassName("madhav")[0].innerHTML);
```

the result would be "This is to test some challenge" on non-IE browsers, but on versions IE8 or older, it would show the following error message: "Object doesn't support property or method 'getElementsByClassName,'" as shown in Figure 1-2.

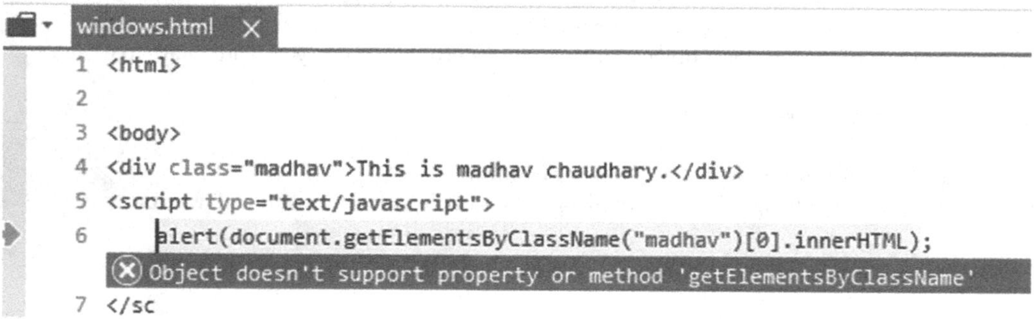

```
  ▼   windows.html   X
  1  <html>
  2
  3  <body>
  4  <div class="madhav">This is madhav chaudhary.</div>
  5  <script type="text/javascript">
  6      alert(document.getElementsByClassName("madhav")[0].innerHTML);
     ⊗ Object doesn't support property or method 'getElementsByClassName'
  7  </sc
```

Figure 1-2. Error shown in older IE browser

Again, the same question looms large: When this property is not supported, how does one get things done? The answer is to write more JavaScript code for browsers that do not support such methods. Writing more code means spending more time and, hence, presents a challenge. More code means challenges in maintaining the code. So, when the getElementsByClassName ceases to work under IE, we can resort to writing

```
alert(document.querySelector(".madhav")[0].innerHTML);
```

and this will make the code behave in the expected way.

Challenges Related to the Globals

Globals in JavaScript are another challenge to understanding and working across browsers. Global variables are the variables that are accessible across all parts of a particular script. They require no reference as such and can be accessed from any scope. The globals are created in JavaScript by writing a simple line of code, such as

```
apressAuthors = "Mukund and Ankur";
```

The internals of globals are important to understand before proceeding to the challenges that this phenomenon present. Because the window is an object that is available by default and contains all the other objects according to a proper hierarchy, whenever a new global is created, it is created as a property of the window object. Thus, the variable apressAuthors is actually not a variable; it is a property of the window object. To understand the difference better, we offer a small demonstration. The following two uses will yield the identical result: display Mukund and Ankur on the output stream (the web browser), as follows:

```
alert(apressAuthors);
```

```
alert(window.apressAuthors);
```

So, once this has become a property of the window object, it can be iterated in a for loop as well, just like other objects can be. So, while the following code is expected to work, it does not for IE8 or older browsers.

```
apressAuthors = "Mukund and Ankur";
for (var variableNames in window) {
    if(variableNames === 'apressAuthors') {
        alert(variableNames) // Would output on Chrome but not on IE8
    }
}
```

Now, about the challenge that appeared. The variableNames did not fulfill the criteria, and, hence, there was no output for IE8. The way globals have been implemented for a browser makes the difference. Under Chrome, Firefox, etc., the globals were enumerable, that is, you could iterate over the elements, but under IE8, this was simply not possible. Again, more work has to be done to confirm to the (business) logic. To eliminate the problem altogether, we can probably declare the globals as follows:

```
var apressAuthors = "Mukund and Ankur";
```

Just the same, there would be problems deleting the implicit globals on IE8 or older versions. So, if there is a need to remove the variable apressAuthors, the following code could create problems. Thus, while

```
delete window.apressAuthors;
```

followed by

```
alert(apressAuthors);
```

would alert "undefined" on Chrome and Firefox, etc., it would show an error, "Object doesn't support this action," under IE.

Again, reworking would be required to overcome this challenge. You could probably use exception handling to solve this problem. So, you could write the following code:

```
try{
    delete window.apressAuthors;
} catch( error ) {
    window['apressAuthors'] = undefined
}
```

There are a number of challenges, then, in working with JavaScript, although it may appear that JavaScript is quite a versatile and powerful language to deal with web development problems web developers face in their day-to-day activities. Therefore, there had to be some way out, and developers had to find the means to eliminate the problems of compatibility and cross-platform functionality.

Need for a Revolution

There was increasing discontent among developers who had to write extra lines of code to achieve the desired functionality across browsers. People used to pay the same amount of money to developers. But since developers had to do more work for less pay, there was a growing demand in the community to have some omnipotent solution.

The document that was rendered in the web browser had to be manipulated by using lengthy JavaScript code, and that, too, without the guarantee of being functional across browsers. Even if the code would work on various browsers, the developers still had to write long lines of code. For example, considering the HTML <div id="test"></div> as in the following code is perfectly okay to create a new container for an error message for all browsers that support JavaScript:

```
var div = document.createElement("div");
    div.setAttribute("class", "error");
    div.innerHtml = "There was an error";
    var testDiv = document.getElementById("test");
    testDiv.appendChild(div);
```

What does the code do? The steps are as summarized.

1. Create a new element in the document (the web page).

2. Set the class attribute of this element to be error. (The CSS for error has already been defined previously. Assume that some external CSS or even some style tag containing the definition has been written elsewhere.)

3. Set the text inside this div as "There was an error."

4. Locate a div in the document that has the id as *test*.

5. Append the newly created div inside this located div. Because this located div is already in the document, the newly created div will also get added to the document.

Let us take up a case in which we have to manipulate some CSS attributes via JavaScript. Let us assume that there is a div with some preset CSS attributes, and we have to change the opacity of the div using JavaScript. Thus, the code snippet that follows is worth looking at.

```
var div = document.getElementById("test");
    div.style.opacity = 0.5;
    div.style.filter = "alpha(opacity=50) ";
```

Now, what has happened here is that browsers prior to IE8 did not understand the opacity attribute; they understood filter. So, to achieve a single objective, more code had to be written in the form of code that the individual browser could understand and, therefore, interpret.

You can easily see that the task that was performed was rather simple but that many lines of code still had to be written. This was becoming unacceptable to developers. Someone had to take charge of the situation, and out of the blue, something had to lead the way for web developers. Developers desperately wanted to cut down on the amount of code they had to write. They wanted to be able to focus on the business logic rather than the underlying browser's CSS and JavaScript implementation. They wanted some code that would run across all systems uniformly.

Who Was the Revolutionary?

There was this gentleman, John Resig, who used to write web applications, and he was among the same community of developers who felt the heat writing lengthy JavaScript code, and that, too, without the guarantee of using a hack-less approach. He continued web development and, in the course of doing so, gathered a number of libraries he required and merged them gradually. This merger resulted in a new bundle, and Resig continued to refine the bundle, by making necessary modifications to the existing code. Ultimately a new bundle with the name jQuery became available to the community. Because Resig was targeting the DOM manipulation capabilities significantly, and there was a CSS library with the name cssQuery, the name jQuery became influential and, hence, coined.

Having done the homework all the while, Resig was creating a bundle, which he released as a framework on August, 26, 2006. The world came to know about a new framework that was to revolutionize the way front-end programming for the Web occurred. Even after having revolutionized front-end Web development, Resig did not stop there. He is currently located in Brooklyn, New York, and is working as dean of computer science at an academy while still breaking new barriers to help the web development community a great deal.

■ **Note** You can obtain more information about John Resig from the Wikipedia page located at https://en.wikipedia.org/wiki/John_Resig.

Why jQuery?

An act becomes a revolution when people can see the inherent advantages associated with it. And it takes time as well. Thus, as the word about jQuery started spreading across the web development community, jQuery began to gain importance and popularity. There were a number of reasons web front-end developers started to use jQuery. The most important reasons included the following:

- Minimal and easy coding
- Readable/clean code
- Easy CSS handling
- Animation methods
- Intuitive function calls

We will discuss each of these reasons in the following sections.

Minimal and Easy Coding

jQuery was developed on top of JavaScript, so jQuery can be safely termed a JavaScript framework. But unlike the lengthy coding style inherent in JavaScript, jQuery was designed to be simple. The lengthy JavaScript code can be easily replaced by the compact code of jQuery. Consider the following HTML:

```
<div id="test"></div>
```

and the corresponding JavaScript code:

```
var testDiv = document.getElementById("test");
testDiv.setAttribute("class", "error");
testDiv.innerHtml = "There was an error";
```

The following jQuery code can be written to attain the same result as simply as

```
$("#test").addClass("error").html("There was an error"));
```

The result in both the cases would be the HTML code <div id="test" class="error">There was an error</div>. The jQuery code would work fine, because it looks for the id attribute to search the target element. We will take up in detail the syntax and the semantics that jQuery follows in the coming chapters, but for a quick reference, the ID is selected using the name that has been specified in the id attribute preceded by a hash symbol (#).

Considering another replacement of the lengthy JavaScript code by a smaller and more readable jQuery code, if you have the HTML <div class="apress">Hello Apress!</div> and the JavaScript code to access this HTML node as document.getElementsByClassName("madhav")[0].innerHTML, the same purpose can be achieved by using $(".apress").html(). As a quick explanation of how the same purpose can be served by two different codes (we will take this up in detail in the coming chapters), the jQuery code looks up an element by its class name as well, with the selector defined as dot(.), followed by the name specified in the class attribute. As a keen observer, you will have noted that there have been two uses of the same method (html). On observing the previous code and comparing it with the example immediately preceding, we easily see that the same method html behaved differently on the passed arguments. This makes jQuery easy to write, as a developer does not have to remember a lot of methods and their signatures to achieve similar functionality. Summing up, the html method, when passed no arguments, returns the text that has been written inside the target node, whereas if some valid string is passed as the argument, the same method sets the text inside the target node, as the string that has been passed on.

Readable/Clean Code

Another reason for you to switch to jQuery is the readability quotient that is added to the code that is written using jQuery. Readability is that programming language feature that enables the next person working on a code (which is written by someone else) to be able to read and understand it as much as possible. Thus, jQuery adds readability to the code, because the syntax is quite simple—all elements having an ID attribute that can be selected in the same manner. Similarly, all elements having a specified class attribute can be selected in the same manner. In short, one aspect of jQuery adding readability to the code that is written is the facility with which an element can be selected. The following discussion offers a number of examples to support this assertion.

Taking the HTML `<div class='apress'>Hello Apress Fans!</div>`, the text inside this node can be selected by writing the JavaScript code

```
document.getElementsByClassName("madhav")[0].innerHTML;
```

and the jQuery code as well:

```
$(".madhav").html();
```

Similarly, if there is the following JavaScript code to make all text color inside all divs across the rendered web page red:

```
document.getElementsByTagName("div")[0].style.color = 'red';
```

the same objective can be achieved by writing the jQuery code as

```
$("div").css({'color', 'red'});red'});
```

As further demonstration of its utility, there is a method provided by jQuery that you can use to switch the visibility of certain node(s) identified by some selector from on to off and from off to on. In short, you can hide or show the matched element by using a single method: toggle. A detailed explanation to this method is provided later on. For now, if the HTML code is `<div class="test">This will demonstrate <strong>toggle</strong></div>`, in order to toggle the visibility of the strong HTML node between on and off you just have to write the jQuery code following:

```
$(.test).on('click', function(){
$('strong').toggle();
});
```

It is clearly visible from the examples that jQuery adds readability to the code that you write. Long and error-prone lines of JavaScript do have an alternative in the form of clean jQuery, for solving common problems.

Easy CSS Handling

As stated earlier in the chapter, the motivation and inspiration behind the creation of jQuery was cssQuery. A framework intended to ease the use of CSS, jQuery has been designed to make handling CSS easier. There is a method with the name `css`. In order to be able to use this method, you have only to remember the original syntax, if you can remember the JavaScript way of writing CSS. So, to set a single CSS attribute to some selector available in the document, you only have to choose from among the three usages available:

```
$('html-selector').css('css-property', 'css-value '); // Setting a single attribute
$('html-selector').css({'css-property': 'css-value', ...}); //Setting multiple attributes
the CSS way
$('html-selector').css({cssProperty: 'css-value', ...}), ...}); // Setting multiple
attributes the JavaScript way
```

Thus, all of the CSS manipulation that you can think of is brought about with the help of this method (`css`) itself, ranging from simple text color change to complicated transition effects. All that is required is the plain old CSS attribute and the corresponding required value. The simplicity and ease in CSS handling is as shown following:

```
$("div").css('color', 'red'); //change the text color inside all the divs available inside
the document to red
$("div").css({'color': 'red', 'border': '1px solid #000', 'background-color': '#fefefe'});
// Setting multiple attributes
```

■ **Note**   Multiple CSS properties are passed on as JSON to this method.

Similarly, if there is a need to add some CSS class, there is a method `addClass` that would add some CSS class to some specified selector. The signature of the method is

```
$('html-selector').addClass('some-css-class');
```

The use of the method is quite simple. Let us take one of the previous examples and write it the jQuery way. Considering the HTML code `<div id="test"></div>`, if you want to add a CSS class attribute to this node, you need to write the following jQuery code:

```
$("#test").addClass("error");
```

The effect of the jQuery code would be the modified HTML which would be the same as `<div id="test" class="error"></div>`. Thus, all the properties available with the class error will now be added to the matched div. This easily demonstrates the easy CSS handling provided by jQuery.

Animation Methods

If you ask a web developer for a reason to have started jQuery, the most probable answer would be animation. jQuery provides a number of methods that support some really fantastic animation, including `animate`, `fadeIn`, `fadeOut`, `fadeTo`, etc., which provide handy ways to animate any element you would wish. The most common out of these methods is the `animate` method. The `animate` method has a simple signature, as shown. A detailed description of the method and its uses under various circumstances will come up in the discussion that follows. So, to provide a fade effect to some div, such as `<div class="error">This is some visible text</div>`, you can use the animate method, as follows:

```
$('.error').animate({'color':'red'}, 500, function(){alert('Animation Completed!')});
```

In a nutshell, what the animate method does in the preceding example is

1. Finds out the matching node with the class as error

2. Changes the CSS color attribute to red

3. Takes 500 milliseconds for the animation to complete

4. Provides information that the animation has been completed

In the current example, you will be alerted by your browser with a message "Animation Completed!" once the animation is finished.

Similarly, there is a slideToggle() method available, which web developers find quite handy. As the name suggests, this method alternately collapses an element to hide it completely or slides down an element to make it completely visible to the human eye. You can specify the speed at which the animation takes place by either specifying the number of milliseconds or some predefined constants, such as *slow* or *fast*. You can also set up some callback method, which would be executed once the animation is complete. Thus, for a quick reference, consider the HTML code as

```
<div class="error">There was an error (You would not like to show it to your users for
long!)</div>
<div class="button">Click this button to hide the error message</div>
```

The intended functionality can be achieved by writing the jQuery code as

```
$(".button").click(function(){
    $(".error").slideToggle();
});
```

The default time required in this case would be 400 milliseconds. An alternate way to perform the same action is as shown following, with swing as the default easing:

```
$(".button").click(function(){
    $(".error").slideToggle(400, "swing", function(){
        alert("Animation Completed!");
    });
});
```

In the preceding code snippet, the difference in the usage means that the following tasks are done in the same order in which they are written:

1. On click of the element with the CSS class button, the animation is fired.

2. The element with the CSS class error is animated in a time period of 400 milliseconds and with a swing effect.

3. Upon completion of the animation, a message "Animation Completed!" is displayed in an alert box.

Intuitive Function Calls

The feature that makes jQuery unique is the intuitive way the methods are called (upon some selected element). You could easily make out the actions that will take place by having a look at the jQuery code. Suppose a number of actions are to take place. The way jQuery permits you to write the actions is in sync with the way you would verbalize it to someone else or the way you would think it to take place. Take, for example, the following code snippet (considering the HTML code as `<div id="test"></div>`):

```
//jQuery Longer methods
$("#test").addClass("error");
$("#test").html("There was an error!");

//jQuery Alternate method:
    $("#test").addClass("error").html("There was an error");
```

The alternate method performs exactly the same task as that done by the longer method. This phenomenon provided in jQuery is known as *chaining*, according to which you can assign multiple tasks to a single matched element in just the same way as you would have thought or planned it out. This is another aspect of readability.

Thus, don't assume that you can completely ignore JavaScript and switch to jQuery because jQuery is a library built on top of JavaScript. jQuery uses all the functionality available with JavaScript to provide you more functionality, reduce the amount of time spent in solving already solved problems, and obviously standardize the way web developers write code. After all, jQuery is just a framework.

So, enjoy jQuerying!

Summary

This chapter discussed how jQuery evolved from the challenges faced by web developers, by using JavaScript as a raw language and by the difference in the implementation of JavaScript by various web browsers. The chapter also shed some light on some salient features and some methods provided by jQuery. In the coming chapters, you will be made more familiar with the methods mentioned in this chapter (and many more useful methods in jQuery). The next chapter will guide you in setting up jQuery on your own development system, and, thus, you will be good to go with jQuery as your useful web development technology.

CHAPTER 2

■ ■ ■

Getting Started with jQuery

In the previous chapter, we had discussed the evolution of jQuery and tried to demonstrate the answer to the question Why to use jQuery? Now that you are prepared to go a step further, the time is ripe to set up the development environment. In this chapter, you will become familiar with the fundamentals of jQuery by coming to terms with its workings. By the chapter's conclusion, you will have become familiar with the following topics:

- The Document Object Model's ubiquity in web development

- Downloading and setting up jQuery

- jQuery Fundamentals

- Working with jQuery

Document Object Model (DOM)

We intentionally used the term *ubiquity* to describe DOM, because it is found everywhere in web programming. One of the most prominent aspects of programming in jQuery is that there is a very heavy use of the manipulation of DOM in the programming problems written using jQuery. So, we also can term jQuery as a DOM manipulation library. The term *DOM* stands for "Document Object Model," and it defines a standard for accessing and interacting with the HTML, XTML, or XML that you, the web developer, learn to write.

As per W3C, the Document Object Model is a platform and language-neutral interface that allows programs and scripts to dynamically access and update the content, structure, and style of a document. The nodes of every document are organized in a tree structure and, hence, are referred to as the DOM tree (see Figure 2-1). jQuery comes with a bunch of DOM-related methods, which makes it easy to manipulate elements and attributes. Before we delve into jQuery methods, however, let's take a minute to understand the DOM tree.

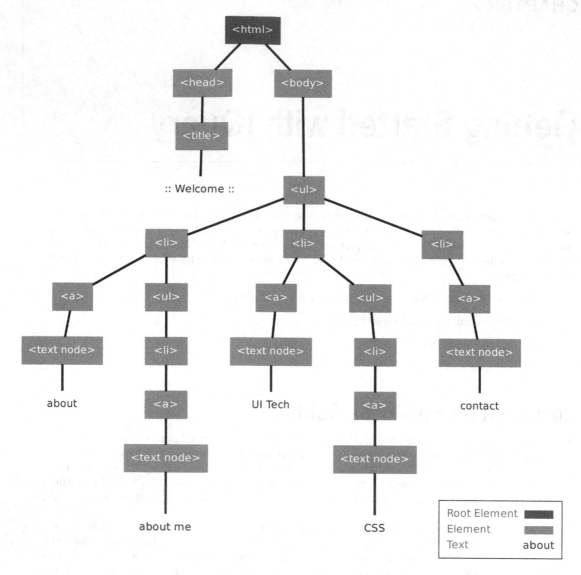

Figure 2-1. *The DOM tree*

html is the root element of any DOM tree. It has two nodes: one is head and other is body. Further, the element ul has li tree children, which are used for navigation. The following code shows a sample fragment from an actual HTML page that uses each of these tree elements.

```
<html>
<head>
    <title> :: Welcome ::</title>
</head>
<body>
<ul class="right">
    <li class="has-dropdown"><a href="#">about</a>
```

```
    <ul class="dropdown">
        <li><a href="#">about me</a></li>
    </ul>
</li>
<li class="has-dropdown">
    <a href="#">UI Tech</a>
    <ul class="dropdown">
        <li><a href="#">CSS</a></li>
    </ul>
</li>
<li><a href="#">contact</a></li>
</ul>
</body>
</html>
```

Downloading and Setting Up jQuery

Now it's time to set up our environment. Downloading jQuery is lot easier than baking a cake. There are several ways to start using jQuery on your web page. You can

- Download the jQuery Library from jQuery.com
- Include jQuery from some content delivery network (CDN), such as Google
- Clone a copy of jQuery from the Git repository

We will go over each of these methods in the following sections.

■ **Note**   You can choose between compressed and uncompressed copies of jQuery. The minified and compressed product copy is suitable for a production environment; a smaller file means less data transmission over the network and, consequently, a faster web site. The uncompressed and readable development copy is suitable for a test or development environment.

Downloading from the Official Web Site

Downloading the jQuery library from the official web site is simple. You can get it from http://jquery.com. If you are not sure which version to download, take the latest stable version from the site. But, if your code will have to work for IE8 or earlier versions, the jQuery site recommends that you use jQuery 1.x. Figure 2-2 shows the jQuery download page.

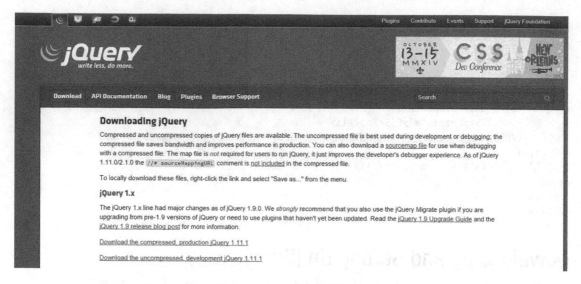

Figure 2-2. *Downloading jQuery*

The jQuery library is a single JavaScript file, and now you have to reference it with a `<script>` tag in your code. For example

```
<head>
<script src="jquery-1.11.1.min.js"></script>
</head>
```

■ **Note**   There is a decision for you to make regarding the placement of the script tag in the web page. For all those tasks that you want to have executed (or ready to be executed) once the entire page is downloaded to the client computer, the old browsers would make you put the script tag after the end of the body tag, so that by the time JavaScript (or jQuery) activities started taking place, each and every DOM element had to have been downloaded. People expert in JavaScript would recommend adding event listeners to initiate the DOM manipulation activity once the DOM was loaded (or using `$(document).ready()`, for that matter). But that is a synthetic solution, and, again, it adds extra programming complexity.

Modern browsers also support `async` and `defer` attributes in the script tag itself. The `async` attribute makes the script loading process asynchronous: whichever script is fetched first is executed first. The `defer` attribute works a bit differently, albeit to achieve the same objective: the scripts are executed in the order in which they are specified, but the browser is not blocked as such. Discussion of these two attributes is beyond the scope of this book, but if you are interested in further details related to these two concepts, you might want to look into the Mozilla Development Network (MDN) at `https://developer.mozilla.org/en/docs/Web/HTML/Element/script`.

Including jQuery from a CDN

If you would like to include jQuery from a CDN, such as one from jQuery or Google, you have to reference the file directly from the URL, as follows:

```
<script src="http://ajax.googleapis.com/ajax/libs/jquery/1.11.1/jquery.min.js"></script>
```

You can also use jQuery CDN from `http://code.jquery.com`.

```
<script src="//code.jquery.com/jquery-1.11.0.min.js"></script>
```

■ **Tip**   If you want to see all the available jQuery versions and files, visit `http://code.jquery.com`.

Clone from GitHub

Assuming that you already have access to GitHub, you can connect to the repository via the command line and clone a copy from there by issuing the following command:

```
$ git clone git://github.com/jquery/jquery.git
```

■ **Note**   If you want to check out and build specific versions of jQuery, let's assume 1.11.0, then use
`$ git checkout 1.11.0`.

---

jQuery Fundamentals

Having downloaded jQuery, we are ready to move ahead and explore the tricks of the trade, by going through the jQuery basics. jQuery is a (JavaScript) library that makes our web development problem solving easier, by enabling us to write less and do more, just as the jQuery tagline says: "write less, do more" (`http://jquery.com`). The methods available in the jQuery framework simplify DOM manipulation. In Chapter 1, we discussed as to *why* to use jQuery. Under the current rubric, we will discuss *how* to use jQuery. So, let us put off all possible doubts and start off with the basic jQuery usage syntax.

jQuery Syntax

We previously stated that jQuery is a DOM manipulation library. So, keeping the current topic in sync with the heading, we will begin by demonstrating and explaining the most basic and common uses of jQuery. In the most basic of the scenarios, you would perform an action in jQuery, such as

```
$(selector).action();
```

Here starts the real lubrication of the jQuery machinery. Let us move toward analysis of the most basic usage that we just mentioned. We have outlined the syntax in list form, as follows:

- The $ (dollar) sign is used to define and access jQuery. If we speak the language of commonly used OOP languages such as PHP, Java, or C++, we would say that the $ symbol is simply a variable in jQuery that represents the jQuery function as such. Another, simpler expression of this statement would be to state that the $ symbol is an alias of jQuery. To state the explanation even more clearly, using `$(selector).action();` would have the same effect as using `jQuery(selector).action();`.

- `(selector)` is used to query (or find) an HTML element. It can be any HTML element—a `<p>` or `<h1>` tag or even a `<script>` tag, and so on. Selectors are quite important to learn and master. If you have a working knowledge of how to use selectors, you will be able to drive through with great ease most of the web development problems you encounter. For the record, we explain selectors in detail in the next chapter.

- `action()` is the jQuery action that must be performed on an element. By *action*, we mean an action to be performed, let's say on a `click` event or a `mouseout` event. We will take up events in the coming chapters, so you can postpone worrying about not knowing about that concept for now.

Here's a specific example, in which you want to hide all the elements that have a class attribute of apress.

```
$(".apress").hide();
```

The `hide()` function is used to hide the element. We will discuss `hide` and how to use it in some depth in Chapter 7.

Document Ready Event

When we were discussing the various JavaScript objects and the related available features that are standard on web browsers, we mentioned the `readyState` attribute available with the `document` object. The jQuery framework makes use of the attribute to "emulate" an event, which is known as the document ready event. The document ready event is important, considering that it provides a time line for certain actions to be executed once the document is downloaded completely to the client web browser. Although abused to a great extent by most web developers, the most common (perceived) usage of this event by web developers is to prevent jQuery code from running before a document is loaded. The ready method available with jQuery helps to manipulate the page safely when a document is ready, by letting you call the methods that you require to be executed upon the occurrence of this event. The syntax follows:

```
$(document).ready(function(){

    // jQuery code go here...
});
```

You can provide a named reference to a method that you might have defined elsewhere (but within the reach of this usage of ready method), as follows:

```
function doSomething(){
...
}

$(document).ready(doSomething);
```

■ **Tip**   You should be extra cautious when following this approach, because once you call a method using the ready method (on the document ready event, as it is commonly called), you are restricting your logic to be used only once, and that, too, is bound by a time line. In addition, it fattens the namespace, because when you add a run-once method, it causes unnecessary memory consumption, and performance takes a hit.

There is also a shorthand method available that accomplishes the same task as the method previously discussed. In the current scenario, it can be used as follows:

```
$(function(){

    // jQuery methods go here...

});
```

jQuery noConflict() Method

At some point, the need may arise to have more than only the jQuery framework on your web page. Another team might be working on another framework, and there may be a possibility that the other framework uses the same $ symbol for some special purpose. Because JavaScript does not discriminate between various frameworks while interpreting, and all the code written in a framework X or Y or jQuery ultimately boils down to JavaScript code, everything will be executed by the JavaScript engine itself. The jQuery code that you might have written could, therefore, cease to work or work incorrectly, if it worked at all. This anomaly in behavior will have been caused by the conflict $ symbol experiences between the other framework and jQuery. In that case, you will have to use the noConflict() method to avoid conflicts. We have already discussed that $ is just an alias of jQuery, so we would have to save the old reference—$ during initialization—and the noConflict() method would be used to restore the reference for use by you. In short, the method would reestablish the fact that $ will be used by the jQuery framework only.

If you are using two versions of jQuery, calling $.noConflict(true) from a second version will return the globally scoped jQuery variable to the first one, and it will work smoothly. The jQuery team recommends that you not do this, however. The following illustrates the syntax for using the noConflict() method:

```
$.noConflict(removeAll)
```

In this code snippet, $ is the usual alias of jQuery; removeAll is the optional parameter that accepts a Boolean value; and the return type of the noConflict method is an object representing jQuery.

Let us look at a specific example. In this case, you will see that we are using the full name instead of the $ alias. The noConflict() method releases the hold on $, as shown in the following:

```
<script src="jQuery.1.10.2.js"></script>
<script src="prototype.js"></script>
<script>
$.noConflict();
jQuery(document).ready(function(){
  jQuery("button").click(function(){
    jQuery("p").text("jQuery is working smoothly");
  });
});

$(document.body).insert("<p>Prototype JS works fine too!</p>");
</script>

<body>
<p>Here comes a paragraph.</p>
<button>Click to test jQuery</button>
</body>
```

In this example, you can see that we have included another JavaScript framework, prototype.js, in addition to the familiar jQuery framework. When this code is executed in your browser, the output will be as follows:

```
jQuery is working smoothly

Click to test jQuery (button)

Prototype JS works fine too!
```

Taking this opportunity to explain the sample code we provided, we would begin by saying that the code is easy to understand (which we always say). Jokes aside, here we are performing an action on the click event taking place on a button. So, when the button (i.e., the button containing the text "Click to test jQuery") is clicked, the action will be performed to change the text inside the paragraph element to "jQuery is working smoothly." The point we wish to make here is that the noConflict method works, and we have demonstrated this by showing that a method from the jQuery framework, as well as a method from another library that we included (prototype.js), were executed successfully.

Because by now you know that the noConflict() method provides a reference to the jQuery object, you can very well think of preserving the reference in a JavaScript variable. Here, we would like to provide you with a demonstration that is closely aligned to one of the software engineering principles: keeping code readable. We are following this principle by making an altogether different reference to the jQuery object. The code, as proposed by us, would be as follows:

```
var muk = $.noConflict();
muk(document).ready(function(){
  muk("button").click(function(){
    muk("p").text("jQuery is still working!");
  });
});
```

```
<body>
<p>Here comes a paragraph.</p>
<button>Click to test jQuery</button>
</body>
```

The output provided by the preceding usage would be exactly the same as that we provided in the example immediately preceding, because we have reused the same example and only changed the reference variable.

■ **Important** The `noConflict()` method is very useful when some other JavaScript library (that uses the $ for its methods and functionalities) is required to work on the same web page. However, the use of two different libraries is not recommended, because one library is as good as another library in some aspect or other. So, the decision to choose a library is to be made wisely, and if there is a need to use more than one framework, this need must be reviewed quite thoroughly.

At this point, you are now familiar with the basic jQuery syntax and the `ready()` and `noConflict()` methods. Assuming you are comfortable with the syntax, we move a step ahead in relating the fundamentals, by providing you a glimpse of selectors in jQuery. We say *glimpse*, because the treatment in the current chapter is only part of the story—the very basics intended to provide general familiarity. The next section covers treats selectors in greater detail.

jQuery Selectors

Let us start with a basic question: What is a selector? A jQuery selector is a functionality that makes use of expressions to find a matching element from the DOM, based on certain criteria. The selectors in jQuery are always specified as starting with a dollar sign ($) followed by an opening parenthesis, followed by the selector expression itself, followed by a closing parenthesis. In short, `$(selector)`, assuming that some code on your web page has not used a reference to the $ symbol. While selecting elements in a document, there are three basic building blocks:

- **Tag name:** This represents the tag that is available in the DOM tree. For example, if we have to select all the h1 headings, this would be done as `$('h1')` or `jQuery('h1')`.

- **Tag ID:** This represents a tag available in the DOM tree with a particular ID. So, `$('#mukund')` will select all elements in the DOM tree that have the ID mukund.

- **Tag class:** This represents a tag available with a given class attribute in the DOM tree. For example, `$('.mukund')` selects all the elements in the DOM that have the class attribute mukund.

Table 2-1 describes the three corresponding selectors and the * wildcard selector.

Table 2-1. *The jQuery Selectors*

Selector	Description
NAME	Selects all the elements that match a given element's name
#ID	Selects a single element that matches a given ID
.CLASS	Selects all the elements that match the given class name
* (asterisk)	Selects all the elements in the DOM

Selector Examples

In this section, we'll consider some common selector use cases. If our treatment seems a bit too complex, we would reiterate what we said previously: our intention is only to make you familiar with the syntax of jQuery. Detailed descriptions of the selectors (what they are, how they are categorized, and much more) is addressed in the next chapter. For now, we suggest that you have a quick look at how the selectors are used, along with the selections that they make (indicated adjacent to the usage).

- **$("ul li:first")**: Gets only the first <li> element of the <ul>

- **$("li > ul")**: Selects all elements matched by <ul> that are children of an element matched by <li>

- **$("p strong, .mukund")**: Selects all elements matched by <strong> that are descendants of an element matched by <p>, as well as all elements that have a class of mukund

- **$(":empty")**: Selects all elements that have no children

- **$("p:empty")**: Selects all elements matched by <p> that have no children

- **$("code, em, strong")**: Selects all elements matched by <code> or <em> or <strong>

- **$("li:not(.mukund)")**: Selects all elements matched by <li> that do not have class of mukund

Selector Fact Files

As its name suggests, jQuery places more emphasis on queries. The jQuery library enables you to search or look up the DOM elements, using a similar syntax to that used in CSS selectors. We have been laying the ground for the next chapter all this while, by hinting about selectors. You will see in the next chapter the way jQuery has been made to select the elements available in the DOM. But for the sake of acclimatization, we will state here that the jQuery framework uses the native browser API methods to traverse the DOM (which will be explained in Chapter 3). In this section of the chapter, we will discuss some of the quick tips taken right from our cheat sheet regarding the use of selectors to keep in mind, which will not only help you to learn about using selectors but will optimize your queries. We list a few of the points from our cheat sheet that we feel will be sufficient to motivate you to move to the next chapter.

- Use ID-based selectors.

- Be specific but avoid excessive specificity.

- Don't repeat selectors.

- Avoid using the universal wildcard (*) selector.

Let us move ahead and have a sneak peek at the ideas conveyed by, and practical demonstrations of, the use of all of these suggestions/tips.

Use of ID-Based Selectors

We all know that ID attributes are created to be unique to each element they are assigned to, and even older browsers can perform searches to find elements specified by an ID attribute. Here, it would be worth taking note that even older browsers are able to use the getElementById, which is very fast. The reason for this freedom with browsers is quite understandable: the method is available in the JavaScript implementation of almost all major browsers available. For a quick refresher, we addressed the getElementById method in Chapter 1.

Let us begin by demonstrating the use of selectors based on ID. A demonstration is as shown in the following example:

```
$("#apress div.mukund");
```

In keeping with the statements we made, this will be a fast lookup operation, because we have used the ID attribute. Having said that, can we move further ahead? You would note that the selector we mentioned seemed more like a CSS selector. As we stated in the previous chapter, one of the reasons for starting to use jQuery is the ease with which you can write selectors in the program, if you have a basic knowledge of CSS. But as everything usually comes at a cost, and nothing in this world is perfect, this ease to writing CSS selectors in jQuery to obtain proper results efficiently comes at the cost of speed. So, having said that, we want to optimize the performance of these selectors further. This is made possible by using the find() method. The demonstration of the usage is as follows:

```
$("#apress").find("div.mukund");
```

The introduction of the .find() method in the selector usage scenario would make the selection faster than the previous example, as the first lookup is handled without going through the Sizzle selector engine. This increase in performance is obtained as a cumulated effect of the speed of the jQuery implementation of the ID-only selectors and the functioning of the find method on the narrowed-down subset of the DOM tree. For the record, and for informative purposes, the implementation of the jQuery selections is known as the Sizzle engine. It is the core component of the jQuery API and is responsible for parsing the DOM to identify the target element. For more information on the Sizzle selector engine, you may want to consult the official web site, located at http://sizzlejs.com.

Be Specific but Avoid Excessive Specificity

To make a selector query fast, you must be specific about the right-hand side of your selector. We would recommend that you use the class names of the DOM elements on the right side of your selector and the tag names only on the left side as, for example,

```
$(".data td.mukund");
```

If you write $('.data tr td.mukund'), it would produce the same effect as $(".data td.mukund"), the reason being straightforward and simple: all TDs come under TRs. Thus, while performing a lookup, the jQuery selector engine will have to search through fewer nodes, which results directly in a performance gain. In short, a flatter selector would be faster than a deeper selector.

Don't Repeat Selectors

You should very rarely repeat a selector to perform some task. Even if it is bound to occur somehow, you should always try to minimize the repetition as much as possible. For every selector that you specify, the jQuery engine has to perform a lookup in the entire DOM tree, which could be quite an expensive operation, considering a full-blown web page. The following example illustrates a scenario in which a div has to be referenced three times for a task that could have been accomplished with only a single reference.

```
$("div").css("color", "red");
$("div").css("font-size", "1.4em");
$("div").text("Ankur is playing football");
```

To improve performance, we can chain the query using the jQuery chaining method. Chaining will be explained in Chapter 3, but for a quick reference, chaining is the phenomenon by which multiple operations are performed on a single object, so that the actions take place in the order in which they are written. So, here is an example of how to do this:

```
$("div").css({ "color": "red", "font-size": "1.4em"}).text("Ankur is playing football");
```

Here, the object returned from the first selector is operated twice, because the first two operations specified in the example are merged into a single function call, and the third operation is performed on the same object that was modified after the merged operation. The main performance gain is obtained by just a single lookup in the DOM tree for searching the element. In the next chapter, you will be guided through writing efficient selectors.

Avoid the Universal Selector

A universal selector is a selector that selects every element universally. So, the use of a universal selector implies side effects, because by selecting *all* elements by the selector, there may be some elements that you do not require, and there would be a very long path to traverse in the DOM tree, which would be quite slow. So, this would suggest that you try to avoid using this type of selector as much as possible. Let us have a look at how to avoid a universal selector in use. Consider the following selector:

```
$( ".buttons > *" );
```

You can avoid selecting all of the descendants of a button element by making use of the jQuery library function `children()`. The selector gets simplified to

```
$( ".buttons" ).children(); .
```

Regarding the use of the `children` method, we would state that the `children` method provided by the jQuery library selects the descendants of the target element (which is specified in the selector expression).

■ **Tip**   The general rule is to keep it simple as much as possible and avoid complex queries, unless your DOM is extremely complicated (or someone else has written it!) and writing complex queries is essential to getting a task done. But we would remind you that being a programmer, you are the best person to know how to simplify the solutions to problems. Just KISS (Keep it simple and straight).

Working with jQuery

With the information conveyed to you through the preceding discussions and demonstrations, you should have a sense of how a problem can be solved using jQuery. When we say that you can solve a problem using jQuery, we do not mean just writing code in jQuery, we mean writing code using the available jQuery library methods. We will consider a real-world example to show how jQuery works. Suppose your boss has asked you to show the terms and conditions of the company on a web site inside a light box window, and you have to produce a quick turnaround time and execute the task in a very short span of time. Here, if you go by our words and wisdom, you do not have to worry and can go ahead and reassure your boss that in the next ten minutes you can implement the requirement.

The Problem Statement

We always recommend planning. We always say that the more you plan, the less you will sweat solving your problems. You should visualize the light box window and how it should look before starting to write the code for the same (see Figure 2-3). You should think about the instruction given by your boss. Try to think about statements such as "When I click the link, it should open the light box window where I can see the terms and conditions," and so on.

Figure 2-3. *A simple sketch that captures the idea of the box you'll create*

To attain your boss's objective, you would need an anchor clicking, for which you would have to show a window located in the center of the web browser screen. There has to be a "close" option to close this window as well. Moving ahead, we put before you the proposed solution to the problem your boss presented you with.

First, let's start with the HTML and CSS for the scenario. Both are straightforward and easy to understand.

```
//HTML
<div class="text-center">
    <a href="javascript:void(0);" class="open-light-window">Terms & Condition</a>
</div>
```

```
<div class="light-box">
    <a href="javascript:void(0);" class="close-box">X</a>

    <h3>:: Terms and Condition :: </h3>

    <p class="text-justify">
This is about the Apress Practical jQuery book. Any text related to it should come here...
    </p>
</div>
<div class="light-bg"></div>

//CSS
<style>
    .text-center{
        text-align:center;
    }
    .light-box, .light-bg {
        display: none;
    }

    .light-bg {
        background: #000;
        width: 100%;
        height: 100%;
        opacity: .8;
        position: fixed;
        left: 0;
        top: 0;
        z-index: 2;
    }

    .light-box {
        background: #fff;
        border: solid 10px #000;
        width: 50%;
        padding: 1em;
        position: absolute;
        left: 50%;
        top:  10%;
        margin-left: -25%;
        z-index: 3;
    }

    .close-box {
        background: #c75f05;
        color: #fff;
        font: bold 2em/1 Arial;
```

```
        position: absolute;
        display: inline-block;
        right: 0;
        top: 0;
        z-index: 4;
    }
</style>
```

Now, if you look at the code, it's quite simple to see that the CSS styling has been added to hide some parts of the light box, so that if a user tries to activate the light box, under the hood, the CSS property will be manipulated, and to the human eye, it will appear as if the light box has come out of nowhere. So, moving quickly to the action part of the code, we propose the following jQuery library functions:

```
<script src="http://ajax.googleapis.com/ajax/libs/jquery/1.11.1/jquery.min.js"></script>
<script>
    $(document).ready(function () {
        function lightWindow() {
            $('.light-bg').fadeIn('slow');
            $('.light-box').slideDown('slow');
        }

        function closelightWindow() {
            $('.light-bg').fadeOut('slow');
            $('.light-box').slideUp('fast');
        }

        $('.open-light-window').on('click', function () {
            lightWindow();
        });
        $('.close-box').on('click', function () {
            closelightWindow();
        });
    });
</script>
```

Let's break down the jQuery:

1. Including the jQuery library to our code. There can be a local copy of the library onto the same server on which the HTML part is kept, or the copy can be fetched from some dedicated server located at some geographically distributed location across the globe.

2. Having a point of time as a reference to trigger the execution of the code. Here, the point of reference is the time in which the DOM tree has been loaded completely onto the web browser. We make use of the jQuery facility $(document).ready(function(){}). Inside the function body, we have provided two functions: lightWindow() and the closelightWindow().

3. The lightWindow() function performs two actions: fading in the light-bg element and slide down of the light box thereafter.

33

4. The closelightWindow() function also performs two actions, albeit ones opposite of those of the lightWindow(): fade out the light-bg and slide up the light box thereafter.

5. In the anchor link, we have attached a CSS class to an anchor element as open-light-window, and some action on the click event would have to be performed, which would take place on this anchor link. Here, the action that we have performed programmatically is to call the lightWindow method.

6. In the end, we have closed the window, and for that, we just called the function closelightWindow().

We hope this example makes sense to you. We will go into further detail concerning light boxes in later chapters.

The Anonymous Function

JavaScript is a different animal from most of the other object-oriented programming languages when it comes to the programming concepts used in it. Even the way classes and objects are handled in JavaScript is done differently. In addition to all these differences, which actually happen to be the character trait of JavaScript, there is a concept in JavaScript known as the *anonymous function*. In the parlance of language-design principles, anonymous functions are first-class functions. First-class functions are those functions that can be passed onto other functions as arguments to it. The anonymous function is a normal function that you declare without any named identifier to refer to it. Reframing the explanation, we can say that a first-class function is one that is not bound to an identifier. An anonymous function is slightly lighter in terms of computation than the normal named function, but it is recommended to be used only when some functionality is required once or twice (i.e., a fewer number of times).

To illustrate this, let us propose a way for you to write an anonymous function. Suppose there is a method with the name doSomething, and suppose you have to initiate the code by some other task. We suggest you use an anonymous function, such as

```
function doSomething(withSomething){
alert(withSomething());
}

doSomething(function(){
return "Homework done!";
});
```

Here, we called the method doSomething by passing an anonymous function (which just returned a message). We made use of the anonymous function by simply calling the parameter with an opening and closing brace (to make it look like a function call).

■ **Note**   Can you try to see what happens when you remove the braces inside the alert statement? Your findings will help you understand the concept of first-class functions from another viewpoint.

Anonymous functions can be used in a number of ways. Let's have a look into a real-world use of anonymous functions, by explaining a use-case involving preloading images with jQuery.

Preloading Images with jQuery

When you want to add some effects to your web page, you cannot resist using jQuery. Adding effects or animation is as easy as making a cup of coffee. We will look at preloading images in following example. We delve into animation in depth in Chapter 7.

You might have come across lots of web sites on which the content gets loaded and images still show a loading icon. If you don't like that situation in which images get downloaded after contents, you might be interested to read the following example of preloading an image.

```
(function($) {
    var cache = [];
    $.preLoadApressImages = function() {
        $.each(arguments, function(i) {
            cache.push($('img').attr("src", arguments[i]));
        });
    }
})(jQuery);
```

This is an anonymous function that is used to preload an image, so that the image will be preloaded in the background. There is nothing special about the code—you can change the name of the useful function from $.preLoadApressImages to any other name and use it outside of jQuery, but to your surprise, doing so will convert this piece of code into somewhat of a plug-in. We cover plug-in development, as well, in Chapters 9 and 10. Before we break down the script, let's see how to make a call to the method we created. The call would be as simple as

```
jQuery.preLoadApressImages("first_image.gif", "/path/to/second_image.gif");
```

Now, let us take time to understand the image preloading code example, by breaking it into understandable chunks, starting with the following:

```
(function($){
...// useful code here
})(jQuery)
```

Here, we wrap the code in an anonymous function and pass it to jQuery using $ as alias. This is done to avoid any conflict with other scripts that might use the $ symbol inside the web page. We covered avoiding (and resolving) conflicts previously when we discussed the method jQuery.noConflict(). You will notice the strange way we have written the anonymous function. This strange way is for a reason: this makes the anonymous function self-executing. This is in sync with our requirement as well. We were required to preload images, so we wanted the functionality to get executed automatically, without the need of some external function call.

Going deeper inside the code to explain its workings, we have defined a variable cache to cache the image(s) that the page in question will be required to load. We warn you that sometimes the image will not be able to get preloaded if you make the variable (or array or any such storage) local to the scope of the loop, because of some browsers' garbage collection mechanism. Because a local variable "dies" once the scope is over, the garbage collector cleans up the local variable upon exit of the scope. So, we make use of the cache variable by iterating through all of the individual elements that were mentioned in the list of images to be preloaded, and we do not worry about the order of images that have been preloaded.

Having said and done everything, we create the image elements and add those images to the browser.

■ **Tip** You will want to set some base URL matching your requirements to the images, so that you can use the images in your web page.

You must have noticed that we used the each() method in the demonstration we provided. We move ahead and provide you with some additional information in that regard.

each() in jQuery

The each() method is used to specify a function to run for each of the matched elements. The syntax is like:

```
$(selector).each(function(index,element){
...// Useful code here
});
```

In the syntax, there are two parameters shown: index and element. The index parameter provides information about the current pointer position in the list of repetitions. The element parameter provides information about the current element that is under the pointer at the current instance. Moving quickly to a demonstration regarding the use of each method, we propose the following:

```
<!DOCTYPE html>
<html>
<head>
<script src="http://ajax.googleapis.com/ajax/libs/jquery/1.11.1/jquery.min.js"></script>
<script>
$(document).ready(function(){
 $( "li" ).each(function( index ) {
   console.log( index + ": " + $( this ).text() );
    });
});
</script>
</head>
<body>


<ul>
  <li>John</li>
  <li>Doe</li>
</ul>

</body>
</html>
```

Here, we are iterating over all the li elements inside the target ul element using the each() method. The output message is logged for each item in the list. Figure 2-4 shows the output containing the text inside each of the li elements inside the ul element in the browser's console.

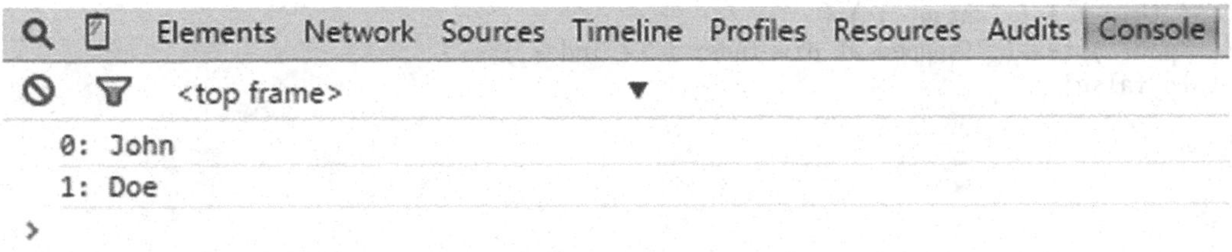

```
Q  ⏸   Elements  Network  Sources  Timeline  Profiles  Resources  Audits  Console

⊘  ⛛   <top frame>                        ▼

     0: John
     1: Doe
  >
```

Figure 2-4. Showing the output of iterating over the li elements inside a ul element

It is not that the loop is uncontrollable upon requirement. Quite like the other loops (for, while, and do-while), it can very easily be stopped, by returning a Boolean false from within the callback function Following is an example:

```html
<html lang="en">
<head>
  <meta charset="utf-8">
  <title>each demo</title>
  <style>
  div {
    width: 30px;
    height: 30px;
    margin: 5px;
    float: left;
    border: 2px gray solid;
    text-align: center;
  }
  span {
    color: red;
  }
  </style>
  <script src="//code.jquery.com/jquery-1.10.2.js"></script>
</head>
<body>

<button>Click to Change colors</button>
<span></span>
<div></div>
<div></div>
<div></div>
<div></div>
<div id="stop">Stop</div>
<div></div>
<div></div>
<div></div>

<script>
$( "button" ).click(function() {
  $( "div" ).each(function( index, element ) {
    // current element is represented by the this
    $( element ).css( "backgroundColor", "green" );
```

```
    if ( $( this ).is( "#stop" ) ) {
      $( "span" ).text( "Stopped at div index #" + index );
      return false;
    }
  });
});
</script>

</body>
</html>
```

We won't go into detail regarding the HTML and CSS code. The preceding code was just for demonstration purposes, and you can very easily understand that it includes a number of div elements having a gray border by default, and there is a span element that has an id attribute as stop and the text color red. If you look at the jQuery code, we are iterating over the div elements available and trying to match the ID selector stop. When the current ID selector is equal to stop, a Boolean false is returned, and the looping code will stop instantaneously. On executing the code in your web browser, you will see the message "Stopped at div index #4" appear with a click of the button element, because the fourth div element in the list contains the id attribute stop.

■ **Note**   The is() method checks the current matched set of elements against a selector, element, or jQuery object and returns true if at least one element in the set matches the given arguments.

Summary

This chapter began with the objective of helping you start working with jQuery. It provided instructions related to setting up the necessary framework. In the course of setting up jQuery, it was established that the essentials of DOM must be known. This chapter made you familiar with jQuery, by taking up some introductory topics, while providing references to future chapters in the book that explain these topics in a more detailed manner. The chapter concluded on a high note, by demonstrating a number of practical working examples, including that of the light box window.

In the next chapter, you will learn about traversing DOM with jQuery and about some standard jQuery concepts, such as using selectors, caching selectors, chaining methods, applying element filtering in jQuery, and many more similar aspects that will help you gain more and more confidence with jQuery.

CHAPTER 3

■ ■ ■

Traversing DOM with jQuery

Having arranged the setup and acquired hands-on knowledge about some of the intricacies of jQuery, can we now ask you to put on your work wear, please? In this chapter, we promise that you will get your clothes dirty with some real-world action sequences. The fortress for you to scale is the DOM (Document Object Model). As you saw in Chapter 2 (refer to Figure 2-1), DOM is an m-ary tree. The best way to reach out to any node is to traverse the nodes and locate the desired node element. In this chapter, you will observe and, therefore, learn how jQuery helps in DOM traversal. By the end of the chapter, you will be familiar with

- Selecting elements with CSS selectors
- Using jQuery selectors
- jQuery traversal methods
- Caching and chaining methods
- jQuery filtering

Selecting Elements with CSS Selectors

In Chapter 2, we discussed the most common methods for selecting CSS elements. We also promised to provide a detailed description of these methods. It is now time to keep that promise. What follows is a series of demonstrations as to how to select elements when you are presented a DOM. The prerequisites are a basic working knowledge of CSS and to have read Chapter 2.

A selector selects. To understand how a selector works, try to understand how a selector is written. In the most common usage, a selector is written as an expression of CSS rules. Let us begin with examples, followed by explanations. To start with, selectors in CSS are recommended (according to the World Wide Web Consortium [www.w3.org]) to be one of the following:

- type selector
- universal selector
- attribute selector
- class selector
- ID selector
- pseudo class selector

Type Selector

A *type selector* is a CSS selector that finds and selects an HTML element in the DOM tree when given the type of HTML node being searched for. So, you can select all HTML input elements by writing input, all HTML span elements by writing span, and so on.

Universal Selector

A *universal selector* is a CSS selector that finds and selects all HTML elements in the DOM tree. For the sake of clarification, let us offer some examples. You can select all the HTML elements available by using an asterisk (*) symbol. For example, you can select all HTML elements inside the body tag by using the * selector.

```
body *
```

Similarly, you can select all elements inside an HTML form element by using the * selector.

```
form *
```

Here, an important and quite interesting aspect to know about universal selectors is that under some conditions, the selectors are implied, and you can achieve functionality even without writing it. For example, if you want to select all HTML input elements having a CSS class of test inside of an HTML form element, you can use

```
form > *.test
```

Or you can do the following as well, to be more specific:

```
form > *input.test
```

But using either of the following without the * selector will also suffice:

```
form > .test
```

```
form > input.test
```

This demonstrates an interesting property exhibited by universal selectors. When a selector expression is composed of a sequence of simple selectors, the asterisk symbol (*) can be omitted altogether.

Attribute Selector

The *attribute selector* finds and selects those HTML elements in a rendered web page that are identified by some attribute. A few of the very commonly available HTML attributes are text, rel, href, title, class, name, and id. So you can specify some HTML attributes to select the desired elements. The demonstration makes this type of selector more clear.

You can select all the text boxes inside a form element using the selector expression

```
input[type="text"]
```

Similarly, you can select some span that has a `title` attribute. Thus, if the HTML is like

```
<span title="Ankur-plays-football">Ankur is playing football</span>
```

you can select all such spans with the `title` attribute set, by using the following selector expression:

```
span[title]
```

As a more complicated usage, you can match against a list of values to be present in the attribute of the HTML elements. You can select the element based on an *exact* match or on *contains* or *contains word* matches. For example, to select an element based on an exact match, you can do this:

```
img[alt="test"]
```

This would select all those image (`img`) elements inside the DOM tree that have "test" as the exact `alt` attribute. This is just another example, as we have already demonstrated the concept via the example of selecting an `input` element of the type `text`.

If you wish to find out more about the contains match, you can do so by writing a selector expression, as follows:

```
img[alt~="test"]
```

Using this selector, you would be able to select those image elements inside the DOM tree that contain the word "test" as a whole. Thus, the preceding written selector would select images that have an `alt` attribute such as "Ankur is writing a test" or "A human is tested at all times during his/her lifetime."

Then there is the contains word selector. Using this type of selector, you can select the HTML elements in which the word *test* occurs, even when part of another word, such as *contest*. An example would make it clearer.

```
img[alt*="test"]
```

This will select all the image elements in which the letters *test* occur. Thus, the selections would include image elements with `alt` attributes such as "Testing is quite important in Software Engineering," "People contesting elections have to pay a security deposit," and so on.

Class Selector

The *class selector* can be used to select the HTML elements from the DOM tree that have some specified CSS class. This is also quite commonly used in day-to-day development activities, and we have mentioned it in the previous chapters as well. As a detailed explanation, the working of the class selector is as follows:

For our first example, let's use the following HTML:

```
<div class="mukesh">The Super Designer</div>
<div class="ankur">The mastermind</div>
<div class="mukund">The boss</div>
```

So, in order to select the class ankur, you would have to do something like

```
.ankur
```

or even this

```
div.ankur
```

Now, let's explore working with multiple classes. If you have assigned more than one CSS class to some HTML elements, you can select those as well, using the class selector.

Starting with this HTML,

```
<div class="mukesh ankur mukund">The web nerds</div>
```

you can select both classes using any of the following selectors:

```
.mukesh.ankur
```

```
.mukund.ankur
```

```
.ankur.mukesh
```

```
.mukund.mukesh.ankur
```

Here, it would be quite interesting to note that the simple class selectors would also work. So, you could select the same div element by using one of the following selectors:

```
.mukesh
```

```
.mukund
```

```
.ankur
```

So, in essence, the class selector attempts to find the HTML element in the DOM tree that has at least the class value mentioned in the selector.

ID Selector

The *ID selector* selects that HTML element from the DOM tree for which the ID attribute matches a given value. This selector has already been mentioned in the previous chapters, and it will continue to be mentioned throughout this book, because this selector is a very common and useful tool. Let us quickly move on to demonstrate how this selector can be used.

Using the HTML

```
<div id="apress">Practical jQuery by Apress Publications</div>
```

you would be able to select this div by using one of the following selectors:

```
#apress
```

```
div#apress
```

If there are CSS classes attached, you can still use the ID selector to select the desired HTML element. You can do so by writing the selector expression, as shown for this HTML:

```
<div id="apress" class="Practical-series">Practical jQuery by Mukund Chaudhary and Ankur
Kumar</div>
```

You can use either of the following selectors:

```
.Practical-series#apress
```

```
div.Practical-series#apress
```

Pseudo Class Selector

Next, we have the *pseudo class selector,* which is used to select HTML elements from the DOM tree that have a pseudo class name attached to them. A pseudo class is a keyword that is appended to some other selector to denote that the element would be selected by the selector upon some special condition. We follow the convention of writing pseudo classes by prepending a *colon* (:) before it. Commonly used pseudo classes include :hover, :visited, :first-child, :nth-child, and :link. A demonstration of a pseudo class selector would make the scenario clear.

With the following HTML,

```
<a href="www.apressmedia.com">The apress official website</a>
```

the selector that selects the link when the mouse hovers over this link node is

```
a:hover
```

Similarly, you can select all of the first children of a particular node type by using the :first-child selector. This scenario, using the following HTML, is as follows:

```
<div>
    <span>This is to test :first-child</span>
    <span><a href="www.apress.com">View more details about Apress Publication</a></span>
</div>
```

So, span :first-child will select the first span element only and not the second element.

Relationship-Based Selectors

Selectors in CSS use some special symbols to denote some special relational hierarchy. Just as you selected the first child, which was of the type span, using the pseudo class :first-child, there are a number of symbols available that enable you to select HTML elements from the DOM tree. Some of them have already been mentioned in Chapter 2. We will discuss others, for the sake of clarity and further elucidation.

- The > symbol
- The + symbol
- The ~ symbol

The > symbol selects the immediate descendants of some HTML element node. The demonstration below will make this more clear.

With this HTML,

```
<div class="apress">
    <p>
    <span>A new author waits to be added to apress.</span>
    <form action="www.apress.com/authors/add" method="post">
    <input type="text" name="new-author" />
    <input type="submit" value="submit" />
    </form>
        <ul>
            <li>Have you done your homework?</li>
        </ul>
    </p>
    <div>
    <p>This is to demonstrate the symbolic selectors present</p>
    </div>
</div>
```

the following selector would select only the p elements that are direct descendants of the following div:

```
div.apress > p
```

■ **Note** If you want to try this yourself, there is a fiddle available at http://jsfiddle.net/ankur6971/6ne8zp9u/17. You can view or perform experiments with the fiddle.

The + symbol is also known as the adjacent selector, because it selects the elements that are adjacent to the target HTML element(s), as identified by the selector. In other words, this selector will select all those elements that are at the same level and adjacent to the element specified by the selector. Being able to foresee the difficulty in understanding this tricky selector, let us demonstrate how to understand this. There is a fiddle at http://jsfiddle.net/ankur6971/6v4bz5u2/1/ that contains the same HTML as in the previous example, but with a different selector:

```
p + div
```

The selected element would be all divs that are at the same level as that of a *p*.

Next, there is the ~ symbol, which selects the elements at the same level, quite like the + symbol, but the difference in its behavior lies in the fact that the elements to be selected need not be adjacent; they can be in any position. To demonstrate, let's have a look at a scenario using the following HTML:

```
<div class="apress">
    <p>
        <span>A new author waits to be added to apress.</span>
    </p>
    <form action="www.apress.com/authors/add" method="post">
        <input type="text" name="new-author" />
        <input type="submit" value="submit" />
    </form>
    <ul>
        <li>Have you done your homework?</li>
    </ul>
    <span>Can this prevent the ~ to work?</span>
    <div>
        <p>This is to demonstrate the symbolic selectors present</p>
    </div>
</div>
```

A selector demonstrating the usage can be

```
p ~ div
```

■ **Note** There is a fiddle for this demonstration available at `http://jsfiddle.net/ankur6971/1u10gw02/`. You can view and perform experiments with this fiddle.

By now, you might be wondering why we have used so much demonstration and explanation to show how you select elements using CSS selectors. The reason behind this is straightforward: jQuery selector functions can use CSS selector expressions to select HTML elements from the DOM tree. This was mentioned in the previous chapters as well, but we will cover this again with a more detailed description in the next section.

Using jQuery Selectors

Selectors are the same—be they CSS or jQuery. It is not that *selectors* were designed that way, it is that *jQuery* was designed that way. As we discussed in Chapter 1, behind the evolution of jQuery was cssQuery, which provided the inspiration for the former. We will extend our discussion now and provide detailed demonstrations, to help you understand how jQuery selectors are used.

To start, let us recall that a selector in jQuery is no special construct. Anything written like `$('.class')` becomes a selector. For the sake of demonstration and full dimensional understanding, we will use the same examples and cases that we did for CSS selectors wherever possible, and we will take up some other examples as well, so that the subject becomes clearer.

Type Selector

Type selectors in jQuery can be used in a very simple way. You just have to know the basic selector and pass on the type of the element to be selected in the form of a single-quoted or double-quoted string: `$('input')`, `$('span')`, and so on.

Universal Selector

Universal selectors in jQuery can be used in a similar way as using CSS. You would have to pass on the universal selector expression as string to the jQuery selector function. A demonstration of this is

`$('body *')`

`$('form *')`

`$('form > *.test')`

Attribute Selector

The *attribute selector* can be used in a similar way to CSS. You would have to pass on the selector expression to the jQuery selector, just as you have been using other selectors. For example, we do the following:

`$('input[type="text"]')`

to select all the input elements for which the type attribute has the value "text." In short, we select all the text boxes present inside the web page.

As another demonstration, you can select all the span elements inside the DOM tree that have the `title` attribute available, by using the selector

`$('span[title]')`

Similarly, jQuery will let you select all those image elements that have the `alt` attribute as the text "test," by allowing you to use the selector, as follows:

`$('img[alt="test"]')`

jQuery will also let you select all those image elements that have the exact word *test* somewhere in the title you used for the selector, as follows:

`$('img[alt~="test"]')`

Similarly, you can select all the image elements in the DOM tree that have the word *test* anywhere— even inside other words—by using the following jQuery selector:

`$('img[alt*="test"]')`

Class Selector

The *class selector* in jQuery is used in much the same way as the type selector, and it selects the element that matches the CSS class attribute as specified in the selector. An example is

```
$('.apress')
```

in which apress would be the name of some CSS class attached to the target HTML element.

ID Selector

Similarly, using an *ID selector*, you can select some HTML element from the DOM tree on the basis of the ID attribute attached to the target element. An example is

```
$('#ankur-pen-color')
```

in which ankur-pen-color is the ID attribute attached to the target HTML element, such as
`<div id="ankur-pen-color">The color of pen does not govern the content it delivers</div>`.

Pseudo Class Selector

Next you have the jQuery selector to select the HTML elements for which some *pseudo classes* have been attached. You can have a selector such as

```
$('span:first-child')
```

which would select the first child of the span element in the HTML we presented to you when we took up the pseudo class selector. You are encouraged to try out more examples on the HTML we provided, because the best learning comes when you learn yourself.

Other jQuery Selectors

Here, we would like to continue the discussion by stating that jQuery selectors are not solely dependent on CSS selectors. There are a number of methods available that *do* take you that extra mile. Walking this extra mile could either have been difficult with CSS or, at most, lengthy and laborious. We will take up some commonly used methods and explain each with an analogy to CSS, so that you will be able to relate jQuery and CSS in this potentially hostile environment!

Let us take up the :eq() selector. This selector works by treating the child elements as indexed from 0, and whatever index you pass on to them, and attempts to select for you that particular element from the DOM tree. As a demonstration, we take up the same HTML as shown in the fiddles in the immediately preceding topic. So, if you want to select the 0 child inside the div with the class value apress, you would have to use

```
$('div.apress:eq(0)')
```

Then, we have the `:gt()` selector, which works in a similar way as `:eq()`, with the exception that this selector will select that HTML element that has the index greater than the value passed on. Thus, in the same example, if you want to select all the p elements that are in an index greater than 0 (because this method has a zero-based index), you would have to use the `:gt()` selector, as follows:

```
$('p:gt(0)').css('background', 'powderblue');
```

If there is a greater than selector, there must be a less than selector as well. So, here is `:lt()`, provided in jQuery, which does the same thing as expected. It selects the elements that are in an index less than the index you specify. So, considering the same example again, here is a demonstration of this selector:

```
$('p:lt(1)')
```

that does the task of selecting all the paragraph elements that are in an index less than 1. Following the HTML example that we have been using for the topics in this chapter, the selection would be as simple as selecting just one paragraph element.

There is additionally the `:has()` selector, which checks if some HTML element has some other HTML element as a child (not necessarily direct) somewhere in the DOM tree. So, citing the same HTML example in the immediately preceding topic, if you had to select the p element that has the span element, the following could be your answer:

```
$('p:has(span)')
```

Besides the previously mentioned selectors available to the web development community, there are some other pseudo-class-type-appearing selectors available in jQuery that are outside the scope of our coverage. If you wish to have information on them (we always recommend acquiring knowledge), you can go to the jQuery official API documentation web site located at `http://api.jquery.com/category/selectors/` to find information on such selectors as `:animated` and `input[name!='newsletter']`.

■ **Note** It is important to to be aware that the selectors provided by jQuery are unable to take advantage of the native DOM implementation. The reason for this is that the CSS selectors have been implemented in the DOM representation of the browsers, so the CSS selectors find their support right from the web browser, and, hence, they get executed much faster. The jQuery-specific selectors are unable to enjoy such freedom. Therefore, it is always recommended that you refrain from using such selectors. Always select something that has native support.

Traversing DOM with jQuery Traversal Methods

As a continuation of our duty to guide you toward the correct path, we now lighten up the ways for you to use the knowledge gained till now (in this chapter) and proceed to apply it in actual scenarios. Because you have a basic knowledge of what selectors are and how you can use them, you will now learn how to traverse the DOM using jQuery. Traversing is not a mistyped word in the current context, because, as we have mentioned earlier, DOM is a m-ary tree and, thus, to reach out to some node programmatically, you must actually move through the correct hierarchy. This phenomenon is known as *tree traversal* and is a vital part of the day-to-day activity of a web developer.

The Curtain Raiser

Before we actually start traversing the DOM tree, let us take up an example for a sample DOM tree. To make this simple, we will use the same HTML example we used to demonstrate some of the selectors.

```
<div class="apress">
    <p>
        <span>A new author waits to be added to apress.</span>
    </p>
    <form action="www.apress.com/authors/add" method="post">
        <input type="text" name="new-author" />
        <input type="submit" value="submit" />
    </form>
    <ul>
        <li>Have you done your homework?</li>
    </ul>
    </p>
    <span>Can this prevent the ~ to work?</span>
    <div>
        <p>This is to demonstrate the symbolic selectors present</p>
    </div>
</div>
```

The reason for taking up the HTML code snippet was to familiarize you with certain buzzwords that are commonly used with tree traversal. Let us try to make some statements regarding the hierarchy. (Please note that the buzzwords have been italicized for emphasis.) The div with the class attribute of apress is the *parent* of all the other HTML elements in the current scenario. This div can also be called as the *ancestor* element of every other HTML element in the example. The immediate *child* elements to this div are p, span, and another div element. These three elements are related to each other as *sibling* elements. All elements other than the div with the class value apress are descendants of this div.

The statements have been grouped to form a paragraph, and it will give you a fair idea of how the tree elements are related to one another. Now, you can easily imagine that because they are related, there would be a phenomenon required to use this relationship and reach out to the appropriate node. A natural question that one could ask is that when we already have the selectors available, why is there a need to worry about traversal? The answer to this question is that using selectors, we reach out to the correct node in the DOM. So, you can assume that selectors and traversal go hand-in-hand. In other words, selectors complement DOM traversal. For a better understanding of the DOM structure and the hierarchy, see Figure 3-1.

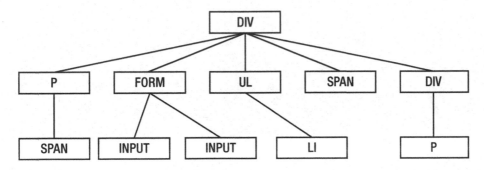

Figure 3-1. *The DOM structure and hierarchy*

jQuery Methods for DOM Traversal

So, jQuery provides a number of methods that assist you in DOM traversal. Some of the commonly used methods include the following:

- parent()
- parents()
- parentsUntil()
- closest()
- children()
- find()
- prev()
- next()
- siblings()

We will provide explanations and demonstrations for these methods in the following sections.

The parent() Method

The parent() method provided in jQuery finds the parent of the target element. Let us consider the same HTML example used in the preceding section. So, if you wish to find out the parent element of the p in the example shown, the jQuery code would be

```
$('p').parent()
```

But, as you can observe in the HTML code, there are multiple occurrences of p, and each has a different element. It is worth noting here that the $().parent() would return more than one object in the current scenario, and, hence, whatever action you attempt to apply to this selected element would be applied across all occurrences. So, if you wished to add a 1px border to the selection, there would be an uneven border; there would be thick borders at some regions. This phenomenon is shown in Figure 3-2.

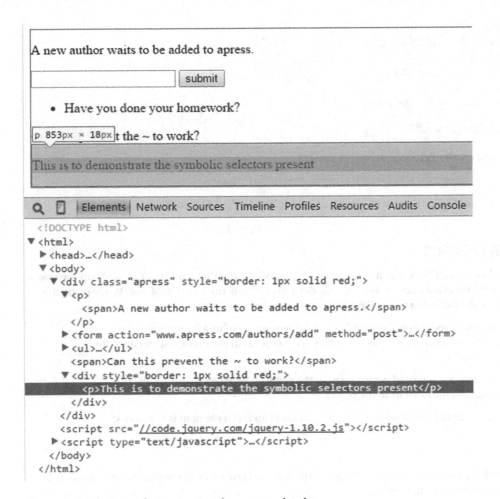

Figure 3-2. The immediate parent and an uneven border

In this condition, the immediate parent of the p element happens to be the ancestor div with the class attribute apress. Therefore, the styling is applied to this div too.

But fear not, you can still select one of the two selections made. The parent() method (optionally) accepts an argument that can be of the type string and which should be a valid selector. So, if you wish to determine the element that has the class apress, you can do so with the following jQuery code snippet:

```
$('p').parent('.apress')
```

For example, if you wanted to apply some styling to the target element, such as the same solid border of 1px width and red in color, you would do something like

```
$('p').parent('.apress').css('border', '1px solid red')
```

Figure 3-3 shows the results of the preceding code.

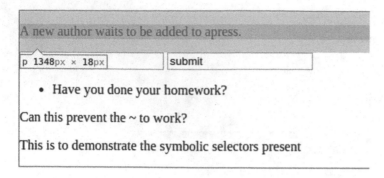

Figure 3-3. The result of `$('p').parent('.apress').css('border', '1px solid red')`

The parents() Method

This method performs a similar action as the `parent()` method, except that `parents()` ascends up the tree to the available height and matches all the available desired elements from the DOM tree. While using the `parents()` method, the following points have to be considered:

- Because the tree traversal occurs bottom up (we are searching for parents), the object that is returned contains the matched elements in the order starting from the closest match.

- When there are repeated occurrences of the same DOM element, the duplicate elements are removed from the object.

The use of the `parents()` method to select the parents of an input element is as follows:

```
$().parents()
```

So, the `parents()` method can be used to give a 1px solid red border to all the parent elements of the input element in the same example as

```
$('input').parents().css('border', '1px solid red')
```

Figure 3-4 shows the border applied to the parent elements.

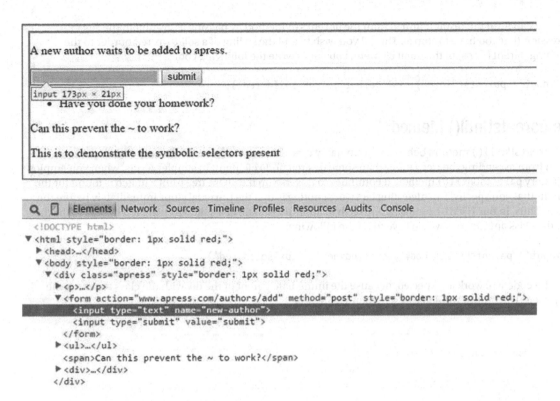

Figure 3-4. *The result of the parents() selector*

As a brief explanation and verification, you can see that all the parents of the input elements named form, div, body, and html obtain the style that you applied via your jQuery method call, because they are the parents of the input element.

■ **Tip**   If you wish to do some tinkering to find out the difference between parent() and parents(), you can try finding the parent of the html element. In doing so, you will observe two completely different and distinctive results. So, if you write

$('html').parent()

you obtain the document object (we covered this in Chapter 1). When you attempt the same using the parents() method

$('html').parents()

you obtain an empty object. This is in accordance with the theory that you have encountered throughout this book till now: jQuery will try to move up to the root element to find the matching element of the type element node. Because the document (which is a parent to the html element) is not of the type element, the returned set is empty. This is quite obvious, as the html element has no parent as such.

You can limit the result returned from the parents() method by passing as argument the selector expression that you have to stop at. Thus, if you wish to add the styling of a solid 1px red border to the matching parent (form) of the input element, you could write the following code:

```
$('input').parents("form").css('border', '1px solid red');
```

The parentsUntil() Method

The parentsUntil() method behaves in a similar way as the parents() method, except that it prevents the search from ascending the tree farther than some desired node element. In simpler terms, when you employ the jQuery parentsUntil() method, it continues to traverse up the DOM tree until a match is found for the element that you specify. An interesting fact worth noting is that the traversal stops immediately before the match. Thus, in our HTML example, if you wish to apply the styling of a solid 1px wide red border to the div with the class apress, you would have to do the following:

```
$('input').parentsUntil("body").css('border', '1px solid red')
```

The code will work as expected, because the immediate parent of the div with the class apress is the body itself. The output would be as shown in Figure 3-5.

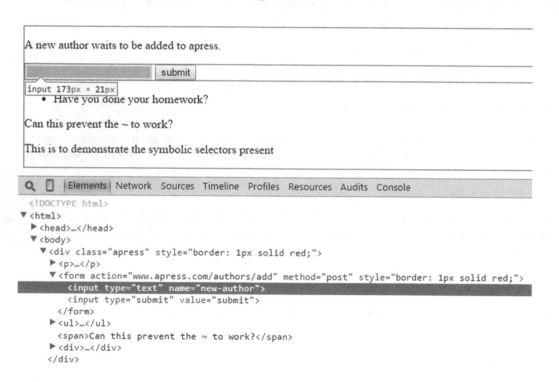

Figure 3-5. *The output of the parentsUntil method*

The closest() Method

There is another method available in jQuery that performs the task of traversing the DOM, starting right from itself and continuing up the DOM until a match is found. This is the closest() method. It includes both ends of the search: itself and the matched elements. The matched elements (if any) are returned in the form of an object containing the elements matched, and that, too, in the actual order in which they appear in the DOM.

You can easily use the closest() method to find and style the div element that is closest to the span inside a p element. To do this, you can write the following jQuery code:

```
$('span').closest('div').css('border', '1px solid red');
```

This would style the closest div in two ways. Because the first span is inside a p that is directly inside a div, the div with the class apress will be styled. Also, the second span is directly inside the div, and, thus, the closest div happens to be the immediate parent itself, so the styling gets repeated. Although this is not a recommended action, because this approach cannot guarantee the correct styling under every other scenario, it is being done here solely for the sake of demonstration. The result of the styling would be like that in Figure 3-6.

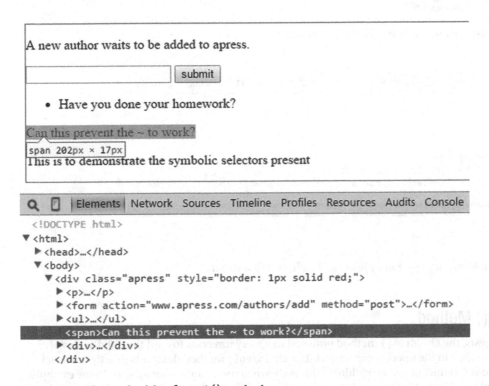

Figure 3-6. *The result of the closest() method*

There is another option available to you for using this method. You can choose to restrict the search within some context by specifying the second argument as some jQuery object. In simple terms, when you specify some context in the form of a jQuery object, you restrict the search to take place within that DOM context as well. To eliminate worry and confusion, here is an example.

```
$('span').closest('p', $('div.apress')).css('border', '1px solid red');
```

What the code does here is traverse up the DOM node, starting from the span, and attempt to find out the closest p that is inside some div with the class apress. Upon finding it, the code attempts to apply the style of a solid 1px border that is red in color. The styling results in something like that shown in Figure 3-7.

Figure 3-7. *The styling result of our sample use of the* `closest()` *method*

The children() Method

As the name suggests, the `children()` method provided in jQuery traverses toward the child nodes of the element as specified in the selector expression. The `children()` method descends exactly one level in the DOM tree to select the immediate children. This is shown in the example that follows. In the example, we have attempted to select all the first-level children of the div with the class attribute equal to apress. The code used to achieve the result is

```
$('div.apress').children().css('border', '1px solid red');
```

The output of the action is as shown in Figure 3-8.

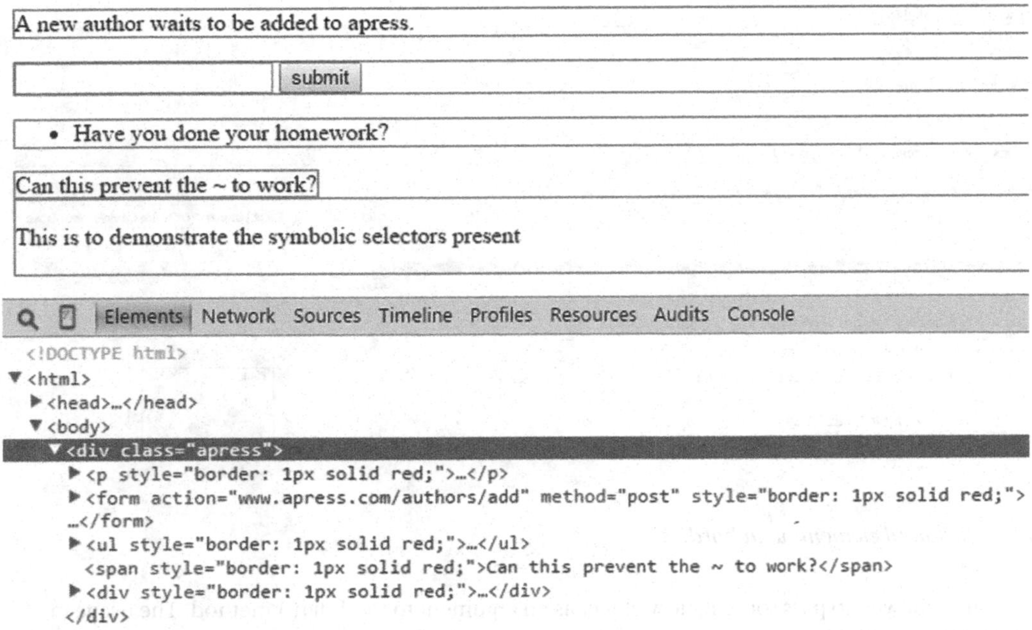

A new author waits to be added to apress.

| submit |

• Have you done your homework?

Can this prevent the ~ to work?

This is to demonstrate the symbolic selectors present

```
Q  🔲  | Elements | Network  Sources  Timeline  Profiles  Resources  Audits  Console
<!DOCTYPE html>
▼ <html>
  ▶ <head>…</head>
  ▼ <body>
    ▼ <div class="apress">
      ▶ <p style="border: 1px solid red;">…</p>
      ▶ <form action="www.apress.com/authors/add" method="post" style="border: 1px solid red;">
      …</form>
      ▶ <ul style="border: 1px solid red;">…</ul>
        <span style="border: 1px solid red;">Can this prevent the ~ to work?</span>
      ▶ <div style="border: 1px solid red;">…</div>
      </div>
```

Figure 3-8. *The result of the* children() *method*

As a continuation of the demonstration of the children() method, we would like to state that you can restrict the selection to find only some element(s) specified in the selector expression. Thus, you can find selected children (p elements) of a specific target element (div.apress) when you use the following jQuery code:

```
$('div.apress').children('p').css('border', '1px solid red')
```

This would, quite understandably, add the desired style to all p elements that are level 1 or immediate children of the div of the class apress.

The find() Method

The find() method, which lives up to its name, finds elements in the DOM tree, and the interesting fact about this method is that it descends the entire available depth in order to match elements. As regards the usage of this method, you only have to remember that you must pass a single argument to it. This single argument can either be a selector expression or some jQuery object representing some DOM element.

To demonstrate, the following jQuery code can be used:

```
$('body').find('p').css('border', '1px solid red')
```

The result of the action is shown in Figure 3-9.

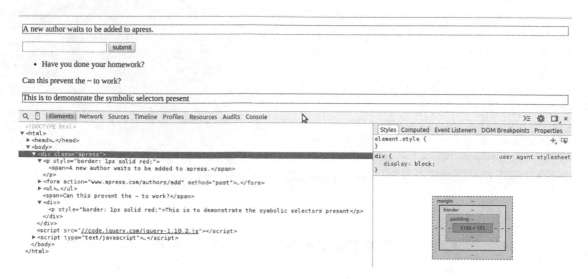

Figure 3-9. *The found elements with borders*

You are also allowed to pass some jQuery object as an argument to the find() method. The usage in that case would be

```
$('body').find($('p')).css('border', '1px solid red')
```

This usage was specially designed to produce the same output as in the previous case. Familiarizing yourself with this method will strengthen your confidence and ability to use jQuery from now on.

The prev() Method

This method does the work of finding the immediately preceding node that matches a desired criteria. As a demonstration, we put up the following jQuery code for you:

```
$('ul').prev().css('border', '1px solid red');
```

which would select the immediately previous sibling to the ul element in the same example we have been considering for other methods. It may surprise you that there is another usage that will yield the same result as this one. This other usage involves passing a selector as an argument to the prev() method. The jQuery code is

```
$('ul').prev('form').css('border', '1px solid red')
```

The next() Method

The next method provided by jQuery is named next(). Quite like its name, it helps you to select the HTML element immediately next in the DOM tree that is at the same level as some desired element specified by you. In other words, the next() method selects the sibling immediately next in the DOM tree. As a demonstration, the following would be the jQuery code:

```
$('div').next().css('border', '1px solid red')
```

Quite surprisingly, the preceding code selects the script tag this time. It also demonstrates that the next() method can select any element available in the DOM tree. For another meaningful example, see the following jQuery code:

```
$('p').next().css('border', '1px solid red')
```

Because, in our example, there are two p elements and there are form and span elements, respectively, as the immediately next elements, the preceding code will add a 1px-wide red border to each of these siblings. The output of the last demonstration is shown in Figure 3-10.

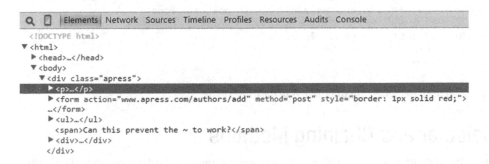

Figure 3-10. *The output of the next() method*

The siblings() Method

If you look carefully, you will see that the function of the next() and prev() methods is to select the sibling elements in the DOM tree. But because the siblings immediately next or previous were selected in those cases, jQuery provides another method, called siblings(), which will select all the nodes at the same level as the desired element you specify. For a demonstration of this, note the following jQuery code:

```
$('ul').siblings().css('border', '1px solid red')
```

This will select and style all the siblings of the ul element in the HTML example we have been using all along.

If you want to limit your selection, you can specify some filter as the argument to this siblings() method. A demonstration of this would be the following jQuery code:

```
$('ul').siblings('p').css('border', '1px solid red')
```

This will select all the p elements that are siblings of the ul element in the DOM tree, with regard to the same HTML example we have been employing throughout the chapter (see Figure 3-11).

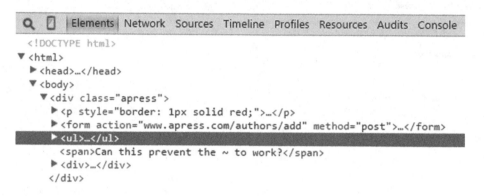

A new author waits to be added to apress.

submit

- Have you done your homework?

Can this prevent the ~ to work?

This is to demonstrate the symbolic selectors present

Figure 3-11. *Selecting all the p elements that are siblings of the ul element*

Caching Selector and Chaining Methods

Whenever you query the DOM tree via some method call, be it some jQuery method or even some JavaScript implementation for the same, it consumes time. The time consumed here is the time taken to traverse the entire DOM tree. Although the tree traversal is optimized for speed during the implementation, be it at the browser level or the programming level, it takes at least some amount of time. So, using the selector methods is a point note, and a fair amount of understanding is required to use the selectors.

There are actually two available approaches that are worth noting: *selector caching* and *method chaining*. We mentioned both of these in Chapter 2. Continuing from where we left off, we will explain and demonstrate why you should take care in handling these selectors. We will also guide you as to what should be your policy to get rid of the problem caused by repeating selectors. Because it is a general principle to optimize something that is working, we advise you to master the use of selectors before moving forward and to adopt optimization.

Selector Caching

Let us begin with selector caching. In simple terms, caching means hiding or storing something at some place. Extending this concept, computer science has assigned the meaning "to store something for quick access." So, when we talk about caching selectors in jQuery, we mean that we store some jQuery object that the selector returns and use the same for referring to the selected DOM node, instead of querying the DOM again and again. Let us stop talking and start doing.

We start this discussion with a small-use case. Considering the same HTML scenario we took up while explaining the DOM traversal methods available with jQuery, let us add some complicated CSS styling, to beautify the HTML and have more functionality via jQuery. Let's try to change the font color of the span element inside of the paragraph element to color code #999 (a shade of gray) and the font family as *sans-serif*. The most probable jQuery code that would be written would be:

```
var spanInParagraph = $('p').find('span');
spanInParagraph.css({'font-family': 'sans-serif', 'color':'#999'});

var form = $('p').siblings('form');
var input = form.find('input');
input.css({'display': 'block', 'border':'1px solid #aaa'});
```

Writing the code would mean that the functionality is achieved, but just compare what happens when you take a closer look at some goods that you have purchased inexpensively. You may begin to notice scratches, defects, etc. In a similar vein, this code has inefficiencies. Let us find out what they are. The jQuery selector for the element p appears more than once. This clearly means that although we wished to refer to the same instance of the p element, we asked jQuery to search for the same element more than once. This effect would not mean much in the present scenario, in which the sample is very small (this being a demonstration), but in real cases, such code would cause browser overload and, consequently, execution speed would slow down. When there is a problem, there has to be a solution. Therefore, we have a solution for this: you have to cache the selector. A demonstration of this follows:

```
var p = $('p');
var spanInParagraph = p.find('span');
spanInParagraph.css({'font-family': 'sans-serif', 'color':'#999'});

var form = p.siblings('form');
var input = form.find('input');
input.css({'display': 'block', 'border':'1px solid #aaa'});
```

What is worth observing here is that the code still works as expected. It required only a small shuffle of variables, but the shuffle was significant. Because the same *p* is being dealt with, we have saved the reference to it in the variable p. Because the p element will never change, the references will not change either. This reference will be used to perform operations in a faster way. This is one approach to selector caching.

Let us consider a complex example. The HTML is as follows:

```
<!DOCTYPE html>
<html>
    <head>
        <title></title>
    </head>
    <body>
        <div class="apress">
            <p>
                <span>A new reader waits to learn jQuery.</span>
                <ul>
                    <li>Have you done your homework?</li>
                    <li>Is it that you are having leisure time?</li>
                    <li>Would you like to have challenges in life?</li>
                    <li>Click here to know the solution.</li>
                </ul>
            </p>
```

```
        <p>If you liked this example, tell others. If not, tell us!</p>
    </div>
</body>
<script src="//code.jquery.com/jquery-1.10.2.js"></script>
</html>
```

Now comes the jQuery part to add functionality to this HTML code. Let us plan to have some interaction between the web page and you, the end user. Let us plan to change the text of the last li element on some interaction. In this example, the jQuery code will bring about a text change after a click event on some HTML element, as follows:

```
$('div.apress').find('ul').children('li').css({'color':'#dedede', 'font-family': 'tahoma,
sans-serif'});
$('div.apress').find('ul').on('click', function(){
    $('div.apress').find('ul').children('li').last().html('All we need is an attentive
    reader!');
    $('ul').children('li').last().css({'color':'seagreen'});
});
```

Figure 3-12 shows the page before the interaction, and Figure 3-13 shows it after the click event.

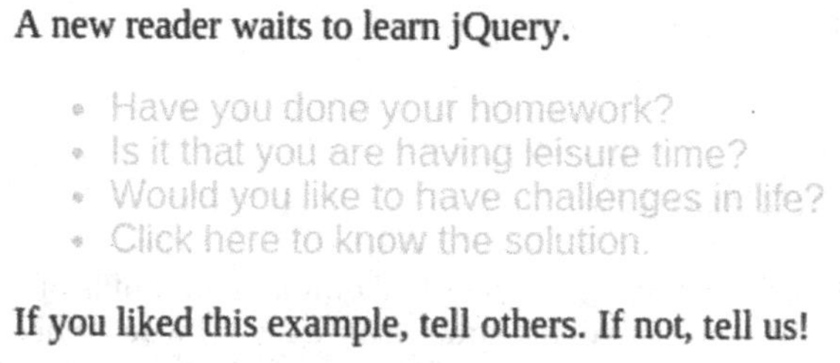

A new reader waits to learn jQuery.

- Have you done your homework?
- Is it that you are having leisure time?
- Would you like to have challenges in life?
- Click here to know the solution.

If you liked this example, tell others. If not, tell us!

Figure 3-12. *The output of the code before a click*

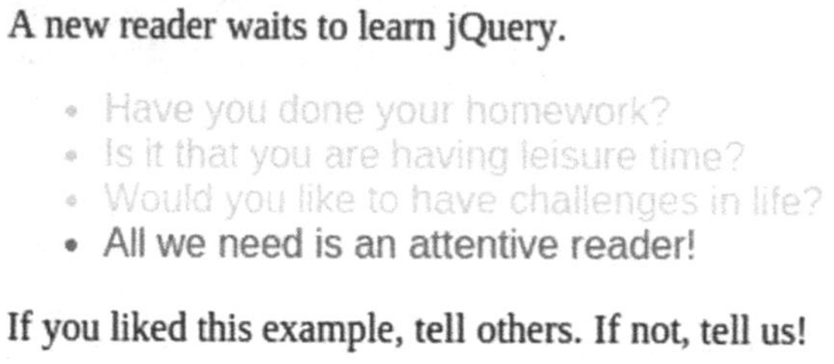

A new reader waits to learn jQuery.

- Have you done your homework?
- Is it that you are having leisure time?
- Would you like to have challenges in life?
- All we need is an attentive reader!

If you liked this example, tell others. If not, tell us!

Figure 3-13. *The output of the code after a click*

Now comes the caching part. You can make out from the example that there are multiple occurrences of the selectors. So, when you make an attempt to cache the repeating selectors, the code will change to

```
var divApress = $('div.apress');
var ulsInsideApress = $('div.apress').find('ul');
var lisInsideUl = $('div.apress').find('ul').children('li');

lisInsideUl.css({'color':'#dedede', 'font-family': 'tahoma, sans-serif'});
ulsInsideApress.on('click', function(){
var lastLi = lisInsideUl.last();
lastLi.html('All we need is an attentive reader!');
lastLi.css({'color': 'seagreen'});
});
```

We term this *code cleansing*. The jQuery people call it *selector caching*. The justification for our term is that, by the action, the code becomes more readable and cleaner. We use the term *cleansing* intentionally, because the performance of this code is not the best as a result of this action. Although it is true that it makes use of caching selectors, there is yet a greater extent to which the performance and cleanup of the code can be enhanced. The cleaner version of the code would look like

```
var divApress = $('div.apress');
var ulsInsideApress = divApress.find('ul');
var lisInsideUl = ulsInsideApress.children('li');

lisInsideUl.css({'color':'#dedede', 'font-family': 'tahoma, sans-serif'});
ulsInsideApress.on('click', function(){
var lastLi = lisInsideUl.last();
lastLi.html('All we need is an attentive reader!').css({'color': 'seagreen'});
});
```

The output remains the same. The aspects of the code that have been cleaned are the following:

- The repeated occurrences have been replaced by the corresponding variables.

- In order to perform more than one action upon the same element, the actions have been chained together.

This leads us to chaining.

Chaining

We mentioned the word *chaining* in Chapter 2. This is another aspect in the code cleaning up process. If you remember what you read in the preceding chapter, you will understand that chaining is a simple process and takes place to reduce the number of times certain code blocks are repeated. Let us take the example of the discussion immediately preceding, wherein some text inside the list item was replaced and provided a text color. The jQuery code was

```
lastLi.html('All we need is an attentive reader!').css({'color': 'seagreen'});
```

Thus far in the book, you have come across method chaining multiple times. Let us refresh your memory by adopting the code snippets and explaining how the scenarios would have been in the absence of chaining. Following, we list a few examples of method chaining used previously, along with the alternative "unchained" means to achieve the same goal.

Chained:

```
$('ul').siblings('p').css('border', '1px solid red');
```

Unchained:

```
var ul = $('ul');
var siblings = ul.siblings('p');
siblings.css('border', '1px solid red');
```

Chained:

```
$('body').find($('p')).css('border', '1px solid red');
```

Unchained:

```
var body = $('body');
var p = $('p');
var pInBody = body.find(p);
pInBody.css('border', '1px solid red');
```

Chained:

```
$('input').parents("form").css('border', '1px solid red');
```

Unchained:

```
var input = $('input');
var form = input.parents('form');
form.css('border', '1px solid red');
```

You could see easily that the phenomenon of chaining cuts down on the number of variables used in the code. Continuing along the same lines that we followed in introducing the current discussion topic, you might quite naturally ask the question, Is it necessary to chain methods? To answer this would take ages, but to make it as concise as possible, we would simply state that to optimize some machinery or algorithm or functionality, it requires effort. For organizations, time means money. Thus, if you make a move to optimize some code, you should consider the time-cost relationship beforehand, failing which, you could easily become a source of expense to your organization.

jQuery Filtering

Whenever we talk about DOM tree traversal, the discussion must include another phenomenon: the phenomenon of filtering the results. Because in a real-world scenario the HTML that gets rendered onto the web browser is composed of a complex and usually large DOM tree, filtering out the unwanted elements from the search result provides significant ease of use to you, the web developer. So, in the current discussion, we will take up filtering, which is provided by thejQuery framework and just as we have been doing all along, we will provide relevant demonstrations, as needed.

The jQuery library provides a number of methods to achieve filtering. We provide a list of some of the most commonly needed and used methods, along with some explanation and some examples. We follow the ascending alphabetical order of the method names. Because by now we have two sample DOMs, we will name the one we mentioned in the beginning of the chapter "jquery-simple" and the one that is newer "jquery-complex." The methods we'll discuss in this section include the following:

- `.eq()`
- `.filter()`
- `.first()`
- `.last()`
- `.has()`
- `.is()`
- `.not()`

The .eq() Method

The `.eq()` method lets you match and filter the elements that are at the specified index in the jQuery object. The indexing is 0-based, meaning that the first element will be at the index 0. Let's consider an example. For the sake of clarity, we will take up both examples we took up while explaining tree traversals.

In case of the jquery-simple DOM, the jQuery code to achieve filtering is

```
$('div').eq(0).css('background', '#efefef');
```

This code filters out all the divs that are at index 0 within the jQuery object that represents a div. Because the div itself is at index 0, the styling is applied to itself. The output is as shown in Figure 3-14.

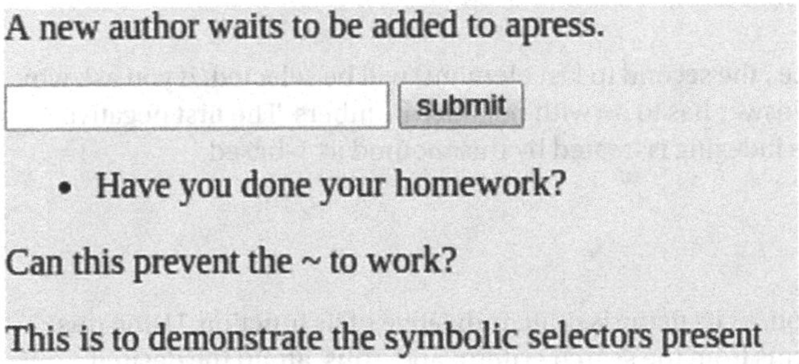

Figure 3-14. The .eq() method output

Now, considering the jquery-complex DOM example, let us try to apply some styling to some list element by first filtering it out. The jQuery code to achieve this functionality is

```
$('li').eq(2).css('color', 'seagreen');
```

Figure 3-15 shows the output.

A new reader waits to learn jQuery.

- Have you done your homework?
- Is it that you are having leisure time?
- Would you like to have challenges in life?
- Click here to know the solution.

If you liked this example, tell others. If not, tell us!

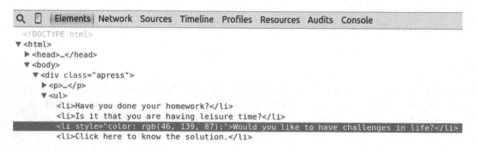

Figure 3-15. *The filtered result*

It is natural for you to ask what will happen if you pass negative numbers to this method. On passing a negative number, the search reverses the order of traversal and starts from the end. Thus, if you write

```
$('li').eq(-2).css('color', 'seagreen');
```

the element at index 2 from the last element (i.e., the second to last element) will be selected. If you ask why it was not the third from the last element, the answer has to do with negative numbers. The first negative number less than 0 is -1. Therefore, the reverse indexing is treated by this method as 1-based.

The .filter() Method

This method does not require much explanation, as its name is quite indicative of its function. Using this method, you can easily filter the desired elements from the search criteria and, thus, attain the desired result. The use of the `.filter()` method is better explained with a demonstration. Let us start with a jquery-simple example.

To add some styling to the div with the class attribute apress, you would use filter as in the following code:

```
$('div').filter('.apress').css({'display': 'block', 'border':'1px solid #aaa'});
```

The output would be like that in Figure 3-16.

A new author waits to be added to apress.

[   ] submit

- Have you done your homework?

Can this prevent the ~ to work?

This is to demonstrate the symbolic selectors present

Q □ | Elements | Network Sources Timeline Profiles Resources Audits Console

```
<!DOCTYPE html>
▼ <html>
  ▶ <head>…</head>
  ▼ <body>
    ▶ <div class="apress" style="display: block; border: 1px solid rgb(170, 170, 170);">
    …</div>
      <script src="//code.jquery.com/jquery-1.10.2.js"></script>
    ▶ <script type="text/javascript">…</script>
    </body>
  </html>
```

Figure 3-16. *The output of* `.filter()`

Considering a more complex usage of `.filter()` in the jquery-simple example, the jQuery code is as follows:

```
$('body').find('form').children().filter($('input[type=text]')).css({'display': 'block',
'border': '1px solid powderblue'});
```

This code

- Starts with the body element

- Finds the `form` element inside the body element

- Finds the children to the `form` element

- Filters all such children that have the type attribute as `text`

- Applies CSS styling to the filtered element

The output that would be produced is as shown in Figure 3-17.

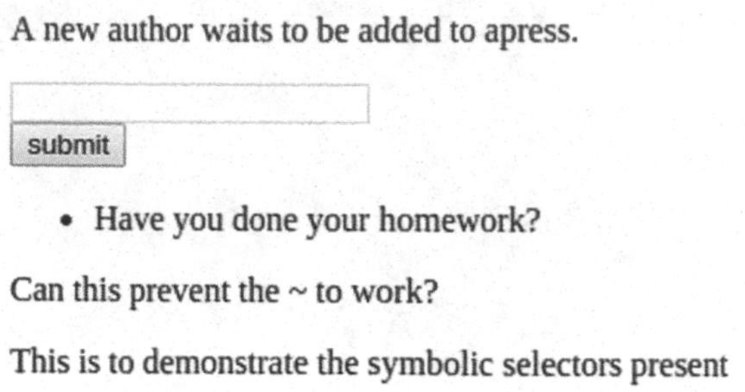

A new author waits to be added to apress.

submit

- Have you done your homework?

Can this prevent the ~ to work?

This is to demonstrate the symbolic selectors present

Figure 3-17. *The filtering result*

To illustrate another use of the .filter() method, we take up a jquery-complex example. The jQuery code to demonstrate this usage is

```
$('div').find('li').filter(function(index){
    return index == 1;
}).css({'font-family': 'serif', 'color': 'powderblue'});
```

The preceding code does the following:

1. Starts with a div element

2. Finds the li elements inside the div

3. Filters all the li elements thus found that have the index as 1

4. Applies CSS styling to the filtered elements

The code will produce the output shown in Figure 3-18.

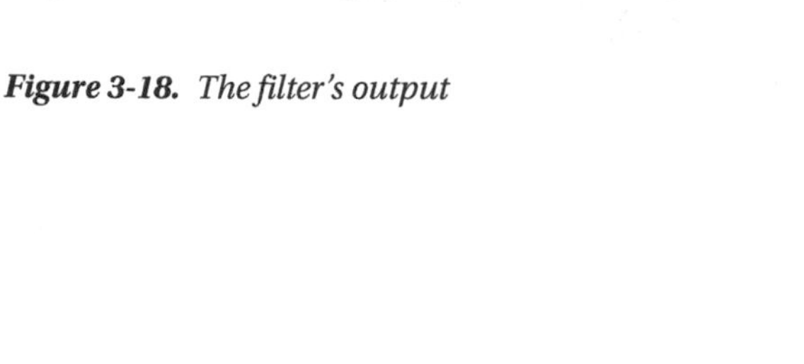

A new reader waits to learn jQuery.

- Have you done your homework?
- Is it that you are having leisure time?
- Would you like to have challenges in life?
- Click here to know the solution.

If you liked this example, tell others. If not, tell us!

Figure 3-18. *The filter's output*

The .first() Method

If you are familiar with the wrapping functions, this method is an appropriate example to demonstrate the same concept. What the method wraps is the .eq() function, with the index as the parameter and the passed value as 0.

With the jquery-simple example, the jQuery code to demonstrate the .first() method is

```
$('div').first().css('background', '#efefef');
```

The output produced is shown in Figure 3-19.

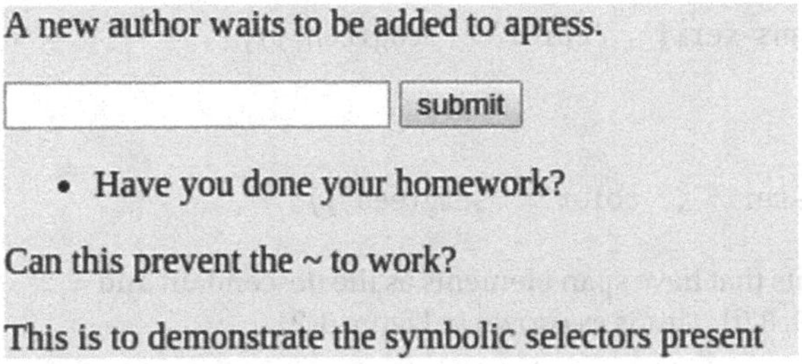

A new author waits to be added to apress.

[   ] submit

- Have you done your homework?

Can this prevent the ~ to work?

This is to demonstrate the symbolic selectors present

Figure 3-19. The output of the .first() method

You can compare this with the code example provided while demonstrating .eq(). You will find that the result is identical, if the code used is

```
$('div').eq(0).css('background', '#efefef');
```

The .last() Method

The .last() method also calls the .eq() method with -1 as the value passed on. As discussed, the number preceding 0 is -1, so this method selects the element at the last index inside the represented jQuery object. The jQuery code considering the example jquery-complex is

```
$('li').last().css('color', 'seagreen');
```

This produces the output shown Figure 3-20.

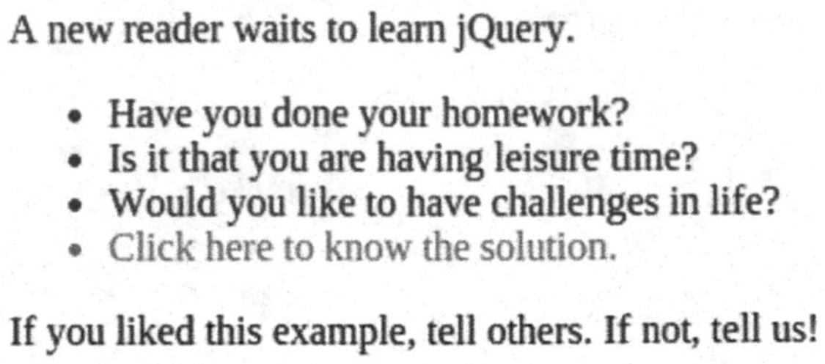

A new reader waits to learn jQuery.

- Have you done your homework?
- Is it that you are having leisure time?
- Would you like to have challenges in life?
- Click here to know the solution.

If you liked this example, tell others. If not, tell us!

Figure 3-20. The output of .last()

Again, you will notice that the output is identical to that produced by the `.eq()` method, with the parameter value as -1. Thus, the output will match the output generated, by using the following jQuery code:

```
$('li').eq(-1).css('color', 'seagreen');
```

The .has() Method

The `.has()` method is used to filter elements based on the descendants contained in it. The descendants are specified in the form of a string or jQuery object. So, to demonstrate this method, you can use the jQuery code with the jquery-simple example, as follows:

```
$('p').has($('span')).css({'font-family': 'sans-serif', 'color': 'seagreen'});
```

Or this code

```
$('p').has('span').css({'font-family': 'sans-serif', 'color': 'seagreen'});
```

would set the font family of all the paragraph elements that have span elements as the descendant and would also set the font color to sea green (rgb[46, 139, 87]). This is as shown in Figure 3-21.

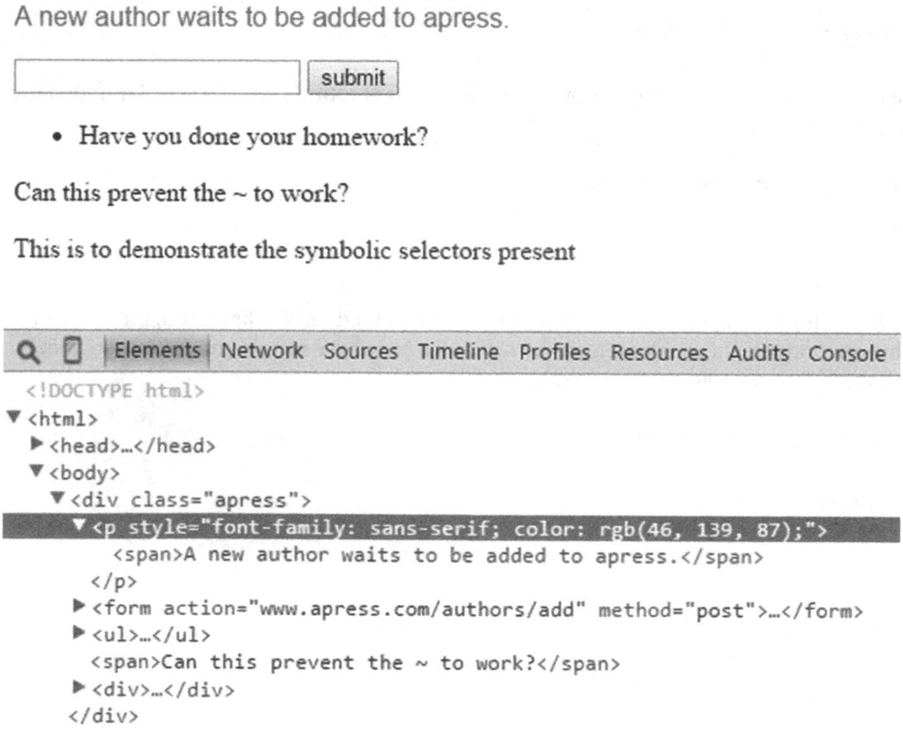

A new author waits to be added to apress.

submit

- Have you done your homework?

Can this prevent the ~ to work?

This is to demonstrate the symbolic selectors present

```
Q  🔲  | Elements | Network  Sources  Timeline  Profiles  Resources  Audits  Console
  <!DOCTYPE html>
▼ <html>
  ▶ <head>…</head>
  ▼ <body>
    ▼ <div class="apress">
      ▼ <p style="font-family: sans-serif; color: rgb(46, 139, 87);">
          <span>A new author waits to be added to apress.</span>
        </p>
      ▶ <form action="www.apress.com/authors/add" method="post">…</form>
      ▶ <ul>…</ul>
        <span>Can this prevent the ~ to work?</span>
      ▶ <div>…</div>
      </div>
```

Figure 3-21. *The effect of* `.has()`

The .is() Method

The jQuery framework provides a method .is() to filter elements, provided they match a given criteria. So, to this .is() method, you can pass a string representing a valid selector expression or a jQuery object, or even some function returning Boolean values. To avoid confusion, let us quickly jump to the demonstrations supporting the aforementioned cases. Let us take up the jquery-simple example and the following jQuery code:

```
if($('span').parent().is('p')){
    $('span').parent('p').css({'font-family': 'sans-serif', 'color':'#999'});
}
```

This code will assign CSS styling to all the p elements that are parent to span elements.
Next, we take up the code for the jquery-complex example.

```
if($('div').children().is('p')){
    $('p').children('span').css({'font-family': 'serif', 'color': 'turquoise'});
}
```

This code checks if the div contains some children that have a *p*, and assigns some CSS styling to those children of the p element that are span. This code produces the output shown in Figure 3-22.

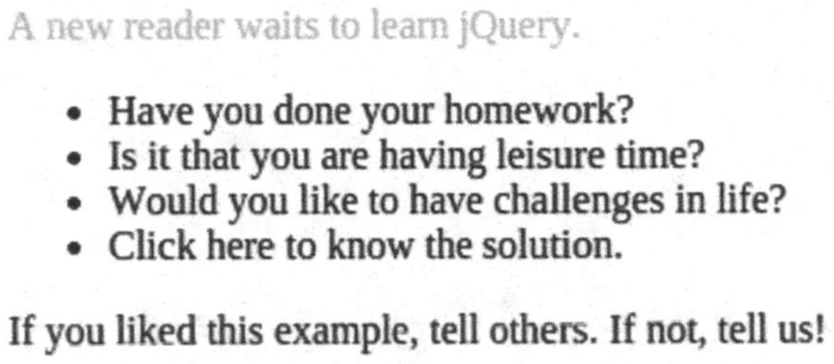

A new reader waits to learn jQuery.

- Have you done your homework?
- Is it that you are having leisure time?
- Would you like to have challenges in life?
- Click here to know the solution.

If you liked this example, tell others. If not, tell us!

Figure 3-22. The .is() method's output

Considering the jquery-complex example again, let us look at the following jQuery code:

```
var isFirstChild = $('ul').is(function(){
    if($('ul').children().length == 4)
        return true;
    else
        return false;
});

if(isFirstChild){
    alert("The UL is a large family with 4 children!");
} else {
    alert("The UL can have more children!");
}
```

When you load the page containing the HTML, the browser will alert a message to your screen, such as "The UL is a large family with 4 children!" because the ul element has, in fact, four li items.

The .not() Method

This method provided by jQuery eliminates (filters out) some (un)desired elements from the target element. The resulting element is a new jQuery object containing the required elements. To demonstrate this, let's take up jquery-simple example once again. The resulting code would be

```
$('div').not('.apress').css({'font-family': 'sans-serif', 'color': 'seagreen'});
```

The code finds all the divs in the DOM tree that do not have the class attribute apress and applies some CSS styling to the resulting set of divs.

The code produces the output as shown in Figure 3-23.

Figure 3-23. *The output of the .not() method*

Summary

With this, we conclude this chapter. In it, you have learned how DOM is used, as well as how you can employ the jQuery framework and the methods available with it. This chapter furthered your understanding of the use of selectors in jQuery by guiding you through the employment of the same selectors, using CSS. In this chapter, you learned how you can cache the jQuery selectors, thereby enhancing script performance. The chapter signed off by explaining in greater depth the technique of filtering by using jQuery, with a handful of demonstrations. The next chapter will teach you how to use jQuery to manipulate the same DOM that you learned to traverse in this chapter.

CHAPTER 4

■ ■ ■

DOM Manipulation with jQuery

In the previous chapter, we discussed traversing the Document Object Model (DOM) with jQuery, and now you have a better idea of the power of jQuery. This chapter will help you to understand the DOM manipulation, to make web pages more efficient. By the end of this chapter, you will be familiar with the following:

- Editing appearance with jQuery CSS methods
- Editing/changing an element's attributes, contents, and position
- Creating and inserting new DOM elements
- Removing and cloning DOM elements
- Working with dimensions

Editing Appearance with jQuery CSS Methods

The CSS methods offered by jQuery provide the control to add/remove CSS classes to/from HTML nodes. Having said that, instead of adjusting the HTML element's style by writing extra lines of CSS code (sometimes inline, as well), you can do this by putting these CSS methods to work. It is easy to change the style of a web page dynamically, but for that, you must be familiar with some of the numerous CSS tricks available with jQuery.

Let us start with the signature `.css()` function.

```
$('jQuery selector').css({"css property name":"css property value"});
```

So, if you would want to change the text color of a paragraph element to blue, for example, you can do that by writing the following code:

```
$('p').css({"color":"blue"});
```

The `.css()` method is a convenient way to set some style or obtain one or more style properties for selected elements. The important thing to note here is that the same `.css()` method can return or set some specific CSS property, depending on its usage. The change in the behavior results from the values that are passed.

Obtaining CSS Properties

To obtain the value of a specified CSS property, you have to use the following signature:

```
.css(propertyName);
```

It can only take one CSS property, and if you want to return an array of one or more CSS properties, you can use *propertyNames* such as

```
.css(propertyNames);
```

For example, to retrieve all of the four rendered border-width values of an element represented by the selector `elem`, you could use the following code:

```
$( elem ).css([ "borderTopWidth", "borderRightWidth", "borderBottomWidth", "borderLeftWidth" ]).
```

■ **Note**   Passing an array of CSS properties to `.css()` will result in an object of property-value pairs. This is available as of jQuery 1.9.

Setting CSS Properties

We stated that the jQuery framework provides a convenient method, `.css()`, which works to set the CSS property on the elements matched by the selector expression. So, for that purpose, you have to make use of the following signature of the `.css()` method:

```
.css(propertyName,value);
```

The two arguments that the `.css()` accepts are described briefly as

propertyName: Name of CSS property and type is string.

value: A value that you must set. The type is string or Number.

Using this information, let us make an attempt to change the background color of a `div` element. The HTML code that we provide for the demonstration is as shown:

```
<!DOCTYPE html>
<html>
<head>
<script src="http://ajax.googleapis.com/ajax/libs/jquery/1.11.1/jquery.min.js"></script>
<script>
$(document).ready(function(){
    $("button").click(function(){
        $("p").css("background-color","red");
    });
});
</script>
</head>
```

```
<body>
<h2>Here Are the Visuals</h2>
<p style="background-color:#ff0000">This is a red p.</p>
<p style="background-color:#00ff00">This is a green p.</p>
<p style="background-color:#0000ff">This is a blue p.</p>
<p>This is a paragraph. Did you notice the change in color? Click on the button to see the
change.</p>
<button>Set background-color of p elements</button>
</body>
</html>
```

In this example, we have used jQuery from the Google library, though you are free to choose from any other content delivery network (CDN), if required. The code is simple to understand, as you now have a basic knowledge of jQuery.

On the click event of button, we are setting the CSS property on all the p elements. Thus, when you click the button, it will make all the paragraphs red. Figure 4-1 shows the output of the mentioned code.

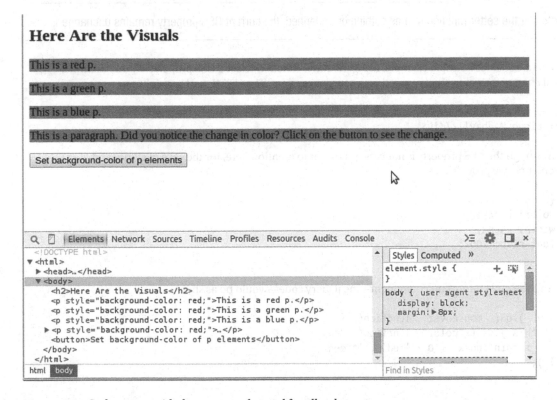

Figure 4-1. *Code output with the property changed for all p elements*

Setting CSS Properties Using Calculations

We have been stating that the jQuery framework provides a very convenient method with which to manipulate the CSS property for the HTML elements. Having said that, this same method, .css(), with another signature, can be made to set the CSS property in DOM elements. It was introduced in version 1.4. The signature of the .css() method in the current context is as shown following, with a brief explanation of the arguments it accepts:

.css(propertyName, function);

> propertyName: The CSS property name to set or change

> function: A function that returns the value to be set as the CSS property. This function receives the index of the element in the set, and whichever value is returned from it, the CSS property is set to that. Also, this represents the current element that has invoked the .css().

■ **Note**   If the setter function returns nothing or undefined, the current CSS property remains unchanged.

Let us consider a simple example, using the setter function to set a CSS property. In this example, we will change the color of a div to red on a mouseover event. The HTML part is as follows:

```
<div>Just roll the mouse over this text to see the color change.</div>
<div> Bingo Madhav!!</div>
```

Although the CSS property is not very important to mention here, for the sake of clarity and convenience, we provide it as

```
div {
    color: black;
    width: 250px;
    font-size: 20px;
}
```

And the most important component—the jQuery code—would be as shown

```
$( "div" ).on( "mouseover", function() {
    $( this ).css( "color", function(index){
        return index == 0 ? 'red' : 'green';
    } );
});
```

The output of this operation would be a change in the color of the text contained inside the div element to red, because there is only a single div when it is being referenced. This is to say that out of the two div elements provided in the example, the text color of that div on which you would hover your mouse would change. Because at that instant, there would just be a single element, the value of the parameter index would be 0, and hence, the function would return red. Thus, the CSS color property would change to red. You can go ahead and play with the code at the fiddle: http://jsfiddle.net/mukund002/5fufr1u4/2/.

Table 4-1 summarizes the various parameters that can be passed to the .css() method to change the CSS properties inside the rendered HTML page.

Table 4-1. *Tabular Representation of Parameters Accepted by the CSS Setter Methods*

Parameter	Description
Property	Specifies a CSS property, such as color, font size, etc.
Value	Specifies the value of a CSS property, such as "red", "1.2 em", etc.
function(index,value)	Specifies the function that returns the new CSS property

Setting Multiple CSS Properties

There are numerous use cases wherein more than one CSS property has to be set. Till this point in time, if you are asked to do so, a very natural approach for you would be to perform a repeated function call to the .css() method with single property-name and property-value pairs. But the jQuery framework has a provision that makes setting multiple CSS properties and values easier than you might think. The following signature should make this clear:

```
.css({property1:value1,property2:value2,property3:value3,...});
```

Again, it is time to show you a simple example to make the usage easier to understand. Let us attempt to change some paragraph text color at the click of a button element. The essential HTML required for the example is as follows:

```
<script src="http://ajax.googleapis.com/ajax/libs/jquery/1.11.1/jquery.min.js"></script>

<body>

<button>Set multiple CSS properties for all p elements</button>
<p>This is a first paragraph.</p>
<p>This is another paragraph.</p>

</body>

jQuery:

$(document).ready(function(){
    $("button").click(function(){
        $("p").css({
            "color":"white",
            "background-color":"#4679BD",
            "font-family":"Arial",
            "font-size":"20px",
            "padding":"5px",
            "margin":"5px"
        });
    });
});
```

The code loads the jQuery from Google CDN and then simply loads the HTML, which looks like Figure 4-2.

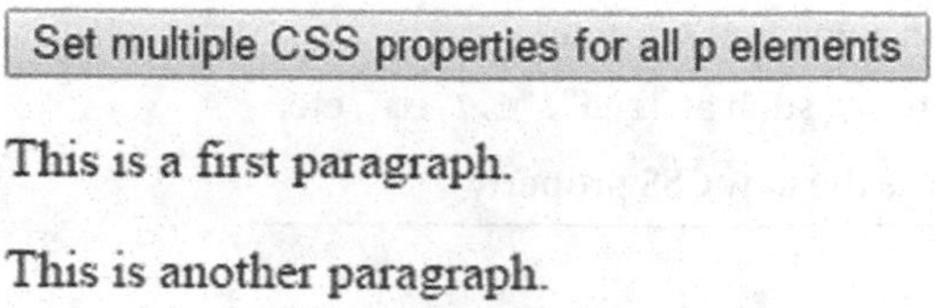

Set multiple CSS properties for all p elements

This is a first paragraph.

This is another paragraph.

Figure 4-2. HTML output before the code has run

Now run the code. Click the button, and you will see the output, which looks like Figure 4-3.

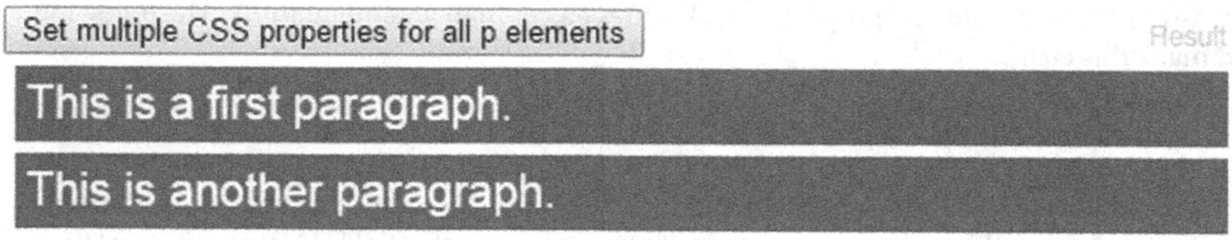

Set multiple CSS properties for all p elements

This is a first paragraph.

This is another paragraph.

Figure 4-3. Output of the code

■ **Note** You can also try it yourself on jsfiddle.net. Go to this URL to test: http://jsfiddle.net/mukund002/6k36eaoL/.

Editing/Changing an Element's Attributes, Contents, and Position

jQuery makes it easy to edit an element's attributes, contents, and position, by providing a number of methods that serve the purpose. It is quite important to note that the attributes of HTML elements are quite useful in developing a satisfactory user experience as well. The title attribute, for example, can be used as a tool tip when the proper CSS styling is applied to it. So, using the methods provided by the jQuery framework, you can modify the attributes, the contents inside the element, and the position of the target element.

Editing Attributes

Before we move on to the topic, let us consider what an attribute is when it comes to HTML. Attributes are extra information that is attached to the HTML element and serves various purposes, depending on the attribute. For example, the alt attribute to the image tag serves the purpose of providing an alternate text, which helps users to see a text when the image is not fully loaded on the browser.

The `attr()` method provided by the jQuery framework is used to set or return attributes and values of selected elements. When this method is used to return the attribute value, it returns the value of the *first* matched element. When this method is used to set attribute values, it sets one or more attribute/value pairs for the set of matched elements.

The signature for the `attr()` method is as follows, with a list containing its salient features:

`.attr(`*`attributeName`*`)`

- This method is used to get the value of an attribute for the first element in a set of matched ones.

- The return type is *string*, and `attributeName` is the name to get.

- This method can be called directly on a jQuery object and can be easily chained to other jQuery methods.

- `.attr()` methods also take advantage of browser compatibility. They eliminate browser compatibility issues, even if the values of some attributes are reported to be inconsistent across different versions of the same browser.

■ **Caution** If you are still using IE 6, 7, or 8, you should avoid attempting to change the type of attribute (or property) of an input element that is in an HTML document. This will result in an error. This is not an issue with new browsers, however.

Before we move to the next signature of the `.attr()` method, it is important to understand the `.prop()` method, as it regards changing DOM properties. Before jQuery 1.6, the `.attr()` method sometimes took a property value when retrieving some attributes, which could sometimes result in inconsistent behavior.

To overcome this inconsistent behavior, jQuery 1.6 comes with the `.prop()` method, which provides a way to retrieve property values, while `.attr()` retrieves the attributes. For example, if we want to retrieve and change the DOM properties, such as checked, selected, or disabled stage, we have to use the `.prop()` method. Let us look at an example to display the checked attribute and property of a check box.

```
//HTML
<input id="chk" type="checkbox" checked="checked">
    <label for="chk"><b>Click here to check me</b></label>
<div></div>
```

```
//jQuery
```

```
<script>
$( "input" )
    .change(function() {
        var $input = $( this );
        $( "div" ).html( ".attr( 'checked' ): <b>" + $input.attr( "checked" ) +
        "</b><br><br>" +
            ".prop( 'checked' ): <b>" + $input.prop( "checked" ) + "</b>");
    })
    .change();
<script>
```

The result will show you how `.prop()` works. It will return a Boolean value. Try it yourself: `http://jsfiddle.net/mukund002/veebLu2p/`.

There are a few more signatures of the `.attr()` that are useful in some cases.

`.attr(attributeName,value)`

- This method is used to set one or more attributes for a set of matched elements. The type is string for attributeName.

- The value parameter sets the value for attribute, and it can take string as well as number.

`.attr(attributeName,function)`

- This is useful when setting multiple attributes or using the values returned by the function.

`.attr(attribute)`

- This is useful when you set an object of an attribute-value pair.

- Return type is a plain object.

Editing Contents

When you want to play with the contents in jQuery, you have to play with the jQuery `.text()`, `.html()`, and `.position()` methods. We will go through each one in the order.

.text()

The jQuery `.text()` method is used to set or return the text contents of selected elements, including descendants. When you use this method to return the content, it returns all the matched elements, and HTML markup will be removed.

Starting with the getter version of the `.text()` method, when you use this method to get the content, the signature is as follows, with a list containing the salient features for the same:

`.text()`

- This method doesn't take any parameter or arguments.

- The result of the `text()` method is a string containing combined text of all elements. The result may vary in different browsers, due to the variation of the HTML parser. The variation may be in the new line or whitespace only.

For example, consider the following HTML:

```
<div class="container">
    <div class="apress">Authors are</div>
    <ul>
        <li>Kumar</li>
        <li>Chaudhary</li>
    </ul>
</div>
```

To see the output of the .text() method, we will use

```
alert($("div.container").text());
```

The result would be something like

```
Authors are
    Kumar
    Chaudhary
```

You can have a look and try out some simple experiments with this code at the fiddle located here: http://jsfiddle.net/mukund002/9h9hsndd/1/.

Now we take up the setter version of the .text() method, as the other signatures for the .text() method. How to use it is as follows, with a list of its salient features:

```
.text(textcontent)
```

- This method is used to set the content of all the matched elements in the set.

- It accepts number, string, or boolean.

■ **Note** If you pass any special character into the arguments, it will be replaced by the appropriate HTML entity.

While working with the text contents contained inside HTML elements in jQuery, it is important to mention, and interesting to note, that the .html() and the .val() methods will also serve similar purposes.

.html()

The .html() method sets or returns the content (the JavaScript equivalent of innerHTML) of the matched elements. When you use it to return content, it will return the contents of the first matched elements. In cases where you use this method to set the content, it overwrites the content of all matched elements.

As with the functionality, the signature for this method is very similar to that of the .text() method. Following, it is as shown, in addition to a salient feature of the method:

```
.html()
```

- This is the first version of the .html() method that does not accept any arguments, and this method is not available on XML documents. This difference is worth taking note of.

The important thing to bear in mind is that if the selector expression matches more than one element, only the first match with HTML contents will be returned. For example, we have the HTML code for which we need the div contents to be retrieved. The code has first div with class="container", and the other has class="apress". This is as follows:

```
<div class="container">
    <div class="apress">Welcome Readers</div>
</div>
```

The jQuery code to demonstrate the `.html()` method is as follows:

```
$("div.container").html();
```

The result would look like

```
<div class="apress">Welcome Readers</div>
```

Similarly, we can use other `.html` signatures, as in the following, which is succeeded by a list citing the purpose of each of the signatures:

`.html(content)`

- Unlike `.html()`, in this signature, the argument is mandatory.

- This `.html(content)` method is used to set the new contents for selected elements and can contain HTML tags.

  `.html(function(index,currentcontent))`

- This method is also used to set the new content, using a function that returns the new content for selected elements.

- `index` returns the index position, and `currentcontent` returns the current HTML content of selected elements.

■ **Tip** If you want to set or return the text content of selected elements, use the `.text()` method instead of `.html()`. This is recommended when HTML content is required.

.position()

While making changes in the text contents, sometime you might need to change the position of some HTML elements as well. For this, the jQuery framework makes provisions for you to use the `.position()` method. Let us consider an example, to make the idea behind using the `.position()` method clearer. Suppose, you have to open a pop up on the web page, and you want to define the position of the pop-up window in the center of the web page. Among the many approaches available to you for showing the pop up in the center, all will have one thing in common: you will make use of the x axis and the y axis.

Having said that, have a look at the way the `.position()` can be written. The signature for `.position()` is as shown, with a list containing the salient features of the method following.

`.position()`

- The `position()` method allows users to retrieve the current position in a set of the matched elements.

- This method returns an object with two properties `top` and `left`.

■ **Note**   jQuery does not return the position of hidden elements. It is also important to note that it will not return the correct coordinates if the page is zoomed (in or out) by the user.

We will now offer an example, which will show us the position (top, left) of a selected element. The HTML part for the example is as follows:

```
<p>This paragraph returns has some X and Y coordinates</p>
<button>Show me the co-ordinates</button>
```

The jQuery code for the same is as shown:

```
$("button").click(function(){
    var position = $("p").position();
    alert("Top: " + position.top + " Left: " + position.left);
});
```

As you can see in the example, we have one `<p>` element and a `button` element. We have called an `alert` on the `click` event of the button element, which returns the position of the `<p>` element. The result will return the position in terms of Top and Left. The output would be Top: 0, Left: 8.

■ **Note**   You can see the resulting position in the fiddle located at `http://jsfiddle.net/mukund002/m2x4kw70/`.

Creating and Inserting New DOM Elements

From all that you've learned so far, you know that it is easy to manipulate DOM elements with the rich library provided by the jQuery framework. Now, we will look into the possibility of creating and inserting new elements into some existing DOM. Here, we would like to underline the fact that creating a new DOM element is quite easy with JavaScript, and, hence, we will compare the way it is done in JavaScript and the way it would be done using jQuery.

Starting off with JavaScript, we use the `document.createElement()` function to create a new element. For example, if you want to create a new `div` element and store the reference in some variable, you use the following:

```
var div= document.createElement('div');
```

In this example, we have created a new element only, but we have not inserted the new element into the document. To insert this new element at the end of the body tag, you have to use the `.appendChild()` function, and the two objectives (creating a new element and inserting it into the existing DOM) in that case is as follows:

```
var div =document.createElement('div');
document.body.appendChild(div);
```

Using jQuery, we will show you that DOM manipulation is just as easy. There is no need to create an element separately. You just have to call the .append() method, as follows:

```
$('body').append('div');
```

Here, the code creates a new element and inserts it just before the closing body tag, and you will notice that using the jQuery method has saved us from writing one line of code as well!

The signature for .append() goes like this:

```
.append(content[,content])
.append(function(index,content))
```

- The .append() function is used to insert the specified content at the end of each element.

- The content in the first signature could be of type htmlString, Element, or an array of objects.

- This method is useful when you have to insert the content as the last child in the element.

■ **Tip** To insert the content as the first child in the element, use the .prepend() method.

.append() vs. .appendTo()

Before we move on to other methods for inserting DOM elements, let's consider the difference between .append() and .appendTo(), another method provided by the jQuery framework that also enables you to insert elements in some existing DOM.

The .append() and .appendTo() methods perform the same task, and the output will be same as well. However, the signature differs with the placement of the content and selector. In .append(), the selector comes first, while with .appendTo(), the content comes first, then the selector expression. Let us look at the two signatures, using the following HTML, to understand the difference:

```
<div class="apress"> It is a container area.</div>
```

For .append(), use the following:

```
$('.apress').append("<div class="author"> It is a container</div>");
```

Or, for .appendTo(), use this:

```
$("<div class="""author> It is a new container</div>").appendTo('.apress');
```

The output in both the cases will be the same and will be the HTML.

```
<div class="apress">It is a container
  <div class="author">It is a new container</div>
</div>
```

Inserting New Elements in Specific Locations

Now it's time to move on to other methods for inserting DOM elements. There will be cases in which you want to insert the new element before and after some specific element, or you have to insert the element, say, to the third or fourth index. In those cases, you have methods such as .before() and .after().

Let us look at the signatures for before() and after(), and then we will see some real-world challenges based on those methods.

.before(*content*[,*content*])

- The .before() method is used to insert the content before each element in the set of matched elements.

- The content type you insert can be one or more additional DOM elements, arrays of elements, or an HTML string or jQuery object.

For example, consider an example using the following HTML:

```
<div class="container">
<div class="apress">Authors<div>
<div>
```

If you use .before() like this:

```
$('.apress').before("<p>How are you?</p>");
```

you get the following result:

```
How are you? Authors
```

On the other hand, the .after() method inserts the contents *after* the set of matched elements. The signature for .after() is the same as that for the .before() method.

If you take the same HTML example using the .after() method,

```
$('.apress').after("<p>How are you?</p>");
```

the result would be

```
Authors How are you?
```

Putting the Methods to Work

Now that you have some understanding of a few methods, it's time to see a real example, in which we'll create a new element and then insert it at the end of the content or before the content. Let's take a look first at the HTML. Then, we'll show the CSS, after which we'll examine the jQuery in a little more detail.

Following is the HTML code to look at:

```
<div class="content-holder">
    <form method="post">
        <fieldset id="payment-slip">
            <legend>CREATING A NEW ELEMENT</legend>
            <div class="row">
```

```
            <div class="large-4 column">
                Upload Slip 1 :
            </div>
            <div class="large-4 column">
                <input type="file" name="Slip1">
            </div>
            <div class="large-4 column">
                <input type="submit" value="Upload">
            </div>
        </div>
    </fieldset>
    <div class="text-right"><a href="javascript:void(o);" class="js-add-new-slip">+ Add
New Slip</a></div>
    <hr>
    <fieldset>
        <legend>inserting HTML elements at the end of the selected element</legend>
        <div class="paragraph-container">
            <p class="paragraph-1">
                Paragraph 1: <br><br>
                Lorem Ipsum is simply dummy text of the printing and typesetting industry.
            </p>
        </div>
    </fieldset>
    <div class="text-right"><a href="javascript:void(o);" class="js-new-paragraph">+
Add New Paragraph</a></div>
    <hr>
    <fieldset>
        <legend>inserting HTML elements at the beginning of the selected element</legend>
        <div class="paragraph-container2">
            <p class="Nparagraph1">
                Paragraph 1: <br><br>
                Lorem Ipsum is simply dummy text of the printing and typesetting industry.
            </p>
        </div>
    </fieldset>
    <div class="text-right"><a href="javascript:void(o);" class="js-new-paragraph2">+
Insert Before Selected ELEMENT</a></div>

    <hr>
    <fieldset>
        <legend>inserting HTML elements after the selected element</legend>

        <p class="After-paragraph1">
            Paragraph 1: <br><br>
            Lorem Ipsum is simply dummy text of the printing and typesetting industry.
        </p>

    </fieldset>
```

```
<div class="text-right"><a href="javascript:void(o);" class="js-after-paragraph">+
Insert After Selected ELEMENT</a></div>

</form>

</div>
```

Because this is pure HTML code, we won't provide an explanation other than to say that this would generate the HTML view. Now, some CSS code will be shown, and like HTML, we are not going to explain it.

```
<style>
    *{
        box-sizing: border-box;
        font-family:Arial;
    }
    .content-holder{
        border:solid 1px #ccc;
        border-radius:5px;
        padding:10px;
        max-width:778px;
        margin:0 auto;
        overflow:hidden;
    }
    h5{
        border-bottom:solid 2px #ccc;
        margin-bottom:10px;
        padding:10px 0;
    }

    .column{
        float:left;
        padding:0 10px 10px 10px;
    }
    .large-4{
        width:33.333%
    }
    .text-right{
        text-align:right;
    }
</style>
```

Now that we are done with the view part of the code, it's time to perform some action. In the following jQuery, you would do the actual task of inserting elements into the DOM.

```
<script>
    (function(){
        var Slipcount = 0,Paragraphcount=0,NParagraphcount=0,aftercount=0;
        $('.js-add-new-slip').on('click',function(){
            Slipcount += 1;
            if(Slipcount<=2){
                var newSlip = '<div class="row">' +
```

```
                  '<div class="large-4 column">Upload Slip '+parseInt(Slipcount+1)+': </div>'+
                  '<div class="large-4 column">'+
                  '<input type="file" name="Slip'+parseInt(Slipcount+1)+'">'+
                  '</div>'+
                  '<div class="large-4 column">'+
                  '<input type="submit" value="Upload">'+
                  '</div>'+
                  '</div>';
            $('#payment-slip').append(newSlip);
        }else{
            alert('You have reached the maximum number of uploads, please refresh
            your browser');
        }
    });
    $('.js-new-paragraph').on('click',function(){
        Paragraphcount += 1;
        if(Paragraphcount<=2){
            var newParagraph = '<p class="paragraph-'+parseInt(Paragraphcount+1)+'">' +
                  'Paragraph '+parseInt(Paragraphcount+1)+':<br><br>'+
                  'It is a long established fact that a reader will be more interested in
                  having illustrations in text explanations.'+
                  '</p>';
            $(newParagraph).appendTo('.paragraph-container');
        }else{
            alert('You have performed the maximum number of uploads, please refresh your'+
                  'browser');
        }
    });
    $('.js-new-paragraph2').on('click',function(){

        NParagraphcount += 1;
        if(NParagraphcount<=1){
            var NParagraph = '<p class="Nparagraph-'+parseInt(NParagraphcount+1)+'">' +
                  'Paragraph '+parseInt(NParagraphcount+1)+':<br><br>'+
                  'This paragraph is coming before selected elements'+
                  '</p>';

            $('.Nparagraph1').before(NParagraph);

        }else{
            alert('You have reached the maximum limit, please refresh your browser');
        }
    });
    $('.js-after-paragraph').on('click',function(){

        aftercount += 1;
        if(aftercount<=1){
            var afterParagraph = '<p class="After-paragraph-
            '+parseInt(aftercount+1)+'">' +
                  'Paragraph '+parseInt(aftercount+1)+':<br><br>'+
                  'This paragraph is coming after selected elements'+
                  '</p>';
```

```
        $('.After-paragraph1').after(afterParagraph);

    }else{
        alert('You have reached the maximum limit, please refresh your browser');
    }
});

})(jQuery);
</script>
```

What we have learned previously in this section is used in the preceding example. In the first paragraph, we are creating a new element, and the important code used to do so is based on the use of the `.append()` method. The code is ensuring that if two elements are created, a third element will not be allowed to be added as another element. In the remaining part of the code, the `.after()` and the `.before()` methods are put to use for the purpose of explanation. We recommend that you try out this code example in your system or even on jsfiddle. The code is located at `http://jsfiddle.net/mukund002/Ldj2sjL9/4/`.

Removing and Cloning DOM Elements

In the previous section, we discussed creating a new DOM element, inserting the DOM element at the beginning of selected elements, and performing the insertions in the DOM at random positions. Sometimes, you need to remove or clone the DOM elements. Let us take a case where this can be useful. Suppose you are working to achieve a functionality whereby on the click of some add button, you have to add a full row, and on click of a delete button, you must remove a full row.

In this situation, you should know that removing and cloning would be a better approach for you. Looking more closely into the problem statement, you will observe that when you are required to add a new row, you can duplicate some already existing row. This is where cloning comes into the picture. Similarly, when you have to delete a row, you must remove the row. Having said that, if you have a working knowledge of the `.clone()` and the `.remove()` methods provided by the jQuery framework, you can go on the hunt!

Here, we will follow a step-by-step approach to help you to learn about the two methods. However, before removing the DOM element, we will show you how to clone it.

First, let's consider the `.clone()` method.

- The `.clone()` method is used to make a deep copy of selected elements. Deep copy means it includes child nodes, text, and attributes.

- The signature is simple and takes a boolean value, i.e., `true` or `false`.

- By default, it takes `false`, which means event handlers should not be copied. In case you have to do that, pass the value as `true`.

- Using the `.clone()` method, you can also modify the cloned element or their content before inserting them into the DOM.

■ **Note** You should avoid using `.clone()` whenever possible, because in some cases, it has the side effect of producing a duplicate `id` attribute if the source element that you cloned contained some `id` attribute. However, if the use is unavoidable, you should use a `class` attribute as an identifier instead of the `id` attribute. A class can be duplicated, but an `id` attribute cannot.

We will take a simple example to illustrate the `.clone()` and `.remove()` methods. But before that, it is the time to consider the `.remove()` method.

The `.remove()` method is used to remove the set of matched elements (including all the text and nodes) from the filtered set. When you use this method, it also removes the data and events associated with that element. The signature is

```
$(selector).remove();
```

Let us take a simple example to understand how this and the `.clone()` methods work. You must delete all the paragraphs from a `div` such as the following one:

```
<div class="apress-container">
    <p>This is a paragraph</p>
    <p>This is second paragraph</p>
    <button class="remove">Remove The Paragraphs</button>
    <button class="add">Clone The Paragraphs</button>
<div>
```

If you write a simple code to delete both paragraphs, you can use the `.remove()` method, as shown following:

```
$('button.remove').on('click',function(){
    $('p').remove();
});
```

Similarly, the code for the `.clone()` method can be written as

```
$('button.add).on('click', function(){
    $('p').clone();
});
```

The result would be very simple. It will show a button, and on the `click` event, the paragraph is removed.

■ **Note** If you want to remove the element without removing data and event, then use the `.detach()` method, and if you only want to remove the content of the selected element, you can use the `.empty()` method. For curious readers, the jQuery official reference is always there. You can read more about the `.detach()` and the `.empty()` methods at `https://api.jquery.com/detach/` and `https://api.jquery.com/empty/`, respectively.

You are now familiar with the signature and use of the `.clone()` and `.remove()` methods. It's now time to carry out an assignment. Suppose you are asked to develop a web page with the option to add and delete rows, and you have the stipulated requirement that it must be completed using jQuery. Here is where your knowledge of jQuery will enter the picture.

First of all, you must create a page with a few elements added and have a button for each, to add and delete the rows. We will go with the code first, and then we will take up the explanations. Let us start with the HTML code, as follows:

```html
<div class="content-holder">

    <div class="apress-container">
        <div class="column"><h4>Add New Candidate</h4>
            <hr>
        </div>
        <div id="callable-row">
            <div class="row">
                <div class="large-4 column">
                    <input name="first-name" type="text" placeholder="First Name">
                </div>
                <div class="large-4 column">
                    <input name="last-name" type="text" placeholder="Last Name">
                </div>
                <div class="large-4 column">
                    <input name="email" type="email" placeholder="Email">
                </div>
            </div>
        </div>

    </div>

    <div class="row lblca">
        <div class="large-4 column ">
            <a href="javascript:void(0);" class="js-add-row">+ Add New Row</a>
        </div>
        <div class="large-4 column">
            <a href="javascript:void(0);" class="js-remove-row">- Delete Row</a>
        </div>
    </div>
</div>
```

You can use the preceding code to generate your HTML page. Now that you have added the HTML, it is time to make this page look slightly better. We will use CSS to beautify our web page.

```css
<style>
    .lblca {
        overflow: hidden;
    }

    .row {
        width: 660px;
        margin: 0 auto;
        clear: both;
    }
```

```css
.column {
    width: 100%;
    float: left;
    padding: 0 10px 10px 10px;
}

.large-4 {
    width: 200px
}

.content-holder {
    padding: 10px;
    border: solid 1px #ccc;
    border-radius: 5px;
    max-width: 680px;
    margin: 0 auto;
}

.content-holder input {
    border: solid 1px #ccc;
    border-radius: 3px;
    font: normal 14px/1.5rem "Trebuchet Ms", Arial;
    width: 100%;
    padding: 2px 8px;

}
</style>
```

Now it's time to see the actual jQuery in action. The following jQuery code is what enables us to add and remove rows:

```html
<script src="http://ajax.googleapis.com/ajax/libs/jquery/1.11.1/jquery.min.js"></script>
<script>
    $('.js-add-row').on('click', function () {
        $('.apress-container').append($('#callable-row').html());

    });
    $('.js-remove-row').on('click', function () {
        var LastSiblings = $('#callable-row').siblings('.row:last-child');
        if (LastSiblings.length != 0) {
            LastSiblings.remove();
        } else {
            alert('Please Add New Row First');
        }
    });
</script>
```

We have used Google CDN to point jQuery; you may use any CDN of your choice or include the jQuery library as of your convenience.

Figure 4-4 shows the output screen for the preceding jQuery.

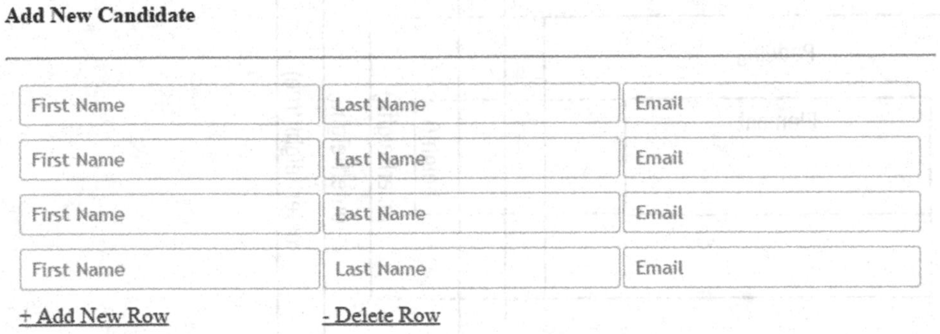

Add New Candidate

First Name	Last Name	Email
First Name	Last Name	Email
First Name	Last Name	Email
First Name	Last Name	Email

<u>+ Add New Row</u>   <u>- Delete Row</u>

Figure 4-4. *Example showing cloning and removing elements*

If you want to see the working demo or want to try, go to the following URL:
`http://jsfiddle.net/mukund002/t6tdp59v/1/`.

Working with Dimensions

Dimensions play an important role in DOM, and it is not difficult to work with them in jQuery. Some of the important methods in jQuery dimensions are

```
width()

height()

innerWidth()

innerHeight()

outerWidth()

outerHeight()
```

Before we start with the dimension methods, let's see how they work in jQuery. Figure 4-5 shows what the different dimension methods apply to.

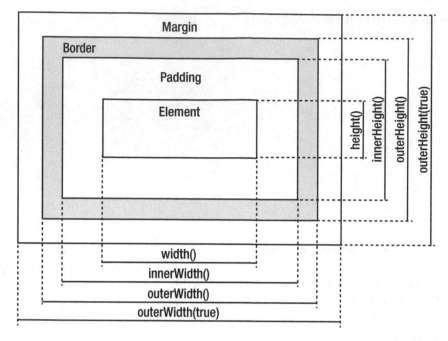

Figure 4-5. *Examples of dimension methods*

We will discuss the various jQuery dimensions in the following sections.

jQuery width() and height() Methods

The width() method is used to set or return the width of an element, and the height() method is used to set or return the height of an element. It is important to note here that neither of the methods includes padding, margins, or borders.

To calculate the width and height of an element, you just need to use selector.width() and selector.height() methods. See the next section for an example of these methods in use.

jQuery innerWidth() and innerHeight() Methods

The innerWidth() method returns the width of an element, including padding, and the innerHeight() method returns the height of an element, including padding. These definitions suffice to explain when you have to use which method. When you want to get the width or height including padding, these are the methods to use.

Let's look at an example in which we calculate the width, height, inner height, and inner width of an element. Let's start with this HTML:

```
<div id="apress" style="height:150px;width:300px;padding:10px;margin:3px;border:2px solid
#4679BD;"></div>
<br>
<button>Show dimensions</button>
```

Here's the jQuery for calculating the dimensions we want:

```
$("button").click(function(){
var txt="";
txt+="<strong>Width of div:</strong> " + $("#apress").width() + "</br>";
txt+="<strong>Height of div:</strong> " + $("#apress").height() + "</br>";
txt+="<strong>Inner Width of div:</strong> " + $("#apress").innerWidth() + "</br>";
txt+="<strong>Inner Height of div:</strong> " + $("#apress").innerHeight();
$("#apress").html(txt);
});
```

The code is simple to understand. We have a `<div>` with `id="apress"`, and we know that these methods will return the required results, which are shown in Figure 4-6.

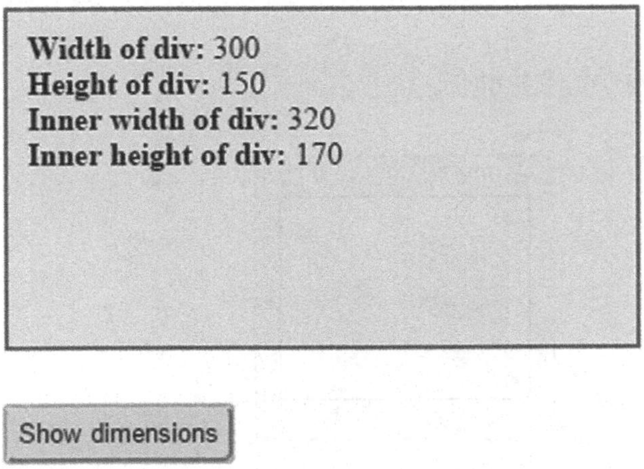

Width of div: 300
Height of div: 150
Inner width of div: 320
Inner height of div: 170

Show dimensions

Figure 4-6. The width, height, inner width, and inner height of an element on a `click` *event*

jQuery .outerWidth() and .outerHeight() Methods

The `.outerWidth()` method returns the width of an element, including padding and the border, and the `.outerHeight()` method returns the height of an element, including padding, a border, and the margin (optional). A brief explanation of the methods and its salient features follows:

.outerWidth()

- This method is used to get the current width for a set of first-matched elements.

- The `.outerWidth()` method also includes padding and a border.

- This method accepts an argument of the type `boolean`. If it is `true`, then it also includes margin; if `false`, then it includes only padding and a border.

.outerHeight()

- This method is used to get the current height for a set of first-matched elements, and it also includes padding and a border.

- As with the .outerWidth() method, the .outerHeight() method also accepts a boolean value (true or false), which decides whether it includes a margin or not.

■ **Note** If you want to get the correct values from the .outerWidth() and .outerHeight() methods, you have to show the parent element first, as the methods do not work perfectly in the case of a hidden element.

If you switch on the developers' view in your browser (we have used Google Chrome for the purpose of demonstration), you can also see the dimensions of the selected element, which look similar to those in Figure 4-7.

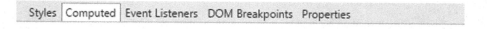

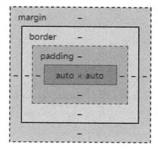

Figure 4-7. *Dimensions viewed in the console*

Summary

In this chapter, you learned a number of jQuery methods used for DOM manipulation. Among the types of manipulation, you learned to change the appearance of an element, create and insert a DOM element, and play with them. You also learned the concept of DOM cloning and how to remove elements, as well as the basics of dimensions in jQuery.

CHAPTER 5

■ ■ ■

Events in jQuery

Events form the core of user interaction in web applications. Web development grows bigger and better day-by-day by making use of events and, hence, benefiting the web developer interested in keeping up with the changing times and maintaining relevance in this era of stiff competition. In this chapter, we will take up the concept of events and explain all their possible aspects. Our focus will be the following topics:

- Introduction to events
- Browsers and events
- Event listeners and event handlers
- The event() method in jQuery
- Binding and unbinding events to DOM elements
- Event propagation and event bubbling
- Callback actions in events

Introducing Events

Events are normal occurrences. As in simple English we say an event has taken place at so and so place and at such and such time, we use the same terminology in web programming. In the context of web programming, web applications are mostly browser-oriented. The most common way for you to add interaction to web sites is to let users perform some action on the web page and program the web page to react to the actions that the user has taken. Because both ends are doing something (action-reaction), humans (the end users) feel that the web page is interactive.

The common means available to a user with which to interact with a web site are through any input device—most commonly the mouse and the keyboard. Some web sites use other input devices, such as the web camera or the microphone, but we will not go into much detail about those, to keep the discussion brief and focused. So, whenever a user moves a mouse pointer over a page, for example, this is a happening for the web page. So, too, is the case in which the user clicks somewhere on the page. Similarly, this is true of all the other user actions, such as mouse right-button clicks, left-button double-clicks, and so on. The web pages treat all these as events.

No explanation is complete without a proper example or examples. We will keep our promise, and, thus, we will inform you about the events that take place on certain user interactions with the web page, along with proper examples wherever possible. For now, have a look at Table 5-1, which lists some common user interactions and their corresponding event names.

Table 5-1. *Common User Interactions and Events*

User Interaction	Event	jQuery Event Name
Moving mouse over the page	Mouse movement	mousemove
Clicking mouse inside web page	Click	click
Placing mouse pointer into DOM element	Focus gain	focus
Pressing some keyboard button	Key press	keypress

You would be surprised to know that events are not caused only when users interact with a web page. Some events take place without user interaction. We will take up the details of those events as well, but for now, you can note that some such events take place when the document is ready, the window has loaded all the components (such as the images), and so on. From Chapter 1, you may recall that the window object represents the instance of a web browser. So, quite intuitively, you can make out that the window load event will be fired when all the images, for example, will have finished loading.

Getting into more detail, an event is a means for the browser to react to the user input. Thus, when an event occurs, the event handler attached to the corresponding element gets activated and executes the task(s) that you have programmed. Now here's a new term: *event handler*. The event handler is a function for which you have to write the appropriate reaction to the user input. Because web programming revolves mostly around web browsers, and web browsers deal in DOM, the events fall within the domain of handling of DOM elements. So, the events get listened to on DOM elements, and the event handler gets activated from the events that take place on DOM elements. In simpler terms, the DOM elements attend to the events by receiving them and calling the associated event handler. Because a picture is worth a thousand words, Figure 5-1 shows a drawing that illustrates how events take place.

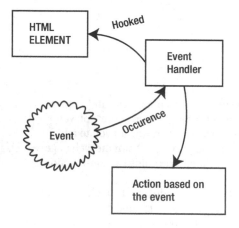

Figure 5-1. *Illustration showing how events take place*

Traditionally, the event is handled using JavaScript code, but as we are demonstrating jQuery, we will show how to write jQuery that will make your web page react to its end users. The jQuery library provides a number of methods, of which we will list and explain the most important ones, including examples wherever possible. All browsers are made differently: some having a particular design, others not. Thus, if we try to use JavaScript to add interactivity to our web pages, we will have to consider each and every browser's architecture, even different versions of the same browser, at times. However, we are strong believers that knowledge brings versatility. So, although we usually would not use JavaScript alone to write event handlers, we will demonstrate how different browsers behave differently while reacting to events. We will explain this to you in the latter sections of this chapter.

As stated a short while ago, DOM elements have to be made to listen to events. It often occurs that the DOM element is tied to some event that will interfere with the default behavior of the DOM element. Let us assume that you have bound some mouse-click event handler to some anchor **(a)** element. The default behavior of the anchor element is to follow the link specified in the href attribute of the tag. So, when the click event takes place, the browser will accept the default action as the final action, as a result of the event. What will happen is that the action you specify will take place, but the default action will very soon (in a fraction of a second) take over from this first action. This can be unpleasant at times. You will have to stop the default action of the DOM element from taking place when the right event is fired. You need not worry. All you have to do is prevent the default event from taking place. This can be done in two ways: by returning a Boolean false value from the event handler function or by preventing the default action of the DOM element altogether. The *prevent default* seems to be the better alternative, as it does not interfere in the behavior of the parent DOM elements, in case of event bubbling. Event bubbling will be explained in detail later in this chapter.

As a quick demonstration of preventing the default action, let us look at some HTML code.

```
<a href="/some-page.html" onclick="showSomeMessage()">Clicking me will say hello to you</a>
```

jQuery

```
function showSomeMessage(){
    alert("Hello Event Handling People");
    return false;
}
```

This code, when run, will show only an alert message and not open the page some-page.html, because the method returns false and, hence, prevents the default behavior of the anchor element from occurring. In case of a prevent default, the code changes to the following:

```
function showSomeMessage(e){
    if (e){
        e.preventDefault();
    } else {
        window.event.preventDefault();
    }
    alert("Hello Event Handling People");
}
```

It is quite natural for the preceding example to have left you with a number of questions. We ask that you be patient until the later parts of this discussion, wherein we will shed more light on what we have just touched upon here.

Browsers and Events

All browsers are unique. This is to say that each browser has its own implementation of DOM and the operations that are possible on the DOM elements. Although a majority of operations behaves the same way, there still remains a number of operations that differ. This difference can often be painful, so much so that it ends up in warning messages to end users. So, better safe than sorry. Before we start talking the language of events, let us take a walk through the common events available. It is quite interesting (and important too) to notice this behavior, because this might give you an insight into some aspects of how browsers are designed.

Let us focus on major browsers. Our motive is simple: there are a huge number of browsers available, and explanations about each of these would end up as numerous books, and we would like to keep the current discussion precise. Throughout this chapter, then, we will focus on the browsers *Chrome* (by Google), *Firefox* (by Mozilla), *Internet Explorer* (by Microsoft), *Opera* (by Opera Software), and *Safari* (by Apple).

We begin this discussion by taking up some extremely common events and see how they fare on our browsers of interest. Some very commonly used events include

- mouse over

- mouse out

- click

- mouse move

- key press

- key release

- input element change

- window resize

- window load

- document ready state change

First, let's consider events directly affected by users.

The mouseover event is supported across all the browsers that we have taken up for discussion. This event is fired whenever the mouse pointer is placed over some DOM element.

When you perform a mouse over, you have to take the mouse pointer away as well. The reason is simple: one cannot keep the mouse pointer on an element forever! So, there is the mouseout event. Like mouseover, this event is supported on all of the major browsers.

An important event is the mouse click event, which is used quite widely by users while interacting with a web page. This event is supported by all the browsers we mentioned. You will easily notice that it is the mouse click event that drives the web, because whatever links are presented on the web browser are followed by clicking them.

Then you have the mousemove event, which gets fired whenever the mouse pointer is moved around the web page. In simple terms, the mousemove event gets fired with the movement of the mouse. If you observe closely, you will see that the mousemove event is fired continuously. So, if you plan to assign some action to your web page when this event gets fired, you have to double-check your algorithm, as users may inadvertently fire events over and over, which can eat up all the computing resources. This is an important aspect to be considered, because an algorithm that runs on will keep the browser busy—busy interpreting the code—and this will result in slow interaction with the user (see Figure 5-2). The mousemove event is supported by all the browsers we have mentioned.

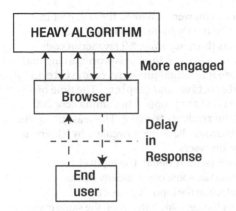

Figure 5-2. Figure showing what happens in the case of a heavy event-handling mechanism

The keypress event gets fired whenever any keyboard button gets pressed. Again, if you wish to attach some functionality to your web page upon this event, you must be careful in doing so, because it may often occur that the web page would require a large amount of data entered by the keyboard. In that case, the algorithm will again slow down the web page, thus resulting in a poorer user experience. The keypress event is supported by all browsers on our list.

Once you press a key (and generate the keypress event), you will have to release it. You cannot hold it pressed forever, however powerful or muscular you may be! So, whenever you release a key you've pressed previously, the keyup event gets fired. This event is supported by all the browsers on our list.

Important

The same number of times that the keypress event gets fired, the keyup event gets fired, so you get two points to monitor and assign interactivity to your web page. Up to now, the events covered were directly influenced by the user. Now we will discuss events that take place through some indirect activity of the user. Let us begin with the input *element change* event. There is an input element to which the input element change event is reported. So, whenever the user makes some change in the input element, this event gets fired. This event is applicable to all the input types to which the user can provide input, and it excludes those input elements that are hidden either through the type="hidden" attribute or through CSS styling. This event is supported by all browsers we have taken into consideration for this discussion.

According to the discussion in Chapter 1, the window object represents an instance of a running browser. There are certain events available that are fired when the user resizes the browser window. You might immediately ask why there would be a need to perform some action when the browser window is resized. The reason becomes clear from the point of view of a user and then that of a front end web developer. A user will want the page to be consistent, irrespective of the size of the browser. Even if the browser window size changes, the user will want the necessary information to be visible at all times. A web developer has to implement such facility to enhance the user experience. This event is supported by all of the browsers we have cited. Because the window object represents a running instance of a browser window, there is an event fired when the window gets loaded completely, including all the resources—external or internal. This event is particularly useful in those case(s) in which you will want to perform some actions on images, for example. Thus, once this window load event is fired, you can be assured that the images are available for the action you want to take. The window load event is available on the browsers we have listed.

The DOM is the pivot to building web-based applications that run on web browsers. Indeed, nothing can be done if the DOM does not allow it. We all should give respect to the DOM. So, when the DOM gets ready on the web browser, there is an event fired that is known as the *ready state*. All JavaScript code (including jQuery) becomes available for execution after the ready state event is fired. It is worth noting that the ready state is not a natural event provided by JavaScript, but there is a natural property, readystate, in JavaScript with a list of values uninitialized, loading, loaded, interactive, *and* complete. The time of the firing of this event (in jQuery) coincides with the value of the readystate property becoming complete. The jQuery community has been continuously encouraging use of the readystate event. The reason is quite simple: the events that would have behaved differently on various browsers have been tweaked by jQuery in such a manner that they all seem to behave the same under various browsers.

Let us consider this benefit provided by the jQuery framework in a little more detail. The input element change event that we addressed in the immediately preceding discussion has some compatibility issues with some older versions of Internet Explorer. The change event is fired when the input (type="text", type="checkbox", or type="radio") is blurred and not when the value changes. Similarly, when the same event is fired when a drop-down menu option is selected, under some browsers, it happens as soon as you select the option, but on other browsers, it happens when you click the drop-down. So, the effect of this will be on user experience, as with some browsers, the user might have to take an extra step to achieve the same functionality.

You have come to know the DOM readystate event (in jQuery) that is fired when the DOM tree is ready to accept user interactions. On the flip side of this, the DOM readystate is available with JavaScript but has a number of anomalies in its behavior across browsers. There is no native browser support for this event, so different browsers treat it differently. For example, on older versions of IE, the method to check is to repeatedly try to execute some insignificant code related to DOM manipulation. So, until some exception was thrown, the page was assumed not to be ready. The insignificant code could be anything from scrolling to the left or scrolling to the top, because this would hardly make a difference under most of the use cases. Because we refrained from using "all cases," you should consider it important that there are use cases in which the difference will matter; even insignificant code could create a side effect.

We just offered a few examples that demonstrate the extra effort you will have to make to achieve the same task if you don't use jQuery; therefore, we advise you to be wise and resort to jQuery!

Event Listeners and Event Handlers

This entire chapter is all about events. To repeat, in order to play with events, there must be a dedicated entity that will wait for the event to take place. Let us take up a real-world analogy to explain event listeners and event handlers in a better way.

Suppose you have a dog. Dogs are considered to be the most faithful creatures on the planet. So, you have a dog that you train to protect your home from intruders. Your dog will happily move around your property, watching the fences, the kids playing in the vicinity, the passersby on the road, and, obviously, a female dog of interest! So far, so good. Whenever someone or something comes near your property, your trained dog will start barking loudly, so that someone in the house (probably you) will realize that something is happening outside that requires your attention. Consequently, you go out of your house and try to sort out the issue—either, for example, by shooing the unwanted animal away from your fence or letting guests into your house by calming down your dog.

With this simple story, you can draw an analogy to a number of facts related to the event listeners and event handlers. Let us start drawing the analogy. Your dog is the entity that will be responsible for providing you the alerts regarding the events that will occur. So, your dog would be the event listener, which keeps looking for events to occur. You can draw an analogy between this event (in English) and the event in web development: the happening that is of interest to you is what you want to monitor. So, the dog (event listener) will provide you notifications about some possible intrusion into your home (the event). You (the event handler) will look into the matter (the event) to decide what action you will take (the action to be taken once the event is fired). To the onlooker, it will appear as though you knew in advance what was going on around your house, in spite of your being absent from the scene. (See Figure 5-3.)

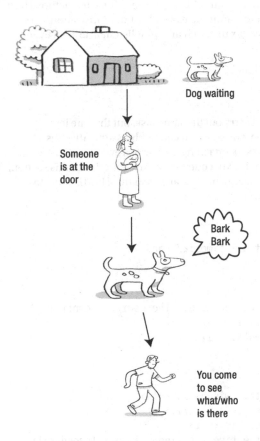

Dog waiting

Someone
is at the
door

Bark
Bark

You come
to see
what/who
is there

Figure 5-3. *Showing the idea behind events*

If we were to say to remove the event handler as soon as you feel that you no longer need it, we would not be incorrect. Memory is a limited resource and will always be. If you wish to remove an event handler, you can use the `removeEventListener()` method provided by the JavaScript library. You can choose which handler to remove, so that the DOM tree does not get overloaded with unnecessary event-handling algorithms. An important fact to know about event handling is that each chunk of assignment to the DOM adds weight to it. The weight addition is in terms of memory consumed. Each object added (yes, you do add objects in JavaScript) increases the memory consumption. Act wisely; preserve the memory footprint!

Being a web developer, by the time you've read this text, you will have generated a question as to what the relationship between an event handler and an event listener is. This is a good question. It is good that our assumption matches yours. The difference between the two terms is substantial, in case of other languages, but in our case—JavaScript—the two are related. So, when you add an event listener, you add a functionality to take some action when some event occurs. In other words, an event listener relates an event and an event handler together. In terms of programming, event listeners are binding entities that bind together some event with some action associated with it. This is where the programming part comes into the picture. Until this point, the discussion was text-based and without any programming example or demonstration, now code snippets will be added for the purpose. The general syntax to attach an event listener (and an event handler) to some DOM element in is

```
$('some-element-selector').on('event-name', function(){
    // Add event handling code here
});
```

There are other methods that are available in jQuery that carry out the same task, but they are less recommended, for reasons we will take up later in this section. For now, you can safely assume that this demonstration will suffice. Let us review a number of use cases for attaching the various events you just learned.

Let us start with the mouseover event. Let us take up an HTML code for all the examples in this section, to simplify our treatment of event handling. We will go on making modifications in this HTML code, to match the context of the example. The starting HTML code is

```
<div class="apress">
    <p>
        <span>Events are something which happen at all times:</span>
    </p>
    <ul>
        <li>You bring about some events.</li>
        <li>Place your mouse pointer here to know common events the user can control.</li>
        <li>But some events happen by other means.</li>
        <li>Click here to know which are those events.</li>
    </ul>
    <p></p>
    <ol>
        <li>The number of times you have resized this window is:</li>
        <li>The number of times you have done a keypress is:</li>
        <li>The number of times a keyup has happened is:</li>
        <li>This content will be alive only till the time the window is not loaded.</li>
        <li>The document is now ready to allow you to play</li>
    </ol>
</div>
```

You can use the event handling mechanism to see how the mouseover event can be used to bring about change in the DOM.

```
var list = $('ul > li:nth-child(2)');
    list.on('mouseover', function(){
        var span = document.createElement('span');
        span.innerHTML = 'The events are: mouseover, mouseout, keypress, keyup and so on.';
        list.append(span);
    });
```

What this code does is find the second child of a ul element (because we kept some meaningful message inside that li element), create a new span element (by JavaScript's createElement method), and, finally, append it to the same child that we selected. The output of the action is shown in Figure 5-4.

Events are something which happen at all times:

- You bring about some events.
- Place your mouse pointer here to know common events the user can control. The events are: mouseover, mouseout, keypress, keyup and so on.
- But some events happen by other means.
- Click here to know which are those events.

1. The number of times you have resized this window is:
2. The number of times you have done a keypress is:
3. The number of times a keyup has happened is:
4. This content will be alive only till the time the window is not loaded.
5. The number of times you have resized this window is:
6. The document is now ready to allow you play

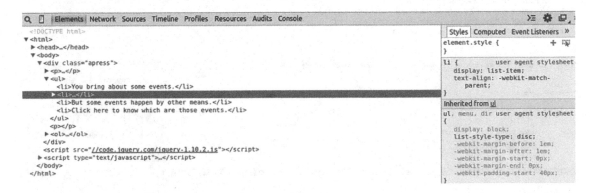

Figure 5-4. *Showing the action taken on a mouseover event*

Let us move on to another event that is closely related to the mouseover event. The relationship is quite straightforward. You will have to do a mouseout if you did a mouseover (you cannot leave the mouse pointer at one location on the screen forever). So, for the purpose of demonstration, let us make some changes in the DOM once a mouseout is fired. We better add some more code to the last example, so that the usage of mouseout is visible.

```
var list = $('ul > li:nth-child(2)');
    list.on('mouseover',function () {
        var span = document.createElement('span');
        span.innerHTML = 'The events are: mouseover, mouseout, keypress, keyup and so on.';
        list.append(span);
    }).on('mouseout', function () {
        list.find('span').remove();
});
```

The result of the code would be to restore the DOM to its original state. This is a very common use case if you look at it that way, because the occurrence of some event should always make some changes to the DOM, with the condition that the changes be undone once the event is complete.

Let us now move on to the next event on our list: the click event. *Clicking* here refers to the click of the mouse's left button. In order to demonstrate the click event, we provide the following sample code:

```
var list = $('ul > li:nth-child(4)');
    list.on('click', function(){
        var span = document.createElement('span');
        span.innerHTML = 'The events are: document ready, window load and so on.';
        list.append(span);
    })
```

The result of this code is similar to that provided by the immediately preceding example on clicking the fourth li. There will be an addition to the DOM tree in terms of a new span containing some text. For clarity, the output is shown in Figure 5-5.

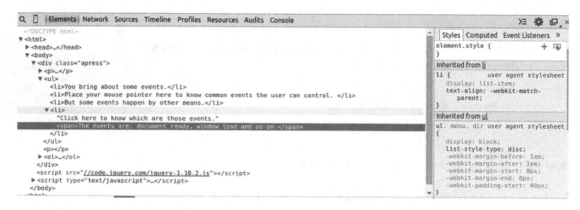

- You bring about some events.
- Place your mouse pointer here to know common events the user can control.
- But some events happen by other means.
- Click here to know which are those events.The events are: document ready, window load and so on.

1. The number of times you have resized this window is:
2. The number of times you have done a keypress is:
3. The number of times a keyup has happened is:
4. This content will be alive only till the time the window is not loaded.
5. The number of times you have resized this window is:
6. The document is now ready to allow you play

Figure 5-5. Showing mouse click event

Next on our list, we have the mousemove method. We must take extra care in demonstrating its use, as the effect will be visible under a real browser as opposed to the other cases, because the effect of a moving mouse cannot be shown in this book. We resort to jsfiddle.net. What we will do is capture the position of the mouse pointer by the x and the y coordinates and show the result on the web page. Consider the following HTML code, which contains some additions, in order to match the current context:

```
<div class="apress">
    <p>
        <span>Events are something which happen at all times:</span>
    <ul>
        <li>You bring about some events.</li>
        <li>Place your mouse pointer here to know common events the user can control. </li>
        <li>But some events happen by other means.</li>
        <li>Click here to know which are those events.</li>
    </ul>
    </p>
    <ol>
        <li>The number of times you have resized this window is:</li>
        <li>The number of times you have done a keypress is:</li>
        <li>The number of times a keyup has happened is:</li>
        <li>This content will be alive only till the time the window is not loaded.</li>
```

```
        <li>The current location of the mouse pointer is:</li>
        <li>The document is now ready to allow you play</li>
    </ol>
</div>
```

The corresponding jQuery code to show the mousemove event is as follows:

```
var list = $('ol > li:nth-child(5)');
    $(document).on('mousemove', function(event){
        var span = document.createElement('span');
        var x = event.clientX;
        var y = event.clientY;

        span.innerHTML = x+" , "+y;
        list.find('span').remove();
        list.append(span);
    })
```

In the preceding code, event is the object provided by JavaScript by default. You can refer to Chapter 1 for more such objects, which are provided by default by JavaScript (and, therefore, have a native support in the browser). Because there is an object, there will be properties associated with it. So, there are properties of our interest as clientX and clientY, which represent the x and the y coordinates of the mouse pointer, respectively. The rest is a plain programming operation, which we have been performing in the examples and in our real lives.

■ **Note**   The output can be viewed at http://jsfiddle.net/ankur6971/wb1m3oyh/1/.

We can modify the mouseout and mouseover events example to demonstrate the keypress and the keyup events. Considering the same HTML example as in the mousemove event example, the jQuery code snippet will look like the following:

```
var list2 = $('ol > li:nth-child(2)');
var list3 = $('ol > li:nth-child(3)');
var countKeyPress = 0;
var countKeyUp = 0;
    $('body').on('keypress',function () {
        var span = document.createElement('span');
        countKeyPress++;
        span.innerHTML = countKeyPress;
        list2.find('span').remove();
        list2.append(span);
    }).on('keyup', function () {
        var span = document.createElement('span');
        countKeyUp++;
        span.innerHTML = countKeyUp;
        list3.find('span').remove();
        list3.append(span);
    })
```

In this example, we are doing the following:

- We are making the body tag listen to keypress and keyup events.

- We are counting the number of times a key has been pressed.

- We are counting the number of times a key has been released.

- We are appending the result to the third and the fourth list elements, respectively, in the ordered list.

There may be questions in your mind. You ask why we make the body listen to the event and not the individual li element. The reason for this is quite simple and straightforward. If we added the event handler to the li element, where would we make the key-based event take place? Because the li element does not take input from the keyboard, the next best solution is to enable the event to be captured from anywhere in the body.

The output and the operational details can be found at http://jsfiddle.net/ankur6971/ pd8xchky/1/. You can see from the fiddle that the number of counts for the keypress and the keyup events gets incremented together every time you hit the keyboard to type something.

■ **Note**   Normally, when you are typing, you will observe that the keyup and the keypress event counts increase together. But when you keep some key pressed, you will see that the keypress event gets fired continuously, until you release the keyboard button, while the keyup will occur only once—when you release the pressed key.

We now take up the $(window).on('load', ...) (commonly known as *window load*) event. If you don't mind going back to the HTML code we used to demonstrate all of the preceding events we've covered, you will notice the fourth li element with some text written inside it. We will make this text disappear as soon as the window load event is fired. The code to achieve this is quite simple.

```
$(window).on('load', function(){
    $('ol').find('li:nth-child(4)').remove();
});
```

The code will become activated on the window load event. The code will find the fourth li element inside the ordered list ol and remove it. The output of the code is as shown in Figure 5-6.

Events are something which happen at all times:

- You bring about some events.
- Place your mouse pointer here to know common events the user can control.
- But some events happen by other means.
- Click here to know which are those events.

1. The number of times you have resized this window is:
2. The number of times you have done a keypress is:
3. The number of times a keyup has happened is:
4. The current location of the mouse pointer is:
5. The document is now ready to allow you play

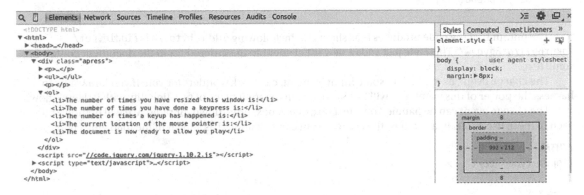

Figure 5-6. *The output of the window load event*

When you resize the browser window, the event that gets fired can be made to do some meaningful task(s) as well. As an example, we will present some jQuery code that gives you a hint as to how can you utilize this event for solving some business problem that may arise in your daily routine. The code for this is

```
var countResize = 0;

$(window).on('resize', function(){
    countResize++;
    var span = document.createElement('span');
    span.innerHTML = countResize;
    list.find('span').remove();
    list.append(span);
});
```

You can view the effect of the code in action from this fiddle: http://jsfiddle.net/ ankur6971/1j027pbz/1/. On executing the code, you will observe that the event is fired continuously, starting from the time you begin resizing the window until the time you stop resizing it. This is another event you should handle with care, as you could easily end up slowing down the user interaction, if you attempt a careless usage.

You can view the effect of the code in action from the following fiddle: http://jsfiddle.net/ankur6971/1j027pbz/1/. On executing the code, you will see that the event is fired continuously, starting from the time you begin resizing the window until the time you stop resizing it. This is another event you should handle with care. You could easily end up slowing down user interaction, if you are not careful with how you use this event. To demonstrate the document ready event in jQuery, we offer the following piece of code, to show you how you can utilize this event:

```
$(document).on('ready', function(){
    var li = document.createElement('li');
    li.innerHTML = 'The document is now ready to allow you play';
    $('ol').append(li);
});
```

The output that the code produces is as shown in the following fiddle: http://jsfiddle.net/ankur6971/qt6gvqvw/. This code just adds a new list element to the ordered list in the document containing some text.

The change event, as applied on some input element, can work wonders for you. If you know how to harness the power of this event, you will be able to attach different types of functionality with it. Here's how.

The change event can be handled on a text box, check box, drop-down, or radio. We will demonstrate each of these use cases. In a text box, the change event can be handled as shown in the following code:

//HTML
```
<input type="text" />
```

//jQuery
```
$('input').on('change', function(){
    alert('Some change has occurred');
});
```

You must know that the change is considered by the browser when you have finished editing the text box. The change is considered once you move out of the text box, after making some change in its contents.

Let's look at one more example related to **input** elements, since we have a number of types of input possible. You will note that the same jQuery code can work on the input types radio and checkbox and the select drop-down. With a slight code change, you can see how events can be captured on the input types just mentioned. So, if your HTML code is

```
<select>
    <option value="1">Option 1</option>
    <option value="1">Option 2</option>
    <option value="1">Option 3</option>
</select>
    <input type="radio" name="radioInput" value="Radio 1" />
    <input type="radio" name="radioInput" value="Radio 2" />
    <input type="checkbox" name="radioInput" value="Checkbox 1" />
```

you would need the following jQuery code:

```
$('input, select').on('change', function(){
    alert('Some change has occurred');
});
```

To clarify, you can make more than one selector work simultaneously, if you write as we wrote. We should have discussed this when we were discussing jQuery selectors...but oversights are never too late to mend!

The Event() Method in jQuery

Before we discuss the `Event()` method specifically, we would like to offer some facts, to enable you to understand frameworks better. Our points are as follows:

- Frameworks are programs written in the same language they are designed for. For example, you can see the Zend framework written in PHP for PHP, the Spring framework written in Java for Java, the jQuery framework written in JavaScript for JavaScript, and so on.

- Frameworks add ease of use for developers by making common functionality available via methods that can be called quite easily. Without frameworks, developers would have to program the solution to common problems repeatedly, causing an inefficient use of bandwidth.

- Frameworks add wrappers to the native objects and methods available in the language in which they are written.

We already took up the first two points, in the preceding chapters. The third point is of interest to us in the current context. Frameworks add wrappers to the native objects and methods to add more functionality to them. The jQuery framework does the same in the case of event handling (and in other scenarios as well, which we will take up later). In the current context, the event object provided by JavaScript is wrapped by jQuery, so that some extra functionality is added and some cross-browser compatibility is achieved. Now, you might ask how events can be non-cross-browser compatible. We would suggest that you recall what we explained in the previous discussions of this chapter: all browsers are unique. Thus, the jQuery framework achieves cross-browser functionality by adopting the W3C standard of the event model and applying it to whichever browser allows the execution of jQuery.

Actually there are three major types of event models.

1. DOM level 0 model

2. DOM level 2 model, or the W3C model

3. Microsoft-specific model, or the MS Internet Explorer model

We will take up these event models in the forthcoming sections of this chapter, but for now, we request that you be content with the names only.

Resuming our discussion, the jQuery framework adds some functionality to the native event object while still maintaining access to those objects which it does not wrap. Shortly, we will provide you a list of the properties and methods wrapped together with the event object. First, however, the wrapping of an event begins with the `Event()` method. You can wrap any native JavaScript event to a jQuery event by using this method. The `Event()` can be called as

```
$.Event('some-javascript-event')
```

or as

```
jQuery.Event('some-javascript-event')
```

So, for example, you can wrap any event, such as `keypress`, `keyup`, `mousemove`, `mouseover`, and so on, using this `Event()` method. Having created the jQuery event, you will obviously want to use it. You will be able to use it by using the `trigger()` method available in jQuery. Summing things up, you can create a jQuery event synthetically and make it occur synthetically on some DOM element. Yes, we are stating the truth. Events can be *made* to happen. Demonstration is better than making statements, so let's consider the same HTML code that we took up throughout our examples of events and add functionality to the web page on the click event, on the fourth list item. The code to achieve this is

```
var list = $('ul > li:nth-child(4)');
    list.on('click', function(){
        var span = document.createElement('span');
        span.innerHTML = 'The events are: document ready, window load and so on.';
        list.append(span);
    })

    var jQueryEvent = $.Event('click');
    list.trigger(jQueryEvent);
```

Comparing the code with the demonstration we made previously, you would notice that we added only two lines of code, the last two of the existing example. The difference that will be created under the current use scenario will be that your code is now free from depending on the user interaction. At any time, you (the developer) can trigger/initiate/make happen a click on the same element to which the same event is attached. Thus, the output of the code will be the same as we saw previously in Figure 5-5.

Another interesting fact is that you can achieve the same effect via another approach—jQuery shorthand methods. Explaining the new term briefly, there are predefined event handlers in jQuery that take similar action as the on() method. The word *similar* is intentional and will be explained later. So, for the click event, there is a click() method; for the mouseover event, there is a mouseover() method; for keypress, there is a keypress() method; and so on. Having obtained this information, let us revisit the example of the click event. The trigger() method can be replaced by the click() method in the preceding example, as follows:

```
var list = $('ul > li:nth-child(4)');
    list.on('click', function(){
        var span = document.createElement('span');
        span.innerHTML = 'The events are: document ready, window load and so on.';
        list.append(span);
    })
list.click();
```

Let us move on to the properties and the methods that the Event() method encapsulates. Because the list is long, for the sake of concision, we will take up only the most commonly used methods and properties.

- event.which
- event.target
- event.relatedTarget
- event.currentTarget
- event.stopPropagation
- event.stopImmediatePropagation
- event.pageX
- event.pageY

The event.which property indicates which element invoked the event. This property provides a numeric value (the corresponding ASCII code) in the case of events that take place as a result of user interaction. If you press the A key on your keyboard, the property will provide you a value 97; in the case of Shift+A, the value would be **65**. If you clicked the left button, the property would provide you with a value of 1, which is the button code for the left mouse button. Time for a demonstration.

We will take up the same mouse click event and the keypress event examples (with subtle modifications) as previously. First is the keypress event. In the following code, the keycode for the keyboard button that you press is indicated. The code for this scenario is as follows:

```
var ol = $('ol');
    $('body').on('keypress',function (event) {
        var span = document.createElement('span');
        span.innerHTML = "The keycode for the key you pressed is: "+event.which;
        ol.find('span').remove();
        ol.append(span);
});
```

What we have done here is explained in the following bullet points:

- We selected the ol element from the DOM, because we want to play with the ordered list. (We did that at the same time.)

- We made the body element respond to the keypress event. (We did that at the same time as well.)

- We created a span element and added some text to it. (We added some counters; here we are adding some text.)

- The text contains the property event.which. (This contains the keycode or the ASCII value of the button you would key in.)

- We first found and removed all span elements that the ol may already have had. (We always do this to avoid repetitions in the DOM.)

- We then appended the newly created span to the ordered list, and our example was complete. (We did this to make the example worth looking at!)

■ **Note**   You can have a look into the output at the fiddle, or give it a try yourself, via http://jsfiddle.net/ankur6971/gaL78k7z/.

When there is a source for an event, there must be a *target* for the event. Following this principle, the jQuery framework provides a target property by the event object that denotes where the event was captured. Because the jQuery framework follows the W3C model (don't worry, we will explain this feature in detail in the coming sections), the event percolates up the DOM tree hierarchy (we will explain this too).

As a quick explanation, *event bubbling* is a phenomenon by which an event takes place and then bubbles or travels up the DOM tree to the parent element, if the event is not captured at the originating level. We will illustrate this point by providing an example. Using the same HTML example, the jQuery code for the same would be

```
var ol = $('ol');
    ol.on('click',function (event) {
        var span = document.createElement('span');
    span.innerHTML = "You just clicked a <strong>" + event.target.nodeName + "</strong>";
        ol.find('span').remove();
        ol.append(span);
});
```

What the code does is display the name of the node where the event took place. The nodeName property of the object represented by event.target provides this information. The output of the code should receive careful consideration. If you click the list element, the nodeName will show LI, but if you click only adjacent to the numbers in the list, the click will be treated as if executed on the ordered list element OL. Why this happens will be explained following. For now, know that the event has bubbled up the DOM tree hierarchy, and this phenomenon is known as event bubbling.

So, there are two direct family members: event.relatedTarget and event.currentTarget. We have intentionally used the term *direct family members* because the behavior of the two go hand-in-hand, but with subtle differences. The currentTarget denotes the DOM element that is directly tied to the event, whereas the relatedTarget denotes the DOM element that has contributed to the event. The difference is quite confusing here, so we will clear the confusion by offering a small example. In keeping with our habit of modifying previous examples, we will take up the same mouseover and mouseout example and manipulate it to work our way. The code is as follows:

```
var list = $('ul > li:nth-child(2)');
    list.on('mouseover',function (event) {
        var span = document.createElement('span');
        span.innerHTML = event.type+" | "+event.relatedTarget.nodeName+" |
        "+event.currentTarget.nodeName;
        list.find('span').remove();
        list.append(span);
    }).on('mouseout', function (event) {
        var span = document.createElement('span');
        span.innerHTML = event.type+" | "+event.relatedTarget.nodeName+" |
        "+event.currentTarget.nodeName;
        list.find('span').remove();
        list.append(span);
    });
```

Here is the formal explanation of what is happening in the example. The events being handled are a simple mouseover and mouseout. There is a reason for this. The relatedTarget works in the event bubbling phase (please have patience, we will explain this very soon). So, in the sample code that we took up, three properties are being explained. If you execute this code, you will observe that the event.type will be either mouseover or mouseout. The relatedTarget.nodeName shows the name of the DOM node where your mouse pointer was previously. So, when you do a mouseover on the li, you must have done a mouseout on some other element. The event.relatedTarget indicates this previous element. Please note that when you do a mouseout on the li (to which you have attached the functionality to react to events), the relatedTarget does not change value, because there was no other DOM element involved at that instant. Another property involved in this scenario, the event.currentTarget, will continue to show the value of the element where the event was tied. So, in our demo, the event.currentTarget will show LI when the event is fired.

■ **Note**   You can view the code in execution at the fiddle: http://jsfiddle.net/6rckdyfh/2/.

Then we have some attributes in the jQuery event object that denote the location of the mouse pointer at all times that the mousemove event is being fired. We mention this because we stated earlier that the mousemove event gets fired continuously, as long as you keep on moving your mouse pointer on the web page. All you require to get this value is to call the property event.pageX or event.pageY, and you will have the x or y coordinates of the mouse pointer relative to the left and top edge of the document. Quickly demonstrating this property is the following code:

```
var list = $('ol > li:nth-child(5)');
    $(document).on('mousemove', function(event){
        var span = document.createElement('span');
        var x = event.pageX;
        var y = event.pageY;

        span.innerHTML = x+" , "+y;
        list.find('span').remove();
        list.append(span);
})
```

If you notice, this is the same example copied and pasted from the mousemove demonstration that was provided earlier in this chapter. The only difference is that we have used the pageX and pageY instead of the clientX and clientY property, respectively. You are encouraged to execute this code and check the output of the code provided.

There are two additional properties, event.stopPropagation and event.stopImmediatePropagation, that we will take up after we discuss binding and unbinding events and the event bubbling phenomenon.

Binding and Unbinding Events to DOM ElementsCareful readers will note that this is not a new topic, because the related concepts have already been taken up while treating other topics. We promised, while treating those other topics, that we would provide a detailed discussion of how events can be bound and unbound to and from DOM elements. We listed all the possible approaches by which it is possible to do so. It's now time to fulfill our promises and explain them.

Binding Events

When we talk of binding events to DOM elements, we mean making an HTML element listen to events and respond to the events by taking some action(s). The actions can range from simple method calls to complex DOM manipulation activities or even asynchronous HTTP requests. Anything that you can imagine possible in JavaScript can be executed as the action to be taken in response to an event.Bearing in mind the discussion we had at the beginning of this chapter, let us take up those events again and try to bind them. Let us also attempt to unbind them. Unbinding is a phenomenon that we will explain in a while. The events which we took up to explain were:

- mouse over

- mouse out

- mouse click

- mouse move

- key press

- key release

- input element change

- window resize

- window load

- document ready state change

117

The jQuery framework provides binding of single as well as multiple events to the same DOM element. In HTML, only a single event could be bound to a single DOM element. If you remember HTML, there were keywords such as onchange, onmouseover, onmouseout, onkeypress, and so on, that you wrote directly within the HTML code. This had a disadvantage: the JavaScript code got mangled with the HTML code, and hence, maintaining such a code was not easy at all. The developer working second on such code would have a nightmarish experience reading and trying to make sense of it. So, jQuery provides a helping hand to developers in this case as well. Let us try to see the difference quickly. Assuming we have a div element that we wish to bind to some event, in HTML code itself, you can do something like the following:

```
<div class='alert-box alert' onclick='sendMail()'>Someone needs to be sent an email on click</div>
```

The JavaScript code for this case can probably be an asynchronous request to some server-side script to initiate sending e-mail. However, that is beyond the scope of our discussion. Let us try to view the same scenario in jQuery. The HTML code would be

```
<div class='alert-box alert' id='mail-send'>Someone needs to be sent an email on click</div>
```

So, the difference in the HTML code is the removal of the event handling portion. Let us move toward jQuery to have the event binding logic in place.

```
$('#mail-send').on('click', function(){
//Some meaningful action
});
```

This was the jQuery section you are familiar with. You can very well observe that the jQuery code has no interference with the HTML code. Let us try some shortcuts. jQuery provides methods that are quick and handy and provide added functionality as well. Let us begin with the mouseover event and the complementary event mouseout. Let us revisit the same HTML code that we used to explain events. The mouseover method can be used as follows:

```
var list = $('ul > li:nth-child(2)');
    list.mouseover(function () {
        var span = document.createElement('span');
        span.innerHTML = 'The events are: mouseover, mouseout, keypress, keyup and so on.';
        list.append(span);
    }).mouseout(function () {
        list.find('span').remove();
    });
```

Quickly walking through the code, we see that it finds out the second li element inside an unordered list ul and adds to the end of it a span element containing some text, once the mouseover event takes place. Once the mouseout event takes place, the same element is searched for the presence of a span, which thereby is removed from the list element li. Besides acting for the regular event binding method, the mouseover and the mouseout event can be used to trigger the mouseover and the mouseout events. As an alternate usage, you can trigger the same event by calling the mouseover() method without any arguments, as list.mouseover(). The mouseout event can similarly be fired by calling the mouseout() method.

The click shorthand method is particularly useful for common scenarios. Revisiting the click event example, you can follow an alternate approach to binding the click() method, as shown in the following:

```
var list = $('ul > li:nth-child(4)');
list.click(function(){
    var span = document.createElement('span');
    span.innerHTML = 'The events are: document ready, window load and so on.';
    list.append(span);
})
```

The output will be exactly the same as it was when .on was used. The actions that are being taken by this method are also the same as those by .on.. Youcan make the click event take place artificially by using the click() method, without using any arguments, as list.click().

Then you have the mousemove event which can be bound to the DOM element to listen to some event. Let us take up the example we took previously. By the end of this example you would understand a very important property about triggering events synthetically. The jQuery code in the current case would be:

```
var list = $('ol > li:nth-child(5)');
    $(document).mousemove(function(event){
        var span = document.createElement('span');
        span.innerHTML = 'Event Triggered';
        if(event.pageX && event.pageY){
            var x = event.pageX;
            var y = event.pageY;
            span.innerHTML = x+" , "+y;
        }
        list.find('span').remove();
        list.append(span);
    });
```

```
    list.mousemove();
```

If you compare the code with the .on version of the mousemove event, you will notice a few changes in the code. The changes are intentional and specific to this scenario. Before explaining the changes, let us quickly walk through the code. The mousemove has been tied to the document. The code creates a span and instantiates it with some self-explanatory text. The text conditionally gets appended with the coordinates of the current position of the mouse pointer. The code removes any previous occurrence of span inside the list element and appends this created span element.

Now, let us try to understand the differences. As was stated, the shorthand event binding methods can trigger the event. In the current scenario, the mousemove() method will work (without supplying any arguments). So, the event will be triggered that way; however, there will be a difference, in that the coordinates will not be visible just after the call to list.mousemove(). So, we have added a message denoting the difference in the behavior. By default, the output will show a message that the event has been triggered, and the mouse coordinates will be visible only once you start moving the mouse pointer on the web page. This is why old and wise people say "Natural is cool!" The keypress and keyup are another pair of events. The keyup occurs mandatorily once the keypress has taken place. We have already stated the reason: one cannot hold a key forever unless one is not using the keyboard for normal activities. Taking up the same example, the jQuery code would be

```
var list2 = $('ol > li:nth-child(2)');
    var list3 = $('ol > li:nth-child(3)');
    var countKeyPress = 0;
    var countKeyUp = 0;
        $('body').keypress(function () {
            var span = document.createElement('span');
            countKeyPress++;
            span.innerHTML = countKeyPress;
            list2.find('span').remove();
            list2.append(span);
        }).keyup(function () {
```

```
            var span = document.createElement('span');
            countKeyUp++;
            span.innerHTML = countKeyUp;
            list3.find('span').remove();
            list3.append(span);
        })

    $('body').keypress();
    $('body').keyup();
```

The changes that we have made here are not much. We have just changed the way the method is called. The `.on` has been replaced by the corresponding shorthand methods: `keypress` and keyup. So, the output will not change much, compared to the previous case. But, yes, there would be a change in the default output now, because we have used the same shorthand method to trigger the two events. Because we had bound some handler to both the events, the count of occurrence of both the events will increase by one. Figure 5-7 shows what the output in the present case would be.

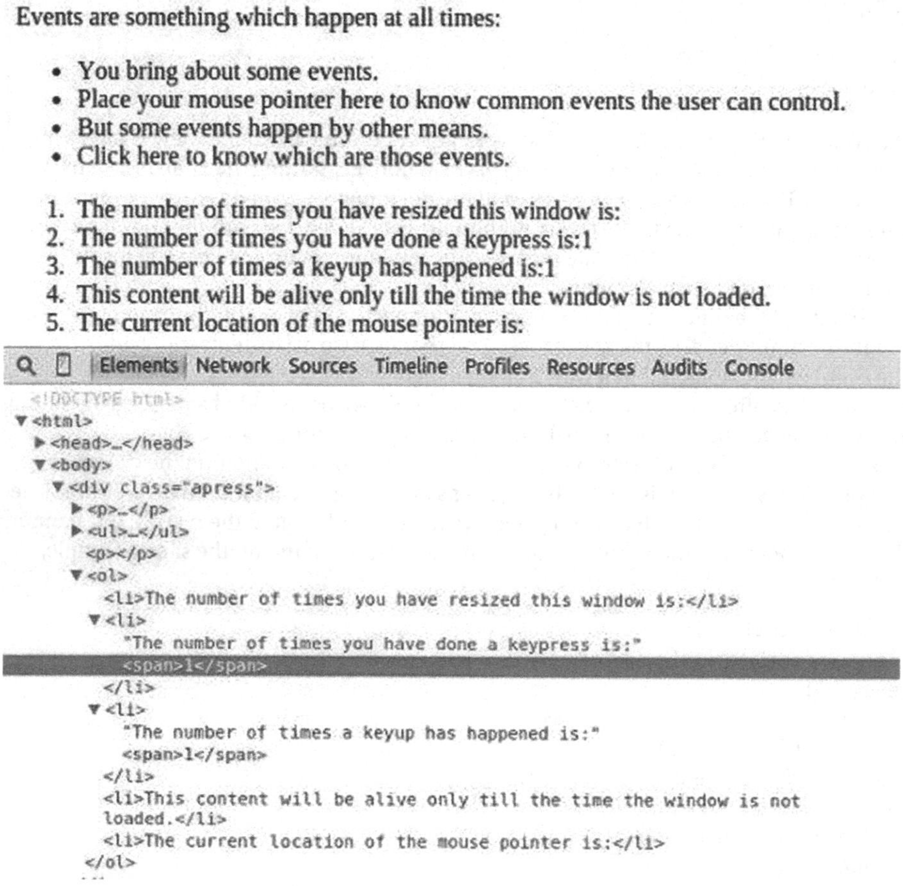
Events are something which happen at all times:
You bring about some events.
Place your mouse pointer here to know common events the user can control.
But some events happen by other means.
Click here to know which are those events.
1. The number of times you have resized this window is:
2. The number of times you have done a keypress is:1
3. The number of times a keyup has happened is:1
4. This content will be alive only till the time the window is not loaded.
5. The current location of the mouse pointer is:
Elements Network Sources Timeline Profiles Resources Audits Console
<!DOCTYPE html>
<html>
<head>…</head>
<body>
<div class="apress">
<p>…</p>
<ul>…</ul>
<p></p>
<ol>
<li>The number of times you have resized this window is:</li>
<li>
"The number of times you have done a keypress is:"
<span>1</span>
</li>
<li>
"The number of times a keyup has happened is:"
<span>1</span>
</li>
<li>This content will be alive only till the time the window is not loaded.</li>
<li>The current location of the mouse pointer is:</li>
</ol>

Figure 5-7. *Count for single `keypress` and keyup events*

We will now consider the case of the input element change event. To be precise, we will take up the same example that we took up earlier in this chapter while considering the change event. The code in this scenario is

```
$('input, select').change(function(){
    alert('Some change has occurred');
});
```

Here, too, you can trigger the change by calling the method change(), as in the following line of code:

```
$('input, select').change();
```

This will trigger the alert message Some change has occurred.

Summing up, having worked with shorthands, it is worth noting that the natural action does not take place once you use the shorthand methods; only the corresponding event is triggered. This triggering of the event takes place in exactly the same way as the trigger method causes it to. Under the hood, the shorthand event binding methods make use of the .on and .trigger methods in sequence, if called without arguments. One notable difference is that the shorthand methods can only be used to trigger those events that take place by user interaction. The facility is not available for events such as window load, document ready, etc. Another difference in the behavior of the shorthand methods and the regular .on method is that by using a single function call of the .on, you can attach multiple events to one single DOM element, whereas the shorthand methods have the capability to attach only one single event at a time, via a single function call. And this triggering of the event via the method call follows the rules of jQuery, as in chaining. So, taking up the last example of the change event, you can chain the triggering of the event with the selected element, as shown in the following code snippet. This will alert a message as soon as the code is executed.

```
$('input, select').change(function(){
    alert('Some change has occurred');
}).change();
```

Obviously, you can perform other tasks instead of the simple alert!

Unbinding Events

Being a web developer is not an easy task at all. You have to consider a number of aspects simultaneously. Despite the client machines becoming stronger, you cannot assume that the code you write will have unlimited memory resources with which to execute. It is particularly important to consider this likelihood, because every time you bind some event to some DOM element, some memory is consumed. So, you cannot go on adding events to DOM and go home when you have hit the target. The DOM gets heavier and heavier. There is, however, a solution available, which is known as *unbinding*. Unbinding is the reverse process of binding, and it is a process that you must always keep in mind while programming events. Thus, if you bind events using the .on() method, you can unbind the same event using the .off() method. The off() method accepts the name of the event as string, the target DOM element selector, and the name of the method that was attached to the event. So, to put up a complete scenario of unbinding events, we would resort to using a jQuery code snippet, as shown following:

```
var clickDemo = function (listElement){
    var span = document.createElement('span');
    span.innerHTML = 'The events are: document ready, window load and so on.';
    listElement.append(span);
}
```

121

```
    var list = $('ul > li:nth-child(4)');
    list.on('click mouseover', function(){
        new clickDemo(list);
})
```

This code binds a click and a mouseover event to some action as specified in the function named clickDemo. So, we have enough material to start demonstrating event unbinding. To unbind the click element, you can use the following code:

list.off('click'); If you try to click the list element, nothing will happen, because now there will be no one to listen to the click event. Neither will the following shorthand work:

```
list.click();
```

However, the mouseover event will continue to be listened to and acted upon by your code. Dismantling the robot further, you can unbind the mouseover event by using the code

list.off('mouseover'); Now the mouseover event will not be listened to, and neither will there be any action taking place when you use the following shorthand:

```
list.mouseover();
```

As a part of fine-grained control over event unbinding, you can unbind all events bound to the list element, by calling the off() method without any arguments, as shown following:

```
list.off();
```

The destruction would be penetratingly deep!

Events Propagation and Events Bubbling

There are promises to keep. We mentioned event models briefly in previous discussions and promised that we would take up those models and their features in detail. It is time for us to explain the phenomena of event propagation and event bubbling. These are important to understand, if you wish to have hands-on information concerning events.

One of the definitions of the term *propagation* is "spreading of something to other regions." There are other meanings, but we will concentrate on this usage, because it is contextual. Just as a belief propagates throughout regions and becomes known among people, events in browsers also propagate to other regions, once they are generated. Following our old habit, let us look at an example. Suppose you have the following HTML:

```
<div class="apress">
    <p>
        <span>Events are something which happen at all times:</span>
    <ul>
        <li>You bring about some events.</li>
        <li>Click here to know which are those events.</li>
    </ul>
    </p>
</div>
```

Continuing where we left off, if you click the second list element, the click event will take place. But there will be event propagation. The event will propagate to other regions the ul, the p, the div, and the body element. This fact may seem surprising to you, but it is genuine: events bubble up the DOM hierarchy. You might question our having started off talking about event propagation while having explained the phenomenon of bubbling. To this we would say that event propagation is a general term for event bubbling: bubbling describes a way by which events get spread to other regions in the DOM tree. So, if someone suggests that event propagation and event bubbling are the same, you can nod your head in agreement!

There are a number of browsers available in this large and unfriendly world, and the browsers are not very friendly either. Browsers follow different event standards, and this makes life miserable for web developers. They do have to write a number of extra lines in order to make the same functionality work on all those browsers that their web site users are expected to make use of. But, for you the silver lining in this dark cloud is that there are a certain set of rules out of which these behaviors arise. Talking mathematically, the set of behaviors that the browsers follow is a finite set. The values contained in the set are event bubbling and the event capturing model. But because we are web developers and not mathematicians, let us move on to talking in plain web development terms.

The Event Capturing and Event Bubbling Models

The event capturing model states that the event propagates down the DOM tree. We intentionally made use of the term *down* because if there is an element A inside an element B, the event that has taken place has taken place inside the element A and moves on to the element B *if* the element A and B both have been attached with the functionality required for the occurrence of the same event. To avoid confusion, let us look at a code snippet and then re-attempt to explain what we just stated. Let us reuse the same (simple) code with a little bit of further simplification. The click event is tied to the div and the second li child of the unordered list li.

```
<div class="apress">
    <p>
        <ul>
        <li>You bring about some events.</li>
        <li>Click here to know which are those events.</li>
        </ul>
    </p>
</div>
```

Resuming our explanation, if the idea of the event capturing model is to be followed, the click event will originate at the div, with the class attribute apress, and travel downward. It will follow the path through the paragraph element p, followed by the unordered list element ul, and finally to the li element. Thus, reiterating what we said, the event capturing model states that the event starts at the top level element in the DOM tree and travels downward, provided there are multiple handlers for the same event (just as raindrops trickle down the leaves of a tree, all leaves are equally needy of water). Old versions of Internet Explorer used to follow this particular model.

The other model is known as the event bubbling model. This is just the reverse of the event capturing model, in the sense that if there are event handlers for the same event defined for DOM elements created in a hierarchy, the event bubbles up the DOM hierarchy. Thus, in the same example we used, the event would originate at the li element and then move up through the ul element to the p and reach out to the div element, where the event handler is attached. This model is followed by newer browsers, but in conjunction with the event capturing model. Mozilla and Opera follow this model, in addition to the event capturing model. Thus, in such browsers, the event will both bubble and capture (not necessarily at the same time).

The W3C Event Model

The W3C standard attempts to resolve the differences between the two models by adopting a middle road. Accordingly, if an event takes place, it will first move downward, until the target element, and from there, it will move upward. Thus, the W3C model is a good example of a hybrid standard containing the best of both worlds. This is a more browser-independent model, and so it is used by the jQuery framework.

This difference in behavior is one aspect. There are numerous others, which we have taken up in the previous chapters and will continue to explore in the coming chapters. If you remember the first chapter of this book, we listed the reasons for using the jQuery framework. We have just provided another reason.

To achieve cross-browser support, use jQuery. The event model that the jQuery framework uses is the W3C model. Thus, the events that have been generated get transferred to the event handler for sure, because the generated events perform bidirectional travel—first toward the descendants, and once the target element is reached, they reverse course to take the direction of propagation toward the original DOM element that created the event. Knowledge is power.With great power comes great responsibility.With great knowledge comes greater confusion.This is our version of the well-known saying. Because you know that the jQuery framework follows the W3C event model, which supports two-way event propagation through event capturing and event bubbling, this presents a new challenge to you, the web developer. If there are multiple event handlers for the same event in the DOM hierarchy, what will happen if all of the DOM elements have been programmed to take different actions on the same event? You might think that you can capture the event at one element and make some modifications in your code, so that the event does not propagate further, in any of the directions—upward or downward. But this would starve the other event handler, because it would not be able to receive notification of the event that it was programmed for. Let us consider an example by going through the following code:

```
//HTML
<div class="apress">
    <p>
        <ul>
        <li>You bring about some events.</li>
        <li>Click here to know which are those events.</li>
        </ul>
    </p>
</div>

//jQuery
var apress = $('div.apress');
apress.on('click', function(){
    alert('A div was clicked');
// Some functionality can be added here
});

apress.find('ul > li:nth-child(2)').on('click', function(){
    alert('The second list element was clicked');
// Some more functionality here
});
```

When you click the second list element, there will be a response on the click event from the list element itself and from the div element as well. This is the point at which you have to focus. You will have to prevent the click event from propagating to the div, in case it was originated on the list element. So, the best solution provided by the jQuery framework is to use the method stopPropagation(), which works well in these situations. Let us have a look into the use of the method. Making changes in the preceding jQuery code, the new code would look like

```
var apress = $('div.apress');
apress.on('click', function(){
    alert('A div was clicked');
});

apress.find('ul > li:nth-child(2)').on('click', function(event){
    alert('The second list element was clicked');
    if(!event)
```

```
        event = window.event;
    event.stopPropagation();
});
```

The code modification is simple. If the event variable is not initialized somehow, the code will initialize it with the event object available by the window object. So, the stopPropagation() method will prevent the click event from propagating to the parent element.

■ **Note**   You can fiddle this example at http://jsfiddle.net/pkz5mhro/1/.

It is quite tempting to get carried away by using return false to stop the event then and there. But a gotcha would be involved in that. So, instead of writing the stopPropagation() method, if you write return false, the code will work in the current case. But it is not to be assumed that such code will have no side effect. The return false is a JavaScript construct that apparently does the work, but under the hood, it makes use of three functionalities:

- Stop the event propagation.

- Stop the default action to be taken.

- Stop the execution flow immediately and exit the current procedure.

A quick explanation of how to prevent the default action from being taken is that the jQuery library provides a method preventDefault(). This method is called in the context of the event object itself, and it prevents the default action of a DOM element from taking place. For example, if you use the preventDefault() method on an anchor element, the anchor element will not direct you to the URL specified in the href attribute. For example, the method usage we are talking about is

```
//HTML
<a href="www.apress.com/authors">Click here to do nothing with the authors!</a>

//jQuery
$(a).click(function(){
    if(!event)
        event = window.event;
    event.preventDefault();
});
```

Thus, if you use return false, that will perform three tasks as opposed to only one, which is what you want. You would not want to prevent the default action from taking place. Sometimes, it may be harmful to your system. You will want to execute some callback methods as soon as the event takes place. If you resort to using return false, you will not be able to call those callback methods, because the return false will return immediately from the current function, which *can* mean that the actions to be taken on occurrence of some event will be stopped immediately. Now this is something that you would never want.

The choice is yours: employ jQuery or makeYourCode('unmaintainable').

Callback Action in Event

We mentioned the term *callback method* at the end of the preceding section. Now we will discuss that method and explain its usages. We will also try to relate the term to other examples or discussions that we have taken up to this point. We will show you how jQuery (JavaScript) can be made to execute a function as soon as an event takes place.

In callbacks, you can perform any regular programming task that you can inside a regular function. If you think that callbacks are rocket science, we can assure you that they are just a methodology to call some function once some other action has been taken place. Thus, in extremely simple terms, a callback is just a function call. In JavaScript, the functions can be of two types: *named* and *anonymous*. The difference between the two is in terms of memory usage and program maintainability. The callback methods consume more memory but for a shorter span of time. The jQuery framework, being written in JavaScript, inherits this feature of JavaScript, and we can use callback functionality in jQuery code as well. Let us move toward a demonstration by taking up an anonymous function. For the sake of simplicity, we will use the same code that we did while treating the `click` event. The code is

```
function clicking(functionObject){
    var span = document.createElement('span');
    span.innerHTML = 'The events are: document ready, window load and so on.';
    list.append(span);
    if(functionObject){
        functionObject();
        }
    }

var list = $('ul > li:nth-child(4)');
list.on('click', function(){
    clicking(function(){
        alert('This would be done at the end.')
        })
    });
```

Taking you through the code, the *parameter* passed on to the `clicking` method is a reference (object) to a function. You can call it a function pointer; we would not bother, and neither would the code! So, when you call the `clicking` function, you are passing it an entire function as the argument. Because the method that was passed was defined at the time of calling, and it has no name of its own, the method will be called as the anonymous method. This anonymous method will be called at the end of the code, once the other lines of code prior to this one have been executed. This is one example of a callback method. Let us move on to another method calling style. Keeping the `clicking` method the same, we will convert the anonymous function to a named function, as shown following:

```
function callbackMethod(){
    alert('This would be done at the end.')
}

var list = $('ul > li:nth-child(4)');
list.on('click', function(){
    clicking(callbackMethod)
});
```

As a word of caution, we would like to state here that the callback functions are just a special case of the regular functions, in that they behave exactly the same way as regular JavaScript methods. Because, in the example we provided, we executed our code without Ajax requests or any such time-bound process, the methods got executed at the end, but in a real-world scenario, the callback methods *can* take more time than usual. So, you can use the event callback methods with added checkpoints, to check if your boss likes your work.

Summary

You likely began this chapter as a novice, with little understanding of events. We explained the core concepts, and you learned about events and how to handle shorthand methods as well. This chapter explained how to program a callback method and familiarized you with the event models that the browsers follow and also how events are treated by browsers. It also taught you which approach jQuery follows to interpret events and make the event handling system cross-browser compatible. Finally, you saw how to create a callback method and use it with events.

In the next chapter, we will continue our discussion of events and walk you through them in more detail, because we believe that events are the most important component of a smart-looking web-based application that runs on a browser.

■ ■ ■

CHAPTER 6

Real World Events in jQuery

In the previous chapter, we discussed events in jQuery, and we will continue that discussion in this chapter, offering real-world events in jQuery. Programming actions taken on events have to be set carefully, and we can assure you that this is no simple matter. If a programmer has limited knowledge or an incomplete understanding of events, this can spell trouble. In order to fully unleash the power of events, a programmer must have a thorough understanding of events. In this chapter, readers will discover the real groundwork required in order to handle events, in addition to gaining hands-on knowledge of the application of events. By the end of this chapter, readers will be familiar with

- Common gotchas in event handling
- Preventing event propagation and bubbling
- Handling the event queue
- Building a jQuery UI accordion
- Validating form elements

Common Gotchas in Event Handling

The previous chapter addressed events, and we assume that you are now familiar with the methods that are required to handle events and that you can now apply those concepts you've learned to implement event handling in real-world applications. But before we guide you on that path, it is worth mentioning that there are a few gotchas in event handling that you, as a web developer, will confront. This section addresses some such cases and suggests solutions.

Handling Dynamic Elements

One of the most common problems that web developers face is how to handle events in the case of elements dynamically added to the Document Object Model (DOM). When we say "dynamically added," we mean those elements that are added to the DOM programmatically, either by using JavaScript code based on some algorithm in the program or by an Ajax call.

The Problem

Having mentioned dynamically adding elements to the DOM, let us take up an example in which we will use an Ajax call to add some element to the DOM and attempt to handle the event on this added element. Consider a very simple HTML code, as follows:

```
<html>
    <head>
        <title>Please make me work...</title>
    </head>
    <body>
        <div id="find-something"></div>
    </body>
</html>
```

Let's see the jQuery code that would work in the case of elements already present in the DOM but not in the current context.

```
$(document).ready(function(){
$('find-something').load('apress.html');

$('#apress').click(function(){
alert('You found me!');
});
});
```

The problem with this code is that when it makes an attempt to select the element with the id attribute apress, it fails to do so, because if you can see the HTML code, you will notice that the desired element is not in the DOM. This will underline a very important fact about the click method: such an event handler only works on elements that are already loaded on the page.

The Solution

This problem can be very easily solved by using a method provided by the jQuery framework that you came across quite frequently in Chapter 5—the on() method. As a quick refresher on the definition of the on() method, it is used to attach one or more event handlers for the selected elements and child elements. The solution to the problem is shown in the following code:

```
$(document).ready(function(){
    $('find-something').load('apress.html');

    $('#apress').on('click', function(){
        alert('You found me!');
    });
});
```

In the code sample we provided, the event handler is bound to the element with an id attribute apress, using the .on() method. Hence, the event handler will be executed once an element with the id attribute apress is loaded in the DOM tree and receives the mouse click event.

■ **Note** In older versions of jQuery (versions previous to 1.7), there was a .live() method that served the same purpose. You could use the .live() method to attach a handler to the event for all the elements that match the current selector in the DOM. This .live() method was deprecated in version 1.7 and removed in the 1.9 version of jQuery.

Handling jQuery Animation Buildup

Using the library methods provided by the jQuery framework, you can program more than one event handler to the same element. While this provides ease of use—you do not have to repeat writing the same selector—this can lead to an unusual behavior when multiple events occur in a short interval of time. This is not an undesired jQuery feature, but at times it can be an eyesore from the end user's perspective.

The Prelude

Before we move deeper into the next problem, we recommend that you look into some related topics via examples. The following discussion will provide examples of two types of event bindings: single event bindings and multiple event bindings. The types are quite intuitive to understand. In single event binding, only a single event is handled on the target element; whereas in multiple event binding, more than one event is handled on the target element.

Consider the following code sample of a single event binding:

```
$('.click-event').on('click',function(){
        alert( 'this element with class click-event was clicked');
    });
```

Also, note the following example, which shows multiple events but only one action to be taken on the event:

```
$('.many-event').on( 'click mouseleave', function() {
        alert( 'mouse hovered over or left a link');
    });
```

The jQuery framework also provides chaining in case of event handling, and this is shown in the example. Here we are chaining many event handlers for a single element (i.e., one function for each event binding).

```
$('.chaining-event').on({
    mouseenter: function () {
        alert('hovered over a link');
    },
    mouseleave: function () {
    alert('mouse left a link');
    },
    click: function () {
    alert('clicked on a link');
    }
});
```

The Problem

Our intention in "The Prelude" was to segue to another discussion related to another potential problem with programming event handling using jQuery. We would like to underline the fact that this is actually a feature provided by jQuery, but as we stated in the chapter's introduction, lack of a proper working knowledge regarding this feature leads to problems. The feature we are talking about is the *jQuery animation buildup*.

Problems arise when a number of events take place on the same element in a quick succession at such a point in time that the preceding event handler has not finished its execution. Let us take the example of a click event. Problems can arise when too many clicks populate a queue. In such cases, you might have to wait for the events to take place, and the page looks worse because it might appear to the end user that the page is working on its own!

The Solution

The jQuery framework provides the .stop() method to stop any queued animation and prevent animation queue buildup. Hence, you can utilize this method to solve the problem we mentioned. The usage is as shown in the following code:

```
$('#anySelector').stop().animate('slow', function(){
    //.. Carry out some task.
});
```

Before jumping directly to the solution, we think you should know about the .stop() method and its signature. The signature is pretty simple.

```
$('#anySelector').stop(clearQueue,jumpToEnd);
```

This methods works well with all the jQuery animation functions, including fading, sliding, and any custom animations. Both the parameters are optional and default to false. The first parameter, clearQueue, specifies whether to remove the queued animation as well as stop the animation. The second parameter jumpToEnd indicates whether the currently executing animation should be completed.

Now you can have a look into the following example, which shows a simple animation using the .stop() method, thereby providing a solution to the problem we mentioned.

```
//HTML
<div id="apress">Click to animate some other div!</div>
<div id="container">Hello Readers!</div>

//jQuery
$(document).ready(function(){
    $("#apress").click(function () {
        $("#container").stop().animate({
            height: '+=50'
        }, 1000);
    });});

//CSS
#container,#apress
{
    padding:5px;
    text-align:center;
    background-color:#4679BD;
    border:solid 1px #c3c3c3;
}
```

```
#container
{
    height: 20px;
}
```

So, in the preceding example, we use the `.stop()` method to stop all the queued animation that might build up if more than one `click` event occurs on the `div` element with the `id` attribute `apress`. Hence, with the use of the `.stop()` method, when `.animate()` is called and there are multiple `click` events in a quick succession, `.stop()` will stop all the previously queued animation and will only respond to the last `click` event that has taken place.

■ **Note**   Try this and check the result at jsfiddle at `http://jsfiddle.net/mukund002/q0umgs29/3/`. We suggest experimenting with and without the `.stop()` method in this example.

Preventing Event Propagation and Bubbling

We discussed the basic concepts of event propagation and bubbling in Chapter 5, but here we will go into further detail. You may recall from Chapter 5 that the concept of event bubbling comes in handy in those situations in which a single event, such as mouse click, may be handled by two or multiple event handlers defined at different levels of the DOM. You may also recall from the previous chapter that event capturing is opposite to bubbling, in terms of how the event gets propagated. In the case of capturing, the event is handled at the first level (highest level) and then it goes to the lower level.

To stop event propagation (either by stopping event capturing or event bubbling), we have to tell the event handler to stop propagating further, and this can be achieved by using the following jQuery code:

```
event.stopPropagation();
```

`event.stopPropagation()` works in all the browsers except for IE prior to version 9.0. For earlier IE versions, you can set the `cancelBubble` property available with IE to `true`, as shown in the following JavaScript code:

```
event.cancelBubble =true;
```

A one-line way to achieve cross-browser code is shown in the following code snippet:

```
event.stopPropagation ? event.stopPropagation() : (event.cancelBubble=true);
```

Now that you are familiar with the functioning of `event.stopPropagation`, we will take up another method provided by the jQuery framework—the `preventDefault` method. This discussion will help you to understand the difference between the two methods, and you will be able to gain a clear understanding of which method to use in which circumstance.

The `preventDefault` method is called on the event object and is used to prevent the default action that the browser takes on at the occurrence of an event.

For example, have a look at the following code, in which we have a button element inside of a `div` element, and we program an event handler to respond to a mouse `click` event on both of the elements:

```
<div id="apress">
    <a id="author">Click Me</a>
</div>
```

The jQuery code supporting the example is as shown:

```
$("#apress").click(function() {
    alert("Apress!!");
});

$("#author").click(function(event) {
    alert("Authors!!");
    event.preventDefault();
});
```

So, in the code setup we provided, when a `click` event occurs, the anchor element's click handler is called, followed by the div's click handler, because the `preventDefault` method only prevents the default action associated with the anchor element from occurring but not the event from propagating to other parts of the DOM. Hence, you will see two alert messages: "Authors!!", followed by "Apress!!".

As a further attempt to clearly demarcate the difference between the uses of the two methods, we recommend that you have a look at the following code snippet (which is just a one-line addition to the previous example):

```
$("#apress").click(function() {
    alert("Apress!!");// mouse click on div element
});

$("#author").click(function(event) {
    alert("Authors!!");
    event.preventDefault();
    event.stopPropagation();
});
```

Here, not only is the default action prevented from occurring, but the event is also stopped from propagating throughout the DOM. The output in this case would just be "Authors!!".

Handling the Event Queue

As you know, a queue in general terms, is a line or sequence of people awaiting their turn to be attended, such as when people line up to board a bus at a bus stop.

In computer science, a queue is an abstract data type in which the first element is inserted at one end, called REAR, and an existing element is deleted from the other end, called FRONT. This makes up a FIFO (First In, First Out) rule, which means the element inserted first will be removed first. Examples of queues can be seen in call center phone systems, serving requests on a single shared resource, such as CPU task scheduling, printer queue, etc.

In terms of event queues, there is/are one or more function/functions waiting to run. A queue can be used for creating animations in most cases, but you can use one anytime you have to run a sequence of functions. Our current context assumes a similar meaning of the term *queue*. In the following text discussion, we provide you additional details about how queues are handled in jQuery.

How Handling Works in a jQuery Event Queue

Event queues can be handled by a jQuery internal queue handler, which is attached to a particular event on a particular element. The first time you bind an event to that element, it initializes the queue and uses the JavaScript method addEventListener to bind the event to jQuery's generic event-handling function. When the event is triggered, the function uses event.target to determine which element it is, and then it finds the queue of handlers associated with it and calls them in the sequence.

The .on() method utilizes this mechanism and takes advantage of event bubbling. When an event occurs, it is triggered on the specific target element and also on all its containing elements, including child elements as well as the dynamically added elements. When you bind the handler to a container, it saves the selector string in the queue entry. When it is processing that entry in the handler queue, it tests whether event.target (which is still the specific element that you clicked) matches the selector and then executes the handler function. This mechanism allows you to bind handlers for elements that have not yet been added to the DOM. This is particularly useful when you have a list of elements that is updated dynamically via an Ajax call (for example, adding rows to a table or adding a particular div on some event).

Now that we have discussed how the internal mechanism of jQuery event queue works, let's discuss the queue() method provided by the jQuery framework.

The jQuery queue() Method

An element can have several queues. The queue() method is used to show the queue of functions to be executed on the set of matched elements.

The signature is pretty simple to understand:

```
$(selectorElement).queue(queueName);
```

In this signature, the parameter queueName is optional.

The default queue in jQuery is fx, and it has some special properties that are not shared with other queues. So, when using the queue method as $(elem).queue(function() {}), the fx queue will automatically de-queue the next function and run it automatically if the queue hasn't started.

■ **Note** The fx queue is used by the .animate() method in particular. In Chapter 7, we will cover in more detail this method and the other methods provided by the jQuery framework to ease creation of animations.

If you are using any custom queue, you must de-queue the function, as it will not start automatically.

Let's consider an example of an event queue that has many events to perform.

```
//HTML
<div class='relative'>
    <a class='event-queue'>Click Here</a>
</div>

//CSS
<style>
    .relative {
        position: relative;
    }
```

```
    .event-queue {
        background: green;
        border-radius: 4px;
        color: #fff;
        display: inline-block;
        left: 0;
        padding: 5px;
        position: absolute;
        top: 60px;
    }
</style>
```

//jQuery

```
        $('.event-queue').on('click', function () {
            $(this).animate({left: '+=400'}, 4000)
                    .slideToggle(1000)
                    .slideToggle('fast')
                    .animate({ left: '-=400'}, 1500)
                    .hide('slow')
                    .show(1200)
                    .slideUp('slow')
                    .slideDown('slow')
                    .animate({ left: '+=400'}, 4000);
        });
```

As you can see from the preceding code, we have set up a queue of events waiting to run at the selector click event. The output of the code is an animated Click Here button that slides from side to side at varying speeds and also appears and disappears. As we mentioned previously in a note, we discuss the `.slideUp()`, `.slideDown()`, `.slideToggle()`, `.hide()` and `.show()` methods in the next chapter.

■ **Note**   You must try this fiddle to see the output: `http://jsfiddle.net/mukund002/d2v7vpyc/`.

Building a jQuery UI Accordion

An accordion is a special type of tab-like UI that can be very useful when showing lots of data in small amounts of space (see Figure 6-1). You can use an accordion, as required, to make any customizations. Before you learn about making custom accordions, we will explore the jQuery UI accordion.

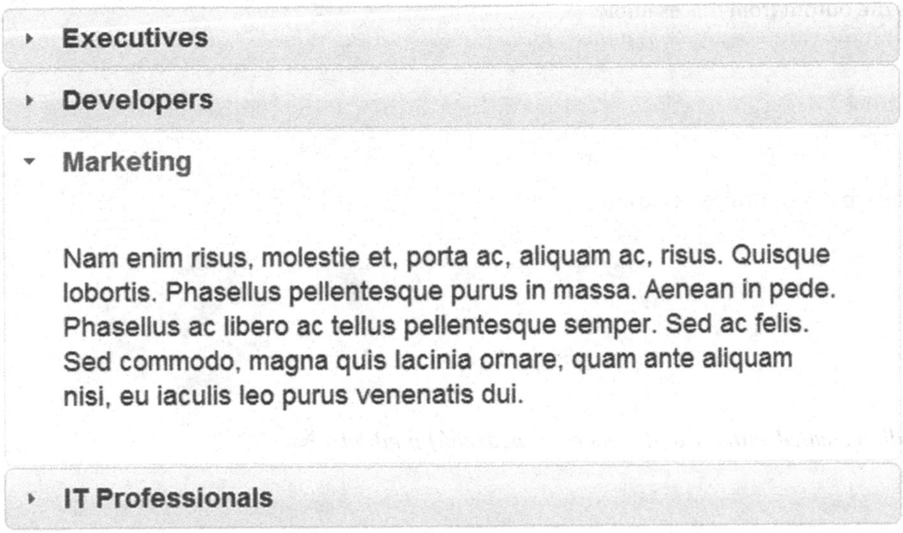

> ▸ **Executives**

> ▸ **Developers**

> ▾ **Marketing**

> Nam enim risus, molestie et, porta ac, aliquam ac, risus. Quisque lobortis. Phasellus pellentesque purus in massa. Aenean in pede. Phasellus ac libero ac tellus pellentesque semper. Sed ac felis. Sed commodo, magna quis lacinia ornare, quam ante aliquam nisi, eu iaculis leo purus venenatis dui.

> ▸ **IT Professionals**

Figure 6-1. A jQuery UI accordion

Using the jQuery UI Accordion

jQuery UI makes it easy to create accordions, and it can be very useful in cases where little space is available but much information has to be shown to the end user. The following example uses a ready-made jQuery accordion that illustrates how easy it is to use one. The jQuery team has already cooked the accordion for you, so all you need to do is serve the dish.

```
//HTML
<div id="apress-accordion">
    <h3>jQuery</h3>
    <div>
        <p> Practical jQuery by Mukund and Ankur </p>
    </div>
    <h3>PhpStorm</h3>
    <div>
        <p>PhpStorm Cookbook by Mukund and Ankur</p>
    </div>
    <h3>PMP (Yet to come)</h3>
    <div>
        <p> Just Planning on this</p>
    </div>
</div>

//jQuery
 $( "#apress-accordion" ).accordion();
```

Figure 6-2 shows the output from this example.

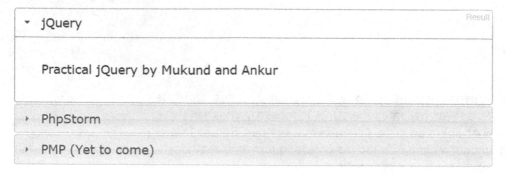

Figure 6-2. *An accordion created with the basic jQuery* accordion( ) *method*

> ■ **Note** You can view this accordion example in action by executing the code using a fiddle located at
> http://jsfiddle.net/mukund002/rn7meh7x/.

The important thing to note here is that you must include the jQuery UI to get the result. For the record, jQuery UI is another framework built with the functionality provided by the jQuery framework. Quoting the official jQuery UI web site,

> *jQuery UI is a curated set of user interface interactions, effects, widgets, and themes built on top of the jQuery JavaScript Library. Whether you're building highly interactive web applications or you just need to add a date picker to a form control, jQuery UI is the perfect choice.*

> ■ **Note** Interested readers may find additional details about jQuery UI from the official jQuery UI web site
> located at http://jqueryui.com/.

Also, the jQuery UI framework can be used for developing web pages, by using the CDN URL inside the desired web page (the appropriate version has to be chosen from http://code.jquery.com/ui/). The jQuery UI framework can also be downloaded and included in the desired web page. Coverage of jQuery UI is provided in Chapter 11.

In the code example we provided earlier in this section, you will have noticed that we just called the ready-made accordion method, which is doing all the work for you. Although this is very convenient, we do not recommend that you create your accordions with the help of the built-in method. The reason we would not recommend using it is because we want you to learn how to create an accordion, as explained in the next section. However, as we noted previously, the built-in method can be useful for meeting very basic accordion requirements.

Customizing an Accordion

An accordion can be customized in various ways to accommodate different requirements, and you need to keep a few things in mind while coding an accordion.

- Only one content section can be active at a time. For example, if you have five blocks in your accordion, then at any point in time, only one will be opened, and the remaining four will be closed.

- You may have to decide whether you want to open the accordion via a click event or on a mouseover, or even on some keyboard key press.

- You can use the .slideUp() and .slideDown() methods for animation, or any other function as well, for animating the accordion close and open activities.

Accordions are most commonly used in FAQs in which you have questions and answers that, if just displayed straight to the normal page, might become incredibly long and potentially cumbersome for users to read or find the answer they are looking for. It would provide a better experience if users could just scroll through the answers and select a topic that would seem to provide the correct answer to the question being considered.

The approach we have taken in this example is that on the click event of the direct children of class "apress-accordion", we remove the "active" class attribute from all dt elements. We then apply the slide-up animation on all direct children of the dd elements.

We will provide an example showing a custom accordion, and then you'll see how it works.

```
//HTML
<fieldset>
    <legend>Custom Accordion</legend>
    <dl class="no-bullets apress-accordion">
        <dt class="active"><strong>Short Description</strong></dt>

        <dd style="display: block">
            <b>About Practical jQuery</b>

            <p>Practical jQuery is your step-by-step guide to learning the jQuery library,
                taking you from downloading jQuery all the way to extending it by writing
                your own plug-ins and testing the DOM using QUnit.</p>
        </dd>
        <dt><strong>Audience</strong></dt>

        <dd>
            <b>Targeted Audience</b>

            <p>Practical jQuery is for web developers who are confident with HTML and CSS
                and familiar with basic JavaScript but struggling to come to grips with
                jQuery. Practical jQuery is great for the developer wanting to enhance
                his/her skillset and wanting to code quicker and efficiently.</p>
        </dd>
        <dt><strong>What You Will Learn</strong></dt>

        <dd>
            <b>Why Practical jQuery.What You Will Learn</b>
```

```html
                <ul>
                        <li>Learn why jQuery is so popular and how to download and install
                            it.</li>
                        <li>Use jQuery's powerful manipulation tools to dynamically update your
                            web site's content.</li>
                        <li>Animate content and build your own image slider with jQuery's
                            animation tools.</li>
                        <li>Extend the library by writing your own custom plug-ins.</li>
                        <li>Use plug-ins created by others in the community and integrate them
                            into your web site.</li>
                        <li>Refactoring and Testing DOM Manipulation using QUnit.</li>
                </ul>

            </dd>
        </dl>
    </fieldset>
```

//CSS
```css
fieldset{
    border-radius:1em;
    border:solid 1px #ccc;
}
.apress-accordion dt {
    font: bold 14px/18px "Trebuchet Ms", Arial, "sans-serif";
    color: #545c60;
    cursor: pointer;
    border: solid 1px #cfcfcf;
    padding: 0.535rem
}

.apress-accordion dt.active {
    background-color: #f1f1f1
}

.apress-accordion dd {
    background-color: #f1f1f1;
    border: solid 1px #cfcfcf;
    padding: 0.535rem;
    display: none;
    margin:0
}

.apress-accordion dd.show {
    display: block
}
```

//jQuery
```javascript
    $('.apress-accordion > dt').on('click', function () {
        $('.apress-accordion > dt').removeClass('active');
        $('.apress-accordion > dd').slideUp('fast');
        $(this).next('dd').slideDown('fast');
        $(this).addClass('active');
    });
```

Now it is the time for some explanation. The CSS is easy to understand. We have one CSS class named "active" through which we assign some background color to differentiate the active part from the nonactive or collapsed part. In the HTML code, you can see that we have one container named "apress-accordion". In the accordion example, when we click the dt element, we remove the active class, use the .slideUp() animation function to animate the dt element downward (to give it an expanding visualization), and mark it as active thereafter. This occurs simultaneously with the removal of the same active class from the previously active element and by using the .slideUp() animation method (to give it a contracting visualization). In simple terms, we just add the active class to the element that we click and remove the active class attribute from the previously clicked element.

Figure 6-3 shows the result of our example.

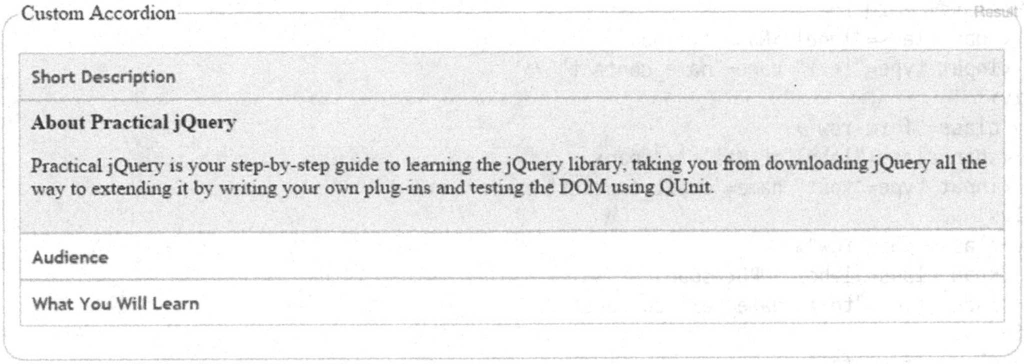

Figure 6-3. *The accordion created with the code in our example*

■ **Note**   You can also see the result on jsfiddle at `http://jsfiddle.net/mukund002/0s71pyax/1/`.

Validating Form Elements

When it comes to validating form elements, different web developers follow and apply various approaches, in addition to sometimes having the need to set the look and feel of form validation per a business requirement. Form validation is helpful when you want to validate the HTML form input data before sending it to the server. The HTML data that are checked by jQuery could be (but are not limited to) the following:

- Required fields are all completed.

- E-mail address is valid.

- Date is in a valid format.

- Fields that require a valid numeric entry do not contain text.

- The field input has a minimum length.

These are a few form validation criteria that we can check using jQuery form validation. Although there could be more things that you can validate, the listed points are the ones very commonly used by web developers. We will provide an example to illustrate the working of the jQuery Validate plug-in.

Using the Validate Plug-in

First of all, we must include the jQuery Validate plug-in, for which we resort to the content delivery network (CDN) URL to include this file. The URL for this is

http://ajax.aspnetcdn.com/ajax/jquery.validate/1.13.1/jquery.validate.js

Next, we write some HTML code to render the form. We then add some CSS to improve the presentation and complete the example with the jQuery code. All this is as shown in the following code:

```
//HTML
<form id="apress_contact" method="post" action="">
    <div class="form-row">
        <span class="label">Name *</span>
        <input type="text" name="name_contact" />
    </div>
    <div class="form-row">
        <span class="label">E-Mail *</span>
        <input type="text" name="email_contact" />
    </div>
    <div class="form-row">
        <span class="label">URL</span>
        <input type="text" name="url_contact" />
    </div>
    <div class="form-row">
        <span class="label">Enter Your comment *</span>
        <textarea name="comment_contact" ></textarea>
    </div>
    <div class="form-row">
        <input class="submit" type="submit" value="Submit">
    </div>
</form>
```

```
//CSS
    * { font-family: Verdana; font-size: 11px; line-height: 14px; }
    .submit { margin-left: 125px; margin-top: 10px;}
    .label { display: block; float: left; width: 120px; text-align: right; margin-right: 5px; }
    .form-row { padding: 5px 0; clear: both; width: 700px; }
    label.error { width: 250px; display: block; float: left; color: red; padding-left: 10px;
}
    input[type=text], textarea { width: 250px; float: left; }
    textarea { height: 50px; }
```

```
//jQuery
$(document).ready(function () {

    $('#apress_contact').validate({ // initialize the plugin
        rules: {
            name_contact: {
                required: true
            },
```

```
        email_contact: {
            required: true,
            email: true
        },
        url_contact: {
            required: true
        },
        comment_contact: {
            required: true
        }
    },
    messages: {
        name_contact: "Please enter your full name.",
        url_contact: "Please enter the valid URL",
     comment_contact: "Please enter some comment."
    } ,
    submitHandler: function (form) {
        alert('valid form submitted');
        return false;
    }
});

});
```

In the HTML, you can see there is a form that has a unique id attribute, "apress_contact", which is used to validate the form The CSS code is added to make the HTML page attractive, by creating proper margins, padding, and by assigning CSS classes containing such CSS code with an input box, text area, etc.

In the jQuery code, you can see that we have used the validate() method, which initializes the Validate plug-in and takes care of the validation conditions that have to be applied. Explaining further, in the preceding example, we have used name="name_contact" for the first element and have applied the required: true rule on it, which shows that the field is mandatory to fill. The email: true rule indicates that you have to enter the e-mail ID in the correct format only. For e-mail, we have two rules: one for validating required value and another for validating correct format. Figure 6-4 shows the completed form, but without a valid e-mail format.

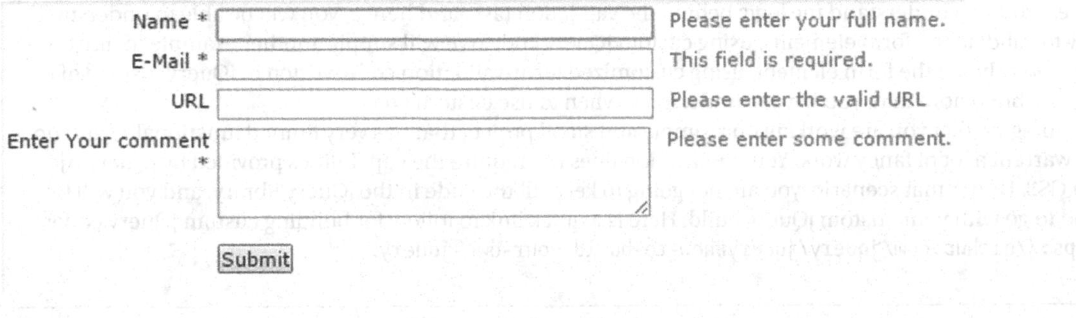

Figure 6-4. *The form created in our example, showing validation at work*

You can set the custom messages for any field. If you don't set any custom message, it will take the default message that is used by the plug-in.

In the preceding example, you have only dealt with rules and messages, but you have more options to explore, such as groups. For example, you may want to use first name and last name and to group your error messages. In such a scenario, you can use groups. A group consists of a logical group name as the key and a space-separated list of element names as the value. You can use errorPlacement to control where the group message is placed.

```
$("#apress_contact").validate({
  groups: {
name_contact: "fname lname"
  },
  errorPlacement: function(error, element) {
    if (element.attr("name") == "fname" || element.attr("name") == "lname" ) {
      error.insertAfter("#lastname"); // Insert the error message related to (first or last)
      name after the lastname
    } else {
      error.insertAfter(element); // Insert the error message after the error creating
      element
    }
  }
});
```

In this code, you can see that if the element attribute name is either equal to fname or to lname, in both cases, we are inserting the error after lastname, and if the condition is not true, then we insert it before the element.

The jQuery Validate plug-in can be particularly useful to novice users, who can employ it to set up form validation in no time at all.

■ **Note**   You can explore this example code on jsfiddle at `http://jsfiddle.net/mukund002/xs5vrrso/124/`.

Validating Form Elements Using Customized jQuery

It is essential to understand the logic behind the validation task, and hence, you will be able to understand how to validate the form elements, using custom jQuery code. We will supply another example to illustrate how you validate the form element, using customized form-validation code written in jQuery instead of a plug-in, but before that, you have to understand when to use custom code.

Imagine that you are working on a simple and small project that has very limited functionality and does not warrant a lot of fancy work. Your application does not require the capabilities provided by jQuery Ajax and CSS. Under that scenario, you are not going to keep all the code in the jQuery library, and you will be good to go with your custom jQuery build. Here is a quick link to follow for building custom jQuery code: `https://github.com/jquery/jquery#how-to-build-your-own-jquery`.

■ **Tip**   It is recommended that you write custom code, as it not only cuts down the number of lines of code but also lets you focus on the main goal you are trying to achieve.

The following HTML code creates the form for our customized form validation:

```
//HTML
<div class="container">
    <form name="myform" action="#" method="post">
        <fieldset>
            <legend>Contact Me</legend>
            <div class="form-group">
                <label>Name</label>
                <input type="text" required name="name" placeholder="Name*"
                    data-error-message="Please Type Your Full Name." />
            </div>
            <div class="form-group">
                <label>Email Address</label>
                <input type="email" required name="email" placeholder="Email Address*"
                    data-error-message="Please Type Your Email Id." />
            </div>
            <div class="form-group">
                <label>Phone Number</label>
                <input type="tell" required name="phone" placeholder="Phone Number*"
                    data-error-message="Please Type Your Phone Number." />
            </div>
            <div class="form-group">
                <label>Message</label>
                <textarea required name="message" placeholder="Message*"
                    data-error-message="Please Type Your Message here."></textarea>
            </div>
            <button type="submit" class="btn btn-success">Submit</button>
        </fieldset>
    </form>
</div>
```

From the preceding code, you can see that we have a form having the elements input type and textarea, as follows:

```
<input type="text" required name="name" placeholder="Name*" data-error-message="Please Type
Your Full Name.">
...
<textarea required name="message" placeholder="Message*" data-error-message="Please Type
Your Message here."></textarea>
```

We have one attribute named required, which we will be using in our jQuery code to check if some element mandatorily requires input. We have another attribute, data-error-message, with which we display an appropriate message, if some mandatory field is left blank.

Next, we add some CSS code to make the HTML elements look better.

```
//CSS
*, *:before, *:after {
    box-sizing: border-box;
}
```

```css
.container {
    max-width: 46em;
    margin: 0 auto;
    width: 100%;
    font: 400 13px/15px Arial;
}

fieldset {
    border-radius: .5em;
    padding: 0 20px 20px 20px;
}

legend {
    font: 800 16px/18px Arial;
}

input[type="text"],
input[type="email"],
input[type="tell"],
textarea {
    background-color: #ffffff;
    border: 1px solid #ccc;
    border-radius: 4px;
    box-shadow: 0 1px 1px rgba(0, 0, 0, 0.075) inset;
    color: #2c3e50;
    font: 400 13px/15px Arial;
    padding:10px;
    transition: border-color 0.15s ease-in-out 0s, box-shadow 0.15s ease-in-out 0s;
    width: 100%;
}

input:focus {
    border-color: #2c3e50;
    box-shadow: 0 1px 1px rgba(0, 0, 0, 0.075) inset, 0 0 8px rgba(44, 62, 80, 0.6);
    outline: 0 none;
}

.btn {
    background-color: #009948;
    border: 1px solid #18bc9c;
    border-radius: 4px;
    cursor: pointer;
    color: #fff;
    display: inline-block;
    margin-top: 20px;
    padding:4px 15px;
    white-space: nowrap;
}

.error {
    color: red;
}
```

```
label {
    display: block;
    font-size: 0.85em;
    line-height: 1.76471em;
    margin: 5px 0;
    opacity: 0;
    transition: top 0.3s ease 0s, opacity 0.3s ease 0s;
}

.fillingStart label {
    opacity: 1;
}
```

Now it's time to see jQuery in action. We have broken the jQuery into several pieces, so that we can explain the code as we go.

```
//jQuery
$(document).ready(function () {
    var fieldElement = $('input,textarea'), errorMessage = '';
    $(fieldElement).on('keyup blur', function () {
        var thisElement = $(this);
        if (thisElement.attr('required')) {
            errorMessage = thisElement.attr('data-error-message');
            if (thisElement.val().length > 0) {
                thisElement.parent('div').addClass('fillingStart');
                if (thisElement.next('.error')) {
                    thisElement.next('.error').remove();
                }
            } else {
                thisElement.parent('div').removeClass('fillingStart');
                if (thisElement.next('.error').length == 0) {
                    thisElement.parent('div').append('<div class="error">' + errorMessage +
                    '</div>');
                }
            }
        }
    }
```

In this part of the jQuery code, we have a variable, fieldElement, in which field elements are stored. In this example, we only have the input and textarea elements. On the keyup or blur event of the form element, a function is called. If the current attribute is required, then we show a message that we have written in data-error-message. If the user starts filling some value to the box, we add a CSS class fillingStart, and the error message is removed from display.

So, in simple terms, we have just checked a few conditions, such as whether the element is blank, and then display some message if it is. If the field has the correct value, we remove that error class, and the error message will be removed.

In the following chunk of code, we check the correct format of the input e-mail ID. If the current element's type attribute is equal to email, then the current element must start with a given regular expression. If the condition is not satisfied, then some error will be displayed.

```
if (thisElement.attr('type') == 'email') {
    if (
        !thisElement.val()
        .toLowerCase()
        .match(/^[_a-z0-9-]+(\.[_a-z0-9-]+)*@[a-z0-9-]+(\.[a-z0-9-]+)*(\.[a-z]{2,4})$/)
    ) {
        if (thisElement.next('.error').length == 0) {
            errorMessage = 'Please Enter Your Valid Email Id';
            thisElement.parent('div')
            .append('<div class="error">' + errorMessage + '</div>');
        }
    }
}
```

The following code will check for a type attribute that equals to tell and will indicate whether the telephone number is valid or not, against some regular expression:

```
if (thisElement.attr('type') == 'tell') {
    if (!thisElement.val()
        .toLowerCase()
        .match(/^((\+[1-9]{1,4}[ \-]*)|(\([0-9]{2,3}\) [\-]*)|([0-9]{2,4})[ \-]*)*?[0-9]
        {3,4}?[ \-]*[0-9]{3,4}?$/)) {
        if (thisElement.next('.error').length == 0) {
            errorMessage = 'Please Enter Your Valid Phone no';
            thisElement.parent('div')
            .append('<div class="error">' + errorMessage + '</div>');
        }
    }
}
```

The following code offers a usage of the :submit selector:

```
$(':submit').on('click', function () {
    var fieldElement = $(this).parents('form').find($('input,textarea')),
        success = true;
    fieldElement.each(function () {
        if ($(this).val() == '') {
            fieldElement.each(function () {
                $(this).focus()
            });
            success = false;
        }
    });
    if (success == true) {
        $(this).parents('form').submit();
    }
});
```

In the preceding code, the `:submit` selector selects the `input` elements with the type attribute `submit` and performs some action on the `click` event. If the form elements are filled, it submits the form. Figure 6-5 shows the rendered form from our example.

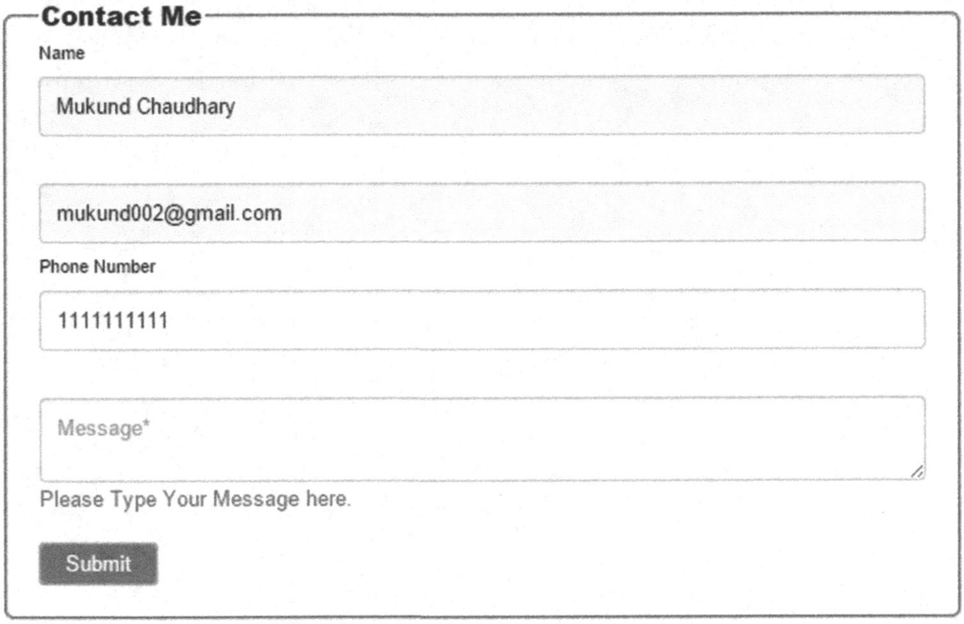

Figure 6-5. *The form used in the example*

■ **Note**   Using `input:submit` as a selector will not select the `button` element. You can go through the code here: `http://jsfiddle.net/mukund002/dmq7rfxb/1/`.

Summary

You already had a basic knowledge of event handling from Chapter 5, but this chapter utilized that knowledge and addressed some common problems and solving them with handling events. It also taught you how to handle the event queue. In due course, the chapter also familiarized you with the jQuery UI accordion, in addition to explaining form validation using jQuery from an event-handling perspective.

In the next chapter, we will address animation in jQuery and take up a number of different commonly used animation applications, such as the slider and light box.

CHAPTER 7

■ ■ ■

Animation in jQuery

One of the (many) reasons for jQuery's popularity in the web development community is its ability to simplify the life of the programmer responsible for creating transition effects on a web page. We will take up this aspect of jQuery in the current chapter. jQuery has a huge, comprehensive set of animation functions with which to perform a number of different animations that are key to a number of features seen on web sites these days, including the fabled slider. In this chapter, we will introduce jQuery's animate function and then look at how we can implement a slider. Covered also are common issues with animations and ways to avoid bugs. By the end of this chapter, you will have learned:

- What the approaches to achieve animation without using jQuery are
- The jQuery animation workhorse: `animate()`
- Common animation types, such as fading or sliding
- The `toggle()` method in jQuery
- How to create a basic light box functionality using jQuery
- How to make the animation behavior work according to specific needs
- How to create a basic image slider

Life Without jQuery

Let us begin this entirely new chapter with a very short and imaginary scenario.

Imagine a parallel universe in which JavaScript technology has already found its niche in the world of web development. Because a substantial amount of time has been spent by people working on JavaScript, they have gained a fair amount of working knowledge in that programming language. There is a person A who has been assigned the work of adding some moving objects to the web site. Because he has a good deal of experience, he will carry out the task using JavaScript.

So, A will go ahead and create an animation procedure to manipulate the *left* and *top* properties provided by CSS for the DOM elements. Because the process of animation requires moving (repositioning) the desired DOM elements, the developer will use such methods as `setTimeout` and `setInterval` to make repeated calls to the animation procedure. Assuming that the task is to start moving some div element along some direction on the screen, A could write some code, as follows:

```
<!DOCTYPE html>
<html>
<head>
    <style type="text/css">
        #to-move-block{
            position: absolute;
            top: 0px;
            left: 0px;
        }
    </style>
    <title>:: Animations and animations ::</title>
</head>
<body>
    <div id="to-move-block">This is a moving block</div>
</body>
<script type="text/javascript">
    var i = 0;
    var blockToMove = document.getElementById('to-move-block');
    setInterval(function(){
        i ++;
        var pixelUnit = i+'px';
        blockToMove.style.left = pixelUnit;
        blockToMove.style.top = pixelUnit;
    }, 5000);
</script>
</html>
```

Let us move back into our world and try to explain what the JavaScript code attempts to do. But we will start off with the HTML part first, so that you get an idea of the HTML code. The HTML code contains just a single DOM element, which is intended to be animated—the div element with the id attribute to-move-block. The CSS code is quite simple to understand. We will explain that the styling has been applied only to the div element present, and the styling securely positions the div at the topmost and left-most corner of the screen.

Now for the animation engine—the JavaScript code. There is a method known as setInterval provided by the JavaScript library. This method performs the task of calling a method specified as the first argument to it at intervals of the number of milliseconds specified as the second argument to it. Here, the setInterval method calls an anonymous function to increment the pixel count by 1 and make it the new left and top positions of the only div available, and it makes the call to this method at intervals of half a second. It will be natural for you to ask whether the same task could be done by using for, while, or do-while constructs, which are already available with such a mature language as JavaScript. To this, we would respond that for, while, and do-while make the CPU remain consistently engaged, and this could mean that the browser that renders the web page you created will freeze, and this can hamper user experience.

So, the animation proceeds when the page is rendered and the developer A was honest in executing the assigned tasks. In Figure 7-1, you can see how the animation proceeds by using the JavaScript code.

Figure 7-1. This frame sequence shows the effect of the animation produced by the JavaScript code

The story is imaginary, but it attempts to convey some causes. It makes us think about the times we are living in. There are people across the globe who are JavaScript experts, with the ability to write any piece of functionality using JavaScript. So far, so good. But consider a fact: every time developers are asked to create a functionality, and they do it their own way, are they not repeating themselves? So, if there are two developers—A and B—working on web development projects, and they follow their own way to program the required functionality, they will be fulfilling the requirements of the company, but doing so by violating a basic principle of software engineering.

Software engineering principles always emphasize that efforts not be repeated. This is termed DRY (Don't Repeat Yourself). We have solid justification for supporting this statement in the current context. Here, an important aspect that we would like to emphasize is that requirements drive the use of technology. So, even if we are trying to demonstrate the use of jQuery, this use might not apply to certain business requirements. There may be those holding a strong belief in the mighty JavaScript who would argue against the use of jQuery for animation, but for us, the decision to choose between the two options is up to you, the developer.

■ **Note**   If you have a chance to have a sneak peek into the source code of the jQuery framework, you will discover that even jQuery makes use of the methods provided by JavaScript. This is quite natural, because, after all, jQuery is just a framework written in JavaScript!

The point that we would like to emphasize is that what you can do in jQuery, you can do in JavaScript, but our concern involves the following two aspects of engineering:

- Writing the same code again and again by people across the globe will not help the developer community at all. Everyone will be stuck writing the basic functionality that jQuery provides by default.

- JavaScript requires expertise, whereas jQuery does not. So, if a developer writes code in JavaScript and does not use jQuery, it is the ethical responsibility of the developer to add proper documentation, because the algorithm implemented in JavaScript may be hard to understand by the next person who is to work on the same project at the same company. This is an aspect of code maintainability. Because jQuery (or any other framework) has standard documentation available, you can at least be assured regarding the amount of effort required by the new person on your team.

jQuery's animate( )

The jQuery framework provides the `animate( )` function, which performs well under most conditions. The process of animation in web pages is principally brought about by modification of the CSS properties. As a part of animation, you will be required to modify the size, or relocate the object in question, by modifying the left and top CSS attributes of the object. The signature of the jQuery method is quite simple. Let's take up the example that we took up in the text immediately preceding. Again, the target that is required to be achieved is "Make a simple block move across the screen in a linear direction diagonally downward." The code that we propose for this purpose is

```
$('#to-move-block').animate({'left': 1000, 'top': 500});
```

Although this code looks simple, there are a number of aspects visible by using it. We will list all that we could zero in on. We encourage you to find additional such clues and remember them for quick reference, once you have a grasp of the idea behind the code.

We must have a DOM selector to be able to call the `animate( )` method. You can specify a class attribute here. So, if your HTML code takes some such form as

```
<div class='about-to-move'>This would be moving at some point in the future</div>
```

you can call the `animate( )` method as

```
$('.to-move-block').animate({'left': 1000, 'top': 500});
```

This code will produce the same effect as when you called the animation using the `id` selector. A selector is an entity that we described in a number of examples in the initial chapters of this book.

The `animate( )` method must have the CSS property as the mandatory argument. The jQuery framework provides the freedom either to provide a single CSS property or a list of CSS properties as the mandatory argument. Because we started with a list of properties, the list of properties has to be passed to this method in a *key:value* format quite similar to that followed by JSON. For the sake of demonstration and explanation, the values passed to the `animate( )` method in the example we took up are

- 1000 pixel value to the CSS left attribute

- 500 pixel value to the CSS top attribute

It is quite apparent from the demonstration and the explanation that the default unit used by the animate( ) method is the pixel (PX)

There is a speed attribute that specifies how long the method will take to complete the process of animation. The unit is milliseconds. You wonder where the speed attribute in the example we took up is. Our answer is that the animate( ) method assumes a default value of 400 milliseconds as the speed attribute. To explain the speed attribute, suppose the left part of the block has to move from the position left = 400 to left = 1000. The path to travel across the screen would be 600 pixels. The time that you will want it complete the length is 400 milliseconds. As *speed=distance/time*, because time is the varying entity, the developer community has coined the term *entity speed* to describe how fast or slow an animation is. Less value means more speed, because the time taken for the animation to complete is less, and more value means less speed, because, quite naturally, more time will be taken by the method to complete the animation.

A slow animation can be brought about by using a large value. So, the animation that we took up in the immediately preceding text can be slowed down by using a speed value of 1000. This can be demonstrated by the following usage:

```
$('#to-move-block').animate({'left': 1000, 'top': 500}, 1000);
```

Similarly, if you want to make the animation faster, you will require a small value. Taking up the same example, the code will be

```
$('#to-move-block').animate({'left': 1000, 'top': 500}, 100);
```

The numbers passed on to animate as the last argument stand for that many milliseconds. Thus, the faster animation will take one-tenth of a second to complete, and the slower animation will take a second to complete. The jQuery framework provides some constants to represent fast and slow animations. So, fast will represent a value of 200 milliseconds, and slow will represent a value of 600. The usage is as follows:

```
$('#to-move-block').animate({'left': 1000, 'top': 500}, 'slow');
```

or

```
$('#to-move-block').animate({'left': 1000, 'top': 500}, 'fast');
```

Animation refers to the state of being alive. The jQuery animate( ) method attempts to "give life," by providing an easing attribute that you can optionally pass on as the third argument to it. The easing attribute provides a better appearance to the motion of the animated object. There are two modes of easing from which you can select: linear and swing.

The linear easing makes the animation follow a regular and a linear time. The animation will run at a consistent speed throughout the duration it is supposed to. To use this effect, you can have the term linear as the third argument. The usage is as follows:

```
$('#to-move-block').animate({'left': 1000, 'top': 500}, 8000, 'linear');
```

Similarly, the animated object can be made to start slowly and then accelerate to the maximum speed exactly midway in the animation from when the animated object decelerates, continuously decreasing the speed until it comes to a standstill, at the end of the animation. This animation effect is brought about by using the term swing as the third argument. The usage is quite similar to what was demonstrated in the immediately preceding example.

```
$('#to-move-block').animate({'left': 1000, 'top': 500}, 8000, 'swing');
```

We would like to emphasize a few points.

- The difference between the two easings will not be visible if you provide a small time duration (a.k.a. speed) value. This is why we specified a large number—eight seconds for the animation to complete.

- If you specify swing easing, the speed of the algorithm increases and decreases by performing some calculation with the mathematical cosine function. If you remember the basics of your mathematical education, this should elicit a smile. For all others, Figure 7-2 represents the speed.

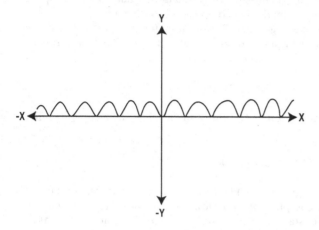

Figure 7-2. *Showing the increase and the decrease of the animation speed as implemented in jQuery*

Another provision of the animate( ) method is the availability of the fourth parameter. The need for this fourth parameter arises from those situations in which you want to perform some action after the animation is complete. As with the usual nature of callbacks, you can pass on a named callback or an anonymous callback. Because you have already gained some familiarity with the callback methods and their use with jQuery methods, we will quickly move on to demonstrate the use of callback in the current context. We assume that you will have to show the left and top coordinates of the block that was animated using the animate( ) method.

```
$('#to-move-block').animate(
    {'left': 1000, 'top': 500},
    8000,
    'linear',
    function(){
        var top = $(this).css('top');
        var left = $(this).css('left');
        alert("The block is now at: ("+top+", "+left+")");
});
```

So, the callback action was quite simple to understand. As soon as the animation was completed, the left and top CSS properties were obtained and composed in a string, which was, in turn, alerted in the (browser) window. You can use named methods in callbacks as well. The usage is as follows:

```
function getCurrentPosition(){
    var blockReference = $('#to-move-block');
    var top = blockReference.css('top');
    var left = blockReference.css('left');
    alert("The block is now at: ("+top+", "+left+")");
}


$('#to-move-block').animate(
    {'left': 1000, 'top': 500},
    800,
    'linear',
    getCurrentPosition
);
```

The example is rather simple. The code is identical to the last example shown, except for some subtle differences. The differences start with the function being named: getCurrentPosition( ). They continue until calling the named method as the fourth argument, in contrast to passing the entire function. The code works as efficiently as it did when we used an anonymous function.

■ **Tip**   You can remember the usage of the animate( ) method as a sequence of four questions: (1) What to animate? (2) How long to animate? (3) How to animate? (4) What to do after animating?

We suggest remembering the method usage as

```
animate('what', 'time-to-take', 'how', 'then-what');
```

Fading in jQuery

After having introduced you to the animate( ) method, we now move on to discuss the applications of animation. As we discussed previously, *animation* is a general term applied to the addition of some movement or activity to some objects. This, in itself, sometimes becomes a programming challenge for web developers who write code for web front ends. But because you have obtained some knowledge of animation with jQuery, we can include animation among the common challenges that we face in our day-to-day web development activities.

One such challenge is how to change the transparency of an element so that its appearance changes. We'll discuss this next. The jQuery framework provides two methods to manage this: fadeOut( ) and the fadeIn( ). The methods are quite self-descriptive. The fadeOut( ) method makes the element look faded, and the fadeIn( ) method returns the faded element to normal. So, we begin with the fadeOut( ) method.

Using the fadeOut( ) Method

We will take up the same HTML example for the sake of clarity and make the method work on that. To recap, the HTML code contains a div element located at the top-left corner of the browser screen. To make it visually appealing, we will add some styling to the div. Or, wait! Let us provide a new HTML code altogether.

```html
<html>
<head>
    <style type="text/css">
        #fading-block{
            position: absolute;
            top: 0px;
            left: 0px;
            height: 200px;
            width: 200px;
            background: powderblue;
            text-align: center;
        }
    </style>
    <title>:: Animations and animations ::</title>
</head>
<body>
    <div id="fading-block">This block would animate on clicking </div>
</body>
</html>
```

Let us quickly walk through the HTML code. The code is quite simple (as usual). The additional CSS styling that we have added is a 100px value to the height and the width attribute. To make the fading effect visible, we have added a background color attribute. Because we have an affinity for lighter shades of blue, we have chosen the shade powderblue. Let us move on to the jQuery code. We have attempted to add an event handler to the div with the id attribute fading-block, such that once the click event takes place on the div, it fades out and becomes invisible. The code that we propose in this case is

```javascript
$('#fading-block').on('click', function(){
    $(this).fadeOut();
});
```

Again, this code is simple (our signature style)! We are just binding the click event to the div in question in such a way that the click event will fade out the element until it disappears completely. Having taken an additional step to use fadeOut( ), let us take more. You have the freedom to select the speed attribute of the fadeOut( ) method. Repeating what we said in the preceding sections, the speed attribute is the time taken (specified in milliseconds) for the fadeOut to be complete. So, this argument will be a numeric value representing the number of milliseconds required for the animation to take place. As an example, you can use the following code:

```javascript
$('#fading-block').on('click', function(){
    $(this).fadeOut(1000);
});
```

This will complete the fadeOut in a matter of a second (or a thousand milliseconds, whichever you prefer). Figure 7-3 shows the effect of this code in a series of frames.

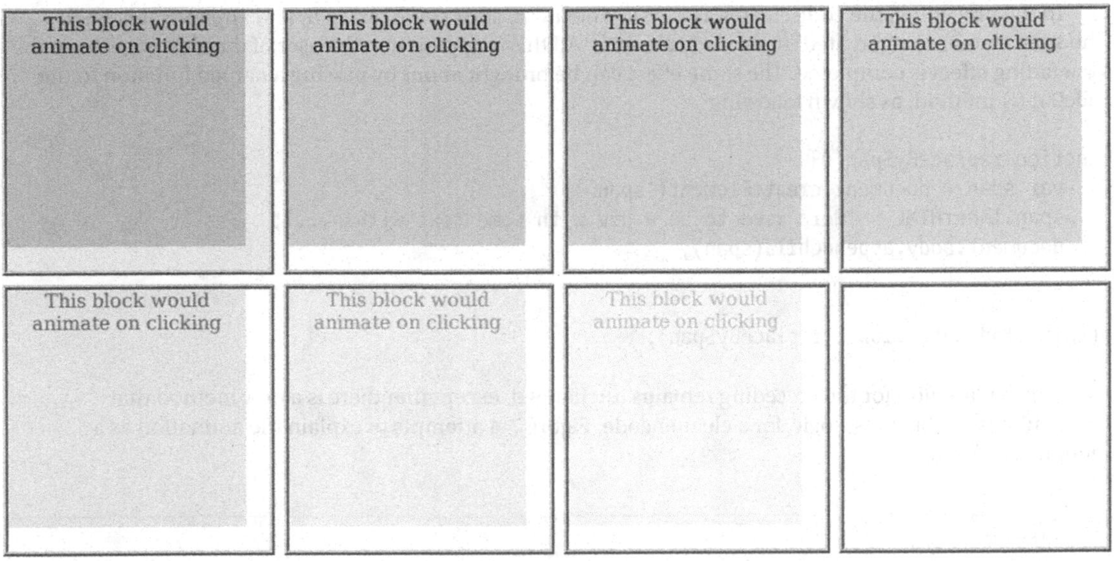

Figure 7-3. Frame sequence showing the effect of the fadeOut

There are predefined constant values as well. Using those constants, you not always have to try and guess the number of milliseconds required to execute, let's say, a fast or a slow fading-out effect. Thus, a slow fading effect can be brought about by specifying the speed as slow. This is as follows:

```
$('#fading-block').on('click', function(){
    $(this).fadeOut('slow');
});
```

Recall that the slow speed refers to a time span of **600** milliseconds, and the fast speed refers to a time span of **200** milliseconds. You can bring about a fast fadeout as follows:

```
$('#fading-block').on('click', function(){
    $(this).fadeOut('fast');
});
```

■ **Note**   As mentioned earlier, a default speed value of **400** milliseconds is used by the fadeOut( ) method, which means that if you do not specify speed value, the animation will take 400 milliseconds to complete.

The jQuery fadeOut( ) method has a provision that enables you to perform some action once the fading out effect is complete. This is the same callback action we have been mentioning throughout this book. You can pass some method itself, or even the name of the method, in case you feel that the business logic could prevent your code from remaining clean. Following are some examples:

```
$(this).fadeOut('slow', function(){
    var span = document.createElement('span');
    span.innerHTML = 'Here used to be a div with some text within...';
    document.body.appendChild(span);
});
```

In the preceding, the code creates a new span element, adds some text to it, and appends this node (the span element just created) to the body element. All this is apparent to the user of the web page, once the slow fading effect is completed. The same effect can be brought about by passing a named function to the fadeOut() method, as shown following:

```
function replaceBySpan(){
    var span = document.createElement('span');
    span.innerHTML = 'Here used to be a div with some text within...';
    document.body.appendChild(span);
}

$(this).fadeOut('slow', replaceBySpan);
```

The explanation for the preceding remains unchanged, except that there is a new method that encapsulates the business logic, for a cleaner code. Figure 7-4 attempts to explain the animation as a sequence of frames.

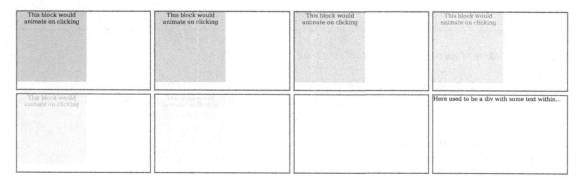

Figure 7-4. *This frame sequence shows the effect of using the fadeIn method*

■ **Note** The fadeOut() method leaves a DOM element intact, without making any changes if the element is hidden from view, via the CSS display: none property. Other conditions under which the fadeOut leaves a DOM element intact are when there is an element with hidden type, when the height and width are set as 0, or when some ancestor of the element is hidden.

Using the fadeIn() Method

The jQuery framework also provides a method that does just the opposite of what fadeOut() does. This will be apparent from the name of the method: fadeIn(). The fadeIn() method changes the display of an element until the element becomes completely visible.

■ **Note** The fadeIn() method requires an element to have the CSS property set as display:none.

Technical discussions require supplementary examples. Therefore, we provide the HTML required for this demonstration.

```html
<html>
<head>
    <style type="text/css">
        #fading-block{
            position: absolute;
            top: 0px;
            left: 0px;
            height: 200px;
            width: 200px;
            background: powderblue;
            text-align: center;
            display: none;
            z-index: -1;
        }
    </style>
    <title>:: Animations and animations ::</title>
</head>
<body>
    <div id="fading-block"></div>
    <span id="to-display-div">Click here to uncover the hidden!</div>
</body>
</html>
```

The HTML is quite similar to that in the example we used for the fadeOut( ) demonstrations, but with a few minor changes, such as addition of display: none to the styling of the only div in the HTML. There is an additional span, which acts as the switch, to enable the effect. So, the plan goes like this: there is be a span element, which upon clicking the span itself disappears, and some other element appears and replaces it. The jQuery code proposed is

```javascript
var div = $('div#fading-block');
var span = $('span#to-display-div');
span.on('click', function(){
$(this).fadeOut();
    div.fadeIn();
});
```

Figure 7-5 illustrates this animation.

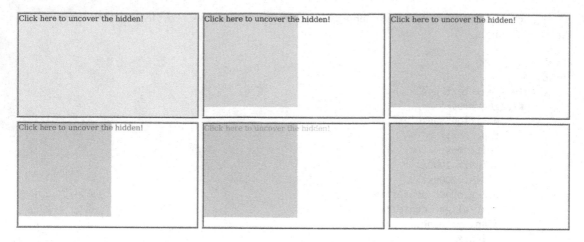

Figure 7-5. *This frame sequence shows the effect of using the* fadeIn *method*

This leaves us open to a number of possible usages, with a number of options to choose from. We can choose the speed or the duration of the animation. We can also choose what action to perform once the fading effect is complete. All this is demonstrated as follows. You can select a slow fadeIn to bring about a 600 millisecond time span.

```
span.on('click', function(){
$(this).fadeOut();
    div.fadeIn('slow');
});
```

You can create a fast animation that lasts for a mere 200 milliseconds, as follows:

```
span.on('click', function(){
$(this).fadeOut();
    div.fadeIn('fast');
});
```

■ **Tip** Having two animation methods in one action provides you a number of effects to choose from, once you toggle the slow and fast animations in the two methods. We encourage you to go ahead and try those combinations.

You can specify the action to be taken once the fading is complete, by choosing from the two demonstrations.

Passing an anonymous function

```
span.on('click', function(){
    $(this).fadeOut();
    div.fadeIn('slow', function(){
        alert('Uncovering complete');
});});
```

Passing a function by name

```
function doSomething(){
    alert('Uncovering complete');
}

span.on('click', function(){
    $(this).fadeOut();
    div.fadeIn('slow', doSomething);
});
```

Figure 7-6 attempts to show the fading animation obtained by using a sequence of frames when either of the alternatives is executed.

Figure 7-6. *This frame sequence shows the fading animation effect using a callback method*

One issue that you might face while using fadeIn( ) with certain elements could be with the display of the element in question. Thus, if the CSS display property is already set to block, or any such value such that the element is already visible, the fadeIn( ) method will cease to work.

Using the fadeTo( ) Method

If you wish to change the opacity of some element to some desired value other than 0 (completely transparent) or 1 (completely opaque), there is a method available: fadeTo( ). This can create good visual effects in a number of cases in which you will be required to assign focus (visual focus) to certain elements in your web page, by fading out some other elements. The fadeTo( ) method accepts two arguments: the speed attribute and the percentage of opacity to be attained by the element, respectively. Keeping the HTML part the same, we propose the following usage of fadeTo( ):

```
var div = $('div#fading-block');
var span = $('span#to-display-div');

span.on('click', function(){
    div.fadeTo('slow', 0.5)
})
```

The code will make the div element half-transparent, by setting the CSS opacity attribute as 0.5. Here, it is worth noting that fadeTo( ) works in both the cases. When you specify the display attribute, the fadeTo( ) can work to make the target element less opaque (as in fadeOut( ) for the element), as shown in Figure 7-7. When you do not specify the display attribute, the fadeTo( ) can work to make the target element more opaque (as in fadeIn( ) for the element).

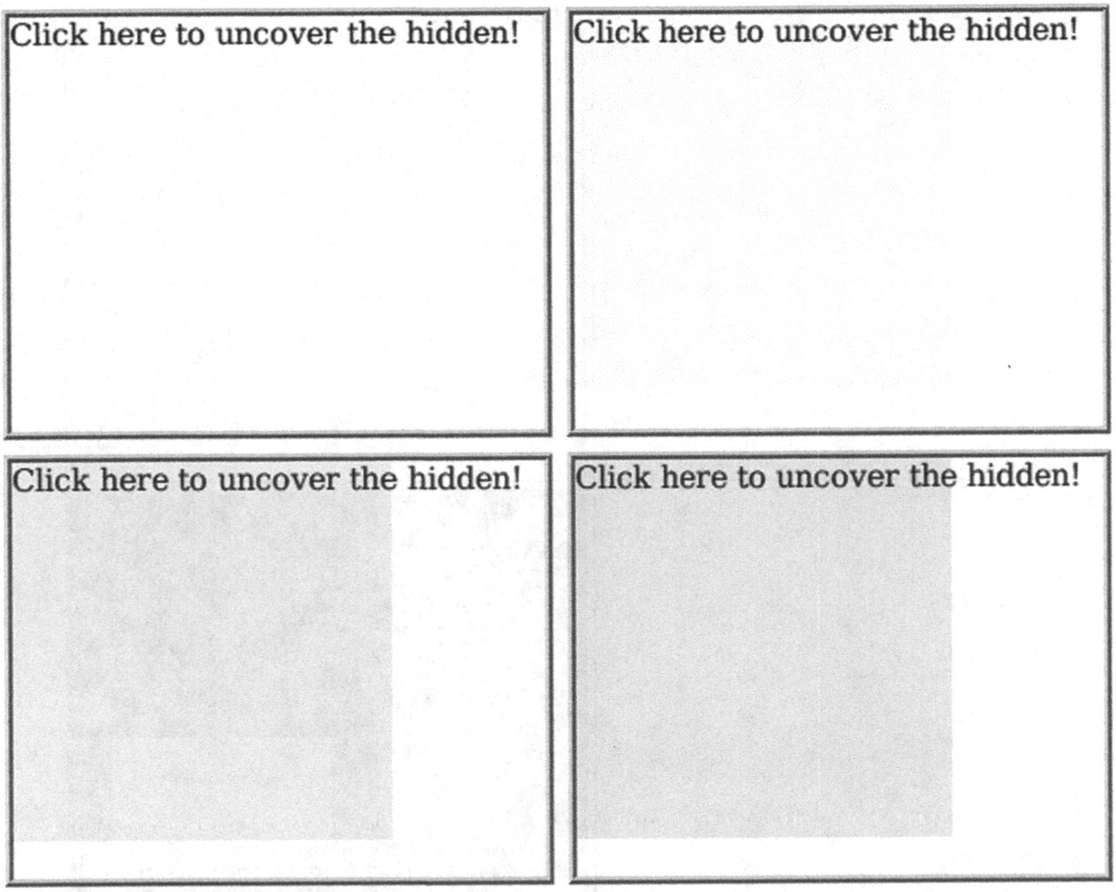

Figure 7-7. This frame sequence shows the change in transparency from 100% to 50%

You can specify some action to be taken once the fadeTo has completed execution, by passing a function or the name of the function as the third argument to the fadeTo( ) method. An example will demonstrate this much better.

```
var div = $('div#fading-block');
    var span = $('span#to-display-div');

    function doSomething(){
    alert('Uncovering complete');
    }

span.on('click', function(){
    div.fadeTo('slow', 0.5, doSomething);
});
```

This is a similar usage to fadeIn( ). Thus, the explanation of the usage is implicit. On clicking a given span element, some div element will fade to 50% opacity. That's it. Have a look at Figure 7-8, to try and understand how the animation takes place, by noting the sequence of frames shown.

Figure 7-8. *This frame sequence shows the same effect using the callback method*

Using the fadeToggle( ) Method

We must also consider a scenario we often face while animating. Frequently, we have to produce an effect of smooth display-switch. By a smooth display-switch, we mean that the animation renders a hidden object visible, or a visible object hidden, in a smooth transition. The effect is similar to what a dimmer switch does to a lightbulb. The name of the method you will find useful in such instances will be the jQuery fadeToggle( ) method. This method works on a selector and accepts three arguments—all optional. We start the demonstration by passing no arguments. The jQuery code is

```
var div = $('div#fading-block');
var span = $('span#to-display-div');

span.on('click', function(){
    div.fadeToggle();
})
```

This is the most simple usage demonstration. Let us make things a bit more complicated. Let us try some speed value. Like fadeIn( ) and fadeOut( ), jQuery supports the keywords slow and fast for fadeTo( ). So, the following code will work fine:

```
var div = $('div#fading-block');
var span = $('span#to-display-div');

span.on('click', function(){
    div.fadeToggle('fast');
});
```

And so will the following code, with a slower fading effect:

```
var div = $('div#fading-block');
var span = $('span#to-display-div');

span.on('click', function(){
    div.fadeToggle(1000);
});
```

You can specify an easing effect, just as you did for animate( ). It would be normal for you to ask us, given that we did not specify the easing attribute, how the method still has something like an easing effect. We will answer by providing a code example.

Note that the jQuery code to attain exactly the same effect as in the preceding example is as follows:

```
var div = $('div#fading-block');
var span = $('span#to-display-div');

span.on('click', function(){
    div.fadeToggle(1000, 'swing');
});
```

This occurs because the default easing value for the fadeToggle( ) method is swing. The other easing value available for use in fadeToggle( ) is linear. You have another option too. Once the fading effect is complete, you can perform an action—the callback action. This can, again, be passed to the fadeToggle( ) method in two ways: either as a named reference to a function or as an anonymous function itself. You have to pass this fadeToggle( ) method as the third argument. We will move ahead with a demonstration that considers the same use case we have been taking up previously to demonstrate the fading effects. Our proposed jQuery code follows:

```
var div = $('div#fading-block');
var span = $('span#to-display-div');

function fadingCallbackAction(){
    if( div.css('display') == 'none' ){
        alert('Div element hidden');
    } else {
        alert('Div element shown');
    }
}
```

```
span.on('click', function(){
div.fadeToggle('slow', 'linear', fadingCallbackAction);
});
```

This example explains another aspect of fadeToggle() that we attempted to state at the beginning of this section—that fadeToggle() switches the display of the target element from on to off and from off to on. In simple terms, fadeToggle() toggles the CSS display property. So, if you keep clicking the text, there will be an alternate display of two messages: "Div element hidden" and "Div element shown," when the div gets hidden and shown, respectively.

Sliding in jQuery

Another very common animation task that web developers are assigned quite frequently is to create a sliding effect in some desired element. Sliding, in the current context, can be understood to be an act of modifying the CSS height property to achieve either of two effects:

1. An increase in the height of the target element, such that it is completely visible

2. A decrease in the height of the target element, such that it is completely hidden

If we talk about sliding in the context of animation, the effects we mentioned have to be achieved in a seamless manner, such that the animation appears to be continuous.

The jQuery framework provides three methods that help us to attain this functionality: slideDown(), slideUp(), and slideToggle(). Let us first explore the slideUp method.

Using the slideUp() Method

The slideUp() method works on a selector and accepts two optional arguments. Let us examine all the combinations that are possible with slideUp by starting with no parameters. The HTML code that we will work with while demonstrating these sliding animations is as follows:

```
<html>
<head>
    <style type="text/css">
        #fading-block{
            position: absolute;
            top: 0px;
            left: 0px;
            height: 200px;
            width: 200px;
            background: powderblue;
            text-align: center;
            z-index: -1;
        }
    </style>
    <title>:: Animations and animations ::</title>
</head>
<body>
    <div id="fading-block">This block would do something on clicking</div>
</body>
```

```
<script src="jquery-1.10.2.js"></script>
<script type="text/javascript">

    var div = $('div#fading-block');

    div.on('click', function(){
        $(this).slideUp();
    });

</script>
</html>
```

The jQuery code proposed by us to slide an element up on clicking the same event is as follows:

```
var div = $('div#fading-block');

div.on('click', function(){
    $(this).slideUp();
});
```

You can have a look into the animation by perusing Figure 7-9.

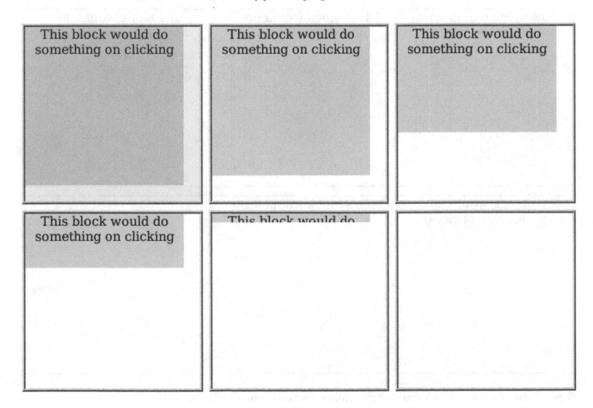

Figure 7-9. *This figure shows the default sliding up animation as a sequence of frames*

You can specify a speed attribute, such as the usual slow or fast, or some number of milliseconds as well, to customize the animation. We choose to pass slow as the speed attribute. This is as shown following:

```
var div = $('div#fading-block');

div.on('click', function(){
    $(this).slideUp('slow');
});
```

The slideUp( ) method can be passed on an easing attribute, which can be either linear or swing. The swing easing effect is something that the slideUp( ) method handles by default. Thus, passing the linear easing effect, we can propose a usage of the slideUp( ) method as follows:

```
var div = $('div#fading-block');

div.on('click', function(){
    $(this).slideUp('slow', 'linear');
});
```

This animation can be seen as a sequence of frames in Figure 7-10.

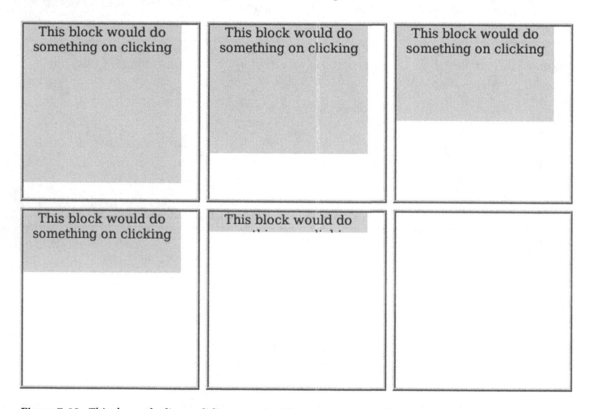

Figure 7-10. *This shows the linear sliding up animation as a sequence of frames*

You can pass on a callback action to take place once the animation is complete. We propose showing an alert message on the browser upon completion of the sliding animation. The method usage could be

```
var div = $('div#fading-block');

div.on('click', function(){
    $(this).slideUp('fast', 'linear', function(){
        alert('Object slid up completely');
    });
});
```

You can see the changes that take place to accomplish this animation by looking at Figure 7-11.

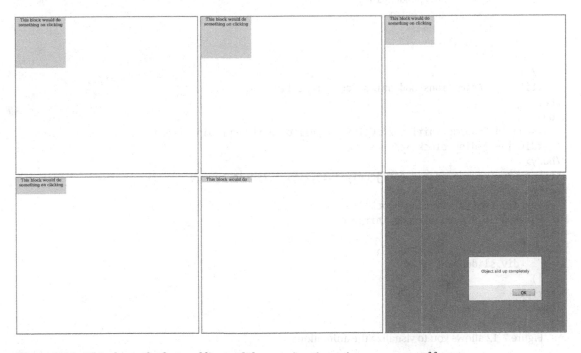

Figure 7-11. *This shows the fast and linear slide up animation using a sequence of frames*

Using the slideDown( ) Method

The slideDown( ) method, on the other hand, does just the opposite of slideUp( ). Working on a selector, it makes an element visible by increasing the height of the target element from 0 (zero) to the actual height of the element. Like slideUp( ), the slideDown( ) method works on a selector and accepts three optional parameters: the duration, the easing effect, and the callback action. The usage is also quite similar to that of the slideUp( ) method. We will demonstrate in order the three usages mentioned, starting from passing no arguments. The usage proposed by us is:

```html
<html>
<head>
    <style type="text/css">
        #fading-block{
            position: absolute;
            top: 0px;
            left: 0px;
            height: 200px;
            width: 200px;
            background: powderblue;
            text-align: center;
            display: none;
            z-index: -1;
        }
    </style>
    <title>:: Animations and animations ::</title>
</head>
<body>
    <span id="fading-initiator">Click to pull down the curtain!</span>
    <div id="fading-block"></div>
</body>
<script src="//code.jquery.com/jquery-1.10.2.js"></script>
<script type="text/javascript">
    var div = $('div#fading-block');
    var span = $('span#fading-initiator');

    span.on('click', function(){
        div.slideDown();
    })
</script>
</html>
```

Figure 7-12 allows you to visualize the animation.

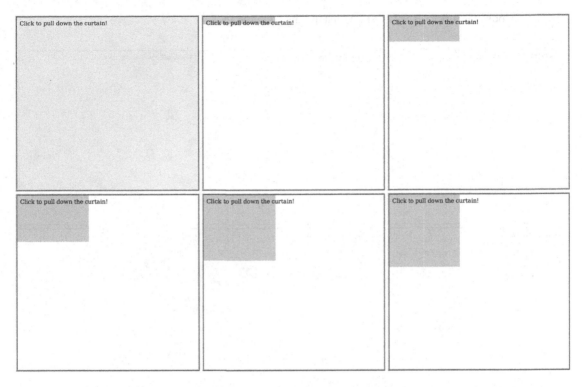

Figure 7-12. *This sequence of frames shows how the mentioned sliding down animation takes place*

Proceeding to another usage, you can pass on a speed attribute to the slideUp method, either as a predefined constant (slow or fast) or some time duration in milliseconds (for example, 600 or 200, representing the slow and fast time durations, respectively, or some other specific duration). We choose a fast animation and propose the following usage:

```
var div = $('div#fading-block');
var span = $('span#fading-initiator');

span.on('click', function(){
    div.slideDown('fast');
});
```

To be able to specify an easing effect, you have to pass on the easing value as the second argument. You could probably add a constant-speed and fast-sliding animation to the div by writing some jQuery code such as the following:

```
var div = $('div#fading-block');
var span = $('span#fading-initiator');

span.on('click', function(){
    div.slideDown('fast', 'linear');
});
```

Have a look at Figure 7-13, to better understand the animation.

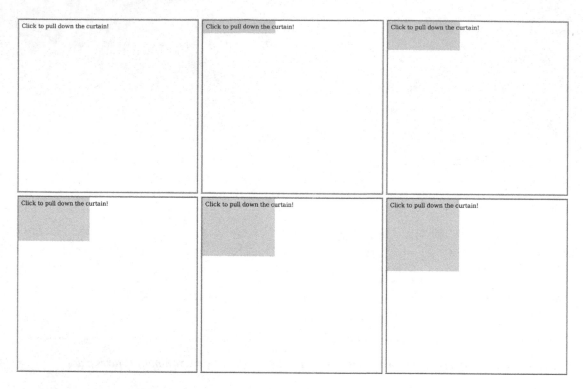

Figure 7-13. *This figure shows the fast and linear animation as a sequence of frames*

There is a provision for a callback action as well. You will have to pass on a name of a function or the function itself (as an anonymous function) to the slideDown( ) method, quite like we did in the case of the slideUp( ) method. We propose the following usage:

```
var div = $('div#fading-block');
var span = $('span#fading-initiator');

span.on('click', function(){
    div.slideDown('fast', 'linear', function(){
        alert('Object slid up completely');
    });
});
```

If you wish to see what the animation looks like in action, see Figure 7-14.

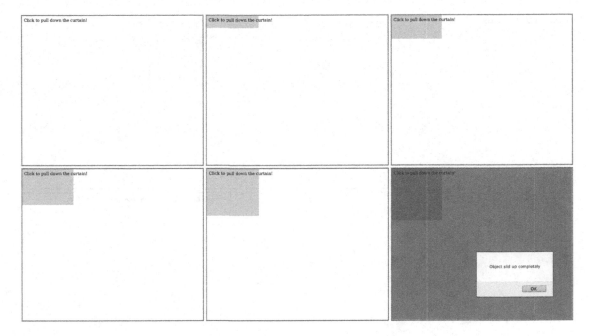

Figure 7-14. *This sequence of frames shows how the fast and linear slide down animation proceeds with a callback method*

■ **Note** The slideDown( ) method requires that the CSS display property be set to none; otherwise, the slideDown( ) function will cease to work.

Using the slideToggle( ) Method

The slideUp( ) and the slideDown( ) methods are rather one-directional. If some element is animated (slid up/down) to bring that same object back to the original state (prior to the animation), you require extra logic. Here, you might consider a method known as slideToggle( ), provided by the jQuery framework. The slideToggle( ) method works much like the fadeToggle( ) method and slides up a visible element by following the same methodology—decreasing the height to make it completely invisible and then turning the display to none. It also makes a hidden element visible by increasing the height to the original height of the element after setting the display to block.

Following is a demonstration of the slideToggle( ) method:

```
var div = $('div#fading-block');
var span = $('span#fading-initiator');

span.on('click', function(){
    div.slideToggle();
});
```

This will slide down the div element that is already hidden and slide up the div element, if it is visible. You can see the animation in Figure 7-15.

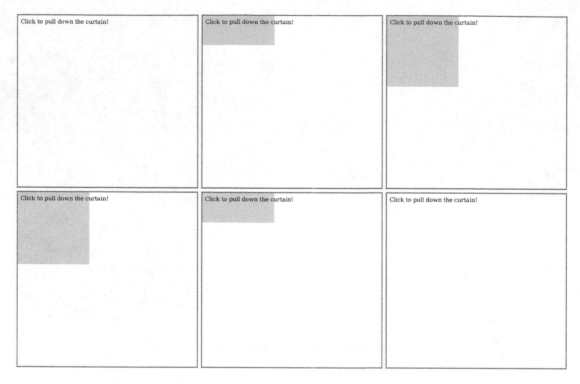

Figure 7-15. *The sliding animation, using a sequence of frames*

You can control the toggling action by passing a speed value as the first argument to the slideToggle() method. The speed values can be either of slow or fast or a positive number specifying the number of milliseconds. By default, slideToggle() assumes slow. The usage in that case would be

```
var div = $('div#fading-block');
var span = $('span#fading-initiator');

span.on('click', function(){
    div.slideToggle('fast');
});
```

Utilizing the full functionality of the slideToggle() method can be achieved by passing the callback action to the slideToggle() method. Let us create a better user experience by adding some interaction to the link that listens to the click event. We propose the following usage:

```
var div = $('div#fading-block');
var span = $('span#fading-initiator');

span.on('click', function(){
    div.slideToggle('fast', function(){
        alert('Object slid up completely');
```

```
        if(span.html() == 'Click to pull down the curtain!'){
            span.html('Click to pull up the curtain!');
        } else {
            span.html('Click to pull down the curtain!');
        }
    });
});
```

Here, once the click event takes place, the text in the span node changes to make the action to take place look relevant.

By now, you will have noticed that all the methods that we mentioned have something in common. Wherever there is a speed attribute to be specified, it is either "slow" or "fast" or some number of milliseconds. Whenever there is some easing effect to be applied, the arguments you pass on to the method are either linear or swing. We ask that you recall the animate() method, in which such arguments are originally described to be passed. All such methods use the animate() method under the hood. To emphasize this point, let's consider the jQuery framework's implementation of these methods.

- The fadeTo() method directly calls the animate() method by forwarding the speed, the target opacity to be attained, the easing to be followed, and the callback action that has to be performed at the end of the animation.

- The slideDown(), slideUp(), and slideToggle() methods set the height and the top and bottom paddings according to their own algorithms and pass on to the animate() method.

- The fadeIn(), fadeOut(), and fadeToggle() methods modify the opacity attribute according to their algorithm and pass on to the animate() method.

Here, you might be very easily tempted to refrain from using the methods provided by jQuery, once you know what is happening under the hood. Relative to this, we would like to draw your attention toward the software engineering principle DRY. When you have included the framework itself, it will not be a wise engineering decision to add extra lines of code to implement what has already been implemented. However, if you think that there are some functionalities that you could implement in a better way than via the framework itself, we encourage you to contact the jQuery developer community. It is the era of open source software, so why not extend a helping hand to the community!

Toggle() in jQuery

The toggle() method is a jQuery process for handling the two basic visibility states—visible and hidden—of an element. Before discussing the toggle() method, however, we would like to make a few points about another approach to visibility states used in jQuery. The jQuery framework provides methods such as show() and hide() that serve the purpose when used independently. The show() and hide() methods are quite like the other methods described in the preceding sections. The show() method sets the *height*, all *margins*, and *paddings* to *show* and thereby calls the animate() method. The hide() method does just the opposite. It sets the height, all margins, and paddings to *hide* and calls the animate() method thereby.

The toggle() method, as already noted, is jQuery's attempt to provide a helping hand to all those scenarios for which you have to select either of the two visibility states for an element—visible or hidden.

Let us start by having a demonstration. We provide the following HTML code, which will be required to support the demonstration:

```
<!DOCTYPE html>
<html>
<head>
    <style type="text/css">
        #fading-block{
            position: absolute;
            top: 0px;
            left: 0px;
            height: 200px;
            width: 200px;
            background: powderblue;
            text-align: center;
            display: none;
            z-index: -1;
        }
    </style>
    <title>:: Animations and animations ::</title>
</head>
<body>
    <span id="fading-initiator">Click to play toggle-toggle!</span>
    <div id="fading-block"></div>
</body>
</html>
```

The main task is done by the call to the jQuery toggle( ) method, which is shown following. The purpose of the code is quite straightforward. Clicking the span will switch the display of the div element from on to off and from off to on, depending on the present display state of the element.

```
var div = $('div#fading-block');
var span = $('span#fading-initiator');

span.on('click', function(){
    div.toggle();
});
```

You can pass on the well-known speed argument to the toggle( ) method, to control the time the method takes to complete. The speed arguments can be either slow, fast, or a number of milliseconds—the default value being 400 milliseconds. The usage with the speed argument set to slow is as shown following:

```
var div = $('div#fading-block');
    var span = $('span#fading-initiator');

span.on('click', function(){
    div.toggle('slow');
});
```

You can control the animation easing behavior much like you could in the case of the sliding and fading animations. The value that controls the easing in this method can be either swing or linear, the default being swing. The usage as proposed by us is

```
var div = $('div#fading-block');
    var span = $('span#fading-initiator');

span.on('click', function(){
    div.toggle('slow', 'linear');
});
```

If you wish, you can specify some callback action, once the toggle is complete, by adopting the usual methodology—passing either the named reference to a method already defined or some anonymous method itself. We demonstrate this in the following code snippet:

```
var div = $('div#fading-block');
var span = $('span#fading-initiator');

span.on('click', function(){
    div.toggle('slow', 'linear', function(){
        alert('Click the span again to continue playing')
    });
});
```

The implementation of the toggle( ) method is similar to the other animation methods that we described in the preceding discussions and demonstrations. However, for the sake of clarity, the toggle( ) method calls the animate( ) method after accepting the speed, easing, and the callback actions (all optional parameters to the toggle( ) method). So, when you call the toggle( ) method, behind the curtains, the values of all four margins, all four paddings, the height, and the opacity attribute to toggle make the animate( ) method work on the resulting object.

■ **Note** There is another toggle method in jQuery that performs an entirely different function, as compared to the toggle( ) method that we have described under the current scenario. The other toggle method is now deprecated (since version 1.8 onward). Just for reference, the deprecated toggle method is used to bind two or more handlers for the click event on the elements, as matched by selectors. The event handlers are used to fire in a cyclic manner. If there were three handlers, the order of execution would be 1-2-3-1, and so on.

Creating a Basic Light Box

All buildings are constructed using small building blocks. Similarly, a complex jQuery functionality can be implemented by using the basic animation methods provided in jQuery. This usage is possible only after having the working knowledge of the methods that contribute to the most commonly used animation methods. So, having discussed the animation methods, we will now take you to the next level in the usage of such methods, to create something useful. We'll assume you want to create a light box, much like those appearing on social sites these days.

Following (at least some) principles of software engineering, before jumping off to write code, we will list the required functionality for our sample light box.

- A light box is a photo album.

- There must be *n* number of photographs for viewing.

- There needs to be a button to start the album.

- There has to be a Next button to move on to the next image available.

- There has to be a Previous button to move to the previous image available.

- There can be a Close button to close the album.

- The transition between the photographs has to be smooth.

- The operation should not end after the last photograph is shown, but, rather, return to the first photograph.

- Similarly, when the user clicks the Previous button when viewing the first photograph, the last photograph should display.

- The photo album should be available on a semitransparent background, to allow maximum eye-focus onto the photographs.

We are developers; we speak code and understand code. So, here is the essential HTML code for a very basic light box functionality, followed by an explanation of what is going on inside and what will be the supplementary jQuery code to get our light box working. We provide the following HTML:

```
<div class="overlay absolute">
    <div class="centered margin-100-auto image-width image-height">
        <div class="image-container">
            <div class="controls absolute image-width white-text">
                <div class="close centered-text float-right">X</div>
                <!--Close the slide show logic is not written here: We have omitted that.-->
                <div class="margin-top-120">
                    <div class="next float-right">&#9755;</div>
                    <div class="previous float-left">&#9754;</div>
                </div>
            </div>
            <img
src="http://mukundtechie.com/wp-content/uploads/2015/05/slide-1.jpg"
class="shown" />
            <img
src="http://mukundtechie.com/wp-content/uploads/2015/05/slide-2.jpg"
class="hidden" />
            <img
src="http://mukundtechie.com/wp-content/uploads/2015/05/slide-3.jpg"
class="hidden" />
            <img
src="http://mukundtechie.com/wp-content/uploads/2015/05/slide-4.jpg"
class="hidden" />
            <img
src="http://mukundtechie.com/wp-content/uploads/2015/05/slide-5.jpg"
class="hidden" />
```

```
            <img
src="http://mukundtechie.com/wp-content/uploads/2015/05/slide-6.jpg"
class="hidden" />
            <img
src="http://mukundtechie.com/wp-content/uploads/2015/05/slide-7.jpg"
class="hidden" />
        </div>
    </div>
</div>
```

The styling used in this light box sample code comes from the CSS code, as follows:

```
html, body, .overlay {
    height: 100%;
    width: 100%;
    padding: 0;
    margin: 0;
    font-family: sans-serif;
}
.overlay {
    background-image: url('http://mukundtechie.com/wp-content/uploads/2015/05/dot.png');
}
.centered {
    overflow: hidden;
}
.image-width {
    width: 570px;
}
.image-height {
    height: 270px;
}
.margin-top-120 {
    margin-top:120px;
}
.margin-100-auto {
    margin: 100px auto;
}
.hidden {
    display: none;
}
.shown {
    display: block;
}
.absolute {
    position: absolute;
}
.centered-text {
    text-align: center;
}
.float-right {
    float: right;
}
```

```
.white-text {
    color: #fff;
}
.controls {
    z-index: 1;
    cursor: pointer;
    font-size: 30px;
    font-weight: bold;
}
.close {
    background: red;
}
```

Now, as for the structure used in this example, we have tried to be as simple and straightforward as possible. We have created an **overlay** (a div with class attribute overlay) to cover the entire area available for the light box functionality. There is an image container (a div with class attribute image-container) inside a container, which strictly makes the light box appear in the exact horizontal center of the screen (a div with class attribute centered). The image container contains the images as well as the Next and Previous buttons. We have added a Close button as well, but we have omitted the functionality, as it can be set according to needs. We have kept all the images that we wished to add to the light box display and have kept the display attribute of all but one image as hidden (by adding the class attribute as hidden). Moving on to the jQuery part, the jQuery code to implement the light box functionality, as proposed by us, is

```
var next = $('div.next');
var previous = $('div.previous');

function LightBox() {
    this.imageContainer = $('div.image-container');
}

LightBox.prototype.getElement = function (currentElement, targetParent, type) {
    if (type == 'next') {
        var nextElement = currentElement.next();
        if (!nextElement.attr('src')) {
            return targetParent.first();
        }
    } else {
        var nextElement = currentElement.prev();
        if (!nextElement.attr('src')) {
            return targetParent.last();
        }
    }
    return nextElement;
}

LightBox.prototype.go = function (where) {
    var imageElement = this.imageContainer.children('img');
    var currentElement = imageElement.filter('.shown');
    var nextElement = this.getElement(currentElement, imageElement, where);
```

```
    currentElement.fadeOut('slow', function () {
        currentElement.removeClass('shown').addClass('hidden');
        nextElement.fadeIn('slow', function () {
            nextElement.removeClass('hidden').addClass('shown');
        });
    });
}

function goNext() {
    var moveAhead = new LightBox();
    moveAhead.go('next');
}

function goBack() {
    var moveAhead = new LightBox();
    moveAhead.go('back');
}

next.on('click', goNext);
previous.on('click', goBack);
```

The light box functionality begins by assigning actions to the click event onto the Next and the Previous buttons. The Next button calls a method goNext( ), whereas the Previous button calls a method goBack( ) when clicked. The goBack( ) and the goNext( ) methods instantiate the LightBox class and call its method go( ) with the arguments 'next' and 'previous', respectively. The go( ) method operates on the argument passed to it and does a sequence of tasks that is described in the following text.

The sequence begins by finding the img children of the image-container and filtering out those img elements that have the class attribute as shown. This filtered element serves as the current element for the light box. Depending on the argument that was passed on to the go( ) method, the go finds the next element (in case of forward movement) or the previous element (in case of backward movement). This discovery is done by a call to the method getElement( ) belonging to the LightBox class. The getElement( ) method accepts the current element (currentElement), a reference to the images in the current light box ecosystem (targetParent), and the direction indicator (type). The getElement( ) method does the task of finding the next element or the previous element, in reference to the current element. If it fails to find the next or the previous element, it returns the last or the first element, respectively, from the list of images, as specified as the second argument to the getElement( ) method. The go( ) method now *fades out* the current element slowly and, upon completion, replaces the class attribute shown with hidden. This is followed by a slow fading in of the next element (as discovered by the getElement( ) method), upon completion of which, the class attribute hidden is replaced by the class attribute shown.

■ **Tip** The light box functionality, as demonstrated in the example, is only for the sake of making you understand how the jQuery animation methods can be used to achieve some larger objective. We encourage you to go ahead and use the demonstration we provided. Try out some changes to make a light box suited to your needs. The fiddle is located at http://jsfiddle.net/ankur6971/uuzdtz84/. Practice makes perfect.

Controlling Animation Behavior

We can safely assume that you have acquired hands-on knowledge of using the animation methods, given that you have reviewed the preceding demonstrations and the explanations of those demonstrations. To control the way the animation works, you must gain some insight into the way the animation is implemented in jQuery. Having provided some insight into the way the animate( ) method has been implemented, we will now provide more insight regarding the way the animation algorithm is implemented. This will give you the added benefit of being able to understand how to control the animation behavior without making changes in the code you have already written.

Smoothing Your Animations

In the jQuery framework, there is a special algorithm, the tweening algorithm, that powers all of the beautiful and effective animation effects. To describe the tweening algorithm exhaustively would almost take another book, but for the sake of the current discussion, we can say that the tweening algorithm attempts to smooth the animation effect, by moving objects or changing the shape of objects smoothly. If you revisit the example that we took up at the beginning of this chapter, you will notice that the increments provided to the CSS left and top attributes were rather discrete—a value of 1px. This discrete value could result in a jagged movement, which could easily spoil the animation's appearance. The tweening algorithm overcomes this jagged movement and provides a smooth appearance to the animating objects. Broadly speaking, the tweening algorithm works on the major values named at the start of the animation, the duration of the animation, and the current time. The algorithm calculates the percentage of time that remains for the animation and inserts some frames representing the moving objects in between the past and the next frames, to give the appearance of a smooth transition. Do not worry if this isn't completely clear yet. As you continue to work with jQuery, you will come to understand these concepts to a greater extent. jQuery is open source, and you have the freedom to view the source code at any time, so we suggest taking the proper time to examine the code and see how jQuery is handling things under the hood.

Using the fx Object to Control Frame Rate

So, you have the freedom to make the animation behavior optimize according to your needs, by setting the value of two parameters to the tweening algorithm. Now, quickly moving toward setting the stage for the demonstration, there is an object with the name fx available inside the jQuery framework. Quite like the other methods available in the framework, such as get, post, and so on, the object can be accessed as $.fx or jQuery.fx or whatever alias you set for the jQuery object. The fx acts as the basis of all the animation effects available in the framework, such as the animation speed, etc. So, in essence, there are two broad ways to control the animation behavior in jQuery: using the jQuery.fx.interval and the jQuery.fx.off.

We begin the discussion with the jQuery.fx.interval property. The interval property is available by the fx object, which, in turn, is available under the jQuery object. Now, regarding the functionality of the interval property, it is used to set the number of frames per second that would be executed for the animation. The default value provided by the jQuery framework for the number of frames that will be executed per second is 13. Mentioning the tweening algorithm we specified a while ago, this interval indicates that a lower value will indicate a smoother animation, whereas a higher value will mean a less smooth animation (both on browsers running under a faster processing unit). So, you can adjust, let's say, 20 frames to be processed per second in your animations, by using the following jQuery code:

```
jQuery.fx.interval = 20;
```

■ **Tip** Animation algorithms are computing resource-intensive. They require a lot of complex mathematical calculations in order to proceed. So, as a front-end developer, it is your responsibility not to ignore those users who might still be using older computers to surf the Web. Such users could find your animation slowing down their computers, which could even result in hampering the other applications that might be running on their machines. If this occurs, this would create a serious user-experience issue, and your web application could suffer due to this. You definitely do not want this to happen.

We find that the jQuery framework terms its activities in strange ways. For example, it terms the duration as the "speed attribute," and the number of times the animation is to be called repeatedly, the number of "frames per second."

Turning Off Your Animation

There is another way to control the animation behavior—by turning off the animation effect altogether. We will revisit the animation algorithm while remaining on point. As we mentioned, jQuery has the strange (to us) behavior of using the duration and speed in some (very confusing) contexts. If you would write a piece of code such as

```
jQuery.fx.off = true;
```

the framework will treat the duration as having a value of 0 milliseconds and, hence, there will be no speed applied, and the animation will become absent from the screen. Yes, we got that right; the animation will *disappear*, and all the methods—slideUp( ), slideDown( ), animate( ), fadeIn( ), fadeOut( ), and so on— will behave as if they do not know how to animate.

As a word of caution, because the interval and the off properties are used in the global context, you should be careful while setting some arbitrary value to them. Such a change could easily have an effect on other animations across your web page. The ideal way to assign some value to this property would be to ensure that all animations are stopped or not running.

Creating a Basic Image Slider

Next, our focus is on another problem frequently faced by front-end web developers and for which a number of code samples probably exist across the Internet. The problem is to create an image slider. We do not prevent you from following other examples, but you should understand what goes on inside. Once you are done, we encourage you to pick up any related code and make a sincere attempt to make that particular code better. It is only in this manner that open source software development advances.

We respect software engineering. We preach software engineering principles. So, in order to solve our next problem, let us first move toward understanding the requirements of a basic form of image slider. We list its properties.

- An image slider is another type of photo album.

- Any image in the image slider can be accessed at random.

- There are three operations possible with an image slider: move to the next image, move to the previous image, and move to any random image.

- The default operation should be moving to the next image, starting from the first image, if no image is selected. If some image is selected, the default operation continues from the selected image.

- The next operation makes the image slide from right to left.

- The back operation makes the image slide from left to right.

- The random selection operation moves that many images from right to left.

- The operation should not end after the last photograph is shown, but, rather, should return to the first photograph.

- Similarly, when the user clicks the Previous button when viewing the first photograph, the last photograph should display.

The HTML code to create a basic structure of the slider is as shown following:

```html
<div class="centered margin-100-auto image-height image-width relative">
    <div class="image-container">
        <div class="controls absolute centered-text white-text float-right cursor-pointer">
            <div class="image-width height-35-pixel" >
                <div class="close centered-text text-30-pixel float-right">X</div>
            </div>
            <div id="thumbs" class="image-width margin-top-70 cursor-default">
                <div class="next float-right text-20-pixel margin-top-20
                cursor-pointer">&#9755;</div>
                <div class="previous float-left text-20-pixel margin-top-20
                cursor-pointer">&#9754;</div>
            </div>
        </div>
        <img
class="absolute shown-image"
src="http://mukundtechie.com/wp-content/uploads/2015/05/slide-1.jpg" />
        <img
class="absolute next-image"
src="http://mukundtechie.com/wp-content/uploads/2015/05/slide-2.jpg" />
        <img
class="absolute next-image"
src="http://mukundtechie.com/wp-content/uploads/2015/05/slide-3.jpg" />
        <img class="absolute next-image" src="http://mukundtechie.com/wp-content/
        uploads/2015/05/slide-4.jpg" />
        <img class="absolute next-image" src="http://mukundtechie.com/wp-content/
        uploads/2015/05/slide-5.jpg" />
        <img
class="absolute next-image"
src="http://mukundtechie.com/wp-content/uploads/2015/05/slide-6.jpg" />
        <img
class="absolute next-image"
src="http://mukundtechie.com/wp-content/uploads/2015/05/slide-7.jpg" />
    </div>
</div>
```

The styling part to be used in the slider comes from the CSS code, as follows:

```
html, body, .overlay{
    height: 100%;
    width: 100%;
    padding: 0;
    margin: 0;
    font-family: sans-serif;
}

.overlay{
    background-image: url('http://mukundtechie.com/wp-content/uploads/2015/05/dot.png');
}

.centered{
    overflow: hidden;
}

.margin-100-auto{
    margin: 100px auto;
}

.margin-top-70{
    margin-top: 70px;
}

.margin-top-20{
    margin-top: 20px;
}

.image-height{
    height: 270px;
}

.image-width{
    width: 570px;
}

#thumbs{
    height: 60px;
    background: #999;
}

.thumb-images{
    height: 50px;
    width: 70px;
    margin: 5px 0 5px 5px;
}

.cursor-pointer{
    cursor: pointer;
}
```

```css
.cursor-default{
    cursor: default;
}

.previous-image{
    left: -570px;
}

.shown-image{
    left: 0px;
}

.next-image{
    left: 570px;
}

.absolute{
    position: absolute;
}

.relative{
    position: relative;
}

.centered-text{
    text-align: center;
}

.float-right{
    float: right;
}

.float-left{
    float: left;
}

.controls{
    z-index: 1;
    width: 24px;
    font-weight: bold;
}

.height-35-pixel{
    height: 35px;
}

.text-30-pixel{
    font-size: 30px;
}
```

```
.text-20-pixel{
    font-size: 20px;
}

.white-text{
    color: #fff;
}

.close{
    background: red;
}
```

We believe in following a hierarchical HTML pattern while creating a user interface. We do so mainly for code readability and maintainability. So, we have created an overlay to contain all of the sliders inside it. The slider (image-container) is contained inside a container that will keep it in the horizontal center at all times (centered). The slider contains the slide controls in the form of a Close button, a Next button, and a Previous button. We have created a placeholder for the thumbnails that will assist us in randomly moving to an available image (thumbs). The thumbs will be generated using the images that we specify as the images in the image container. This is to say that you will not have to copy the images to create the thumbnails; our jQuery code will take care of that. Inside the image container, there are two CSS classes attached to the images, to achieve some specific functionality in the slide show. The shown-image has been added to the image that we would like to be shown. The next-image has been attached to make some images stay immediately adjacent to the right-most end of the image with the style attribute shown-image. There is another class attribute to be used—previous-image. The previous-image attribute will be attached to make the image(s) move to the left by the distance equal to its own width. (Here, to keep things simple, we have hard-coded the width to 570px.) To make the overall explanation simpler, there is one image that will be shown; all images to the left of this image will have the style attribute previous-image, and all images to the right of this (shown) image will have the style attribute next-image. The previous images will have the left attribute set as **-570px**, and the next images will have the left attribute set as **570px**, where **570px** is the width of the image we have taken up.

Now, let us look into the actual engine that will run the slider. Although this problem can be solved in multiple ways, we propose the following jQuery code to demonstrate how to implement a slider:

```
var Slider = function(){
    this.imageContainer = $('div.image-container');
    this.checkAndSetLast();
    this.prepareRandomMovement();
}

Slider.getDistance = function(where){
    return (where=='next') ? ['-570px', '570px'] : ['570px', '-570px'];
}

Slider.replaceClass = function(whichElement, cssClassList, byWhat){
    var type = typeof cssClassList;
    if(type == 'object'){
        $.each(cssClassList, function(index, singleCssClass){
            whichElement.removeClass(singleCssClass);
        });
    } else {
        whichElement.removeClass(cssClassList);
    }
    return whichElement.addClass(byWhat);
}
```

```
Slider.prototype.getElement = function(referenceElement, targetParent, type){
    if(type == 'next'){
        var nextElement = referenceElement.next();
        if(!nextElement.attr('src')){
            return targetParent.first();
        }
    } else {
        var nextElement = referenceElement.prev();
        if(!nextElement.attr('src')){
            return targetParent.last();
        }
    }
    return nextElement;
}

Slider.prototype.go = function (where){
    var imageElement = this.imageContainer.children('img');
    var currentElement = imageElement.filter('.shown-image');
    var nextElement = this.getElement(currentElement, imageElement, where);
    var nextToNextElement = this.getElement(nextElement, imageElement, where);

    var distance = Slider.getDistance(where);
    currentElement.animate({'left': distance[0]},'slow', function(){
        Slider.replaceClass(currentElement, 'shown-image', 'previous-image');
    }
);
    nextElement.animate({'left': '0px'},'slow', function(){
        Slider.replaceClass(nextElement, 'next-image', 'shown-image');
        Slider.replaceClass(nextToNextElement.css({'left': distance[1]}), 'previous-image',
        'next-image');
    });
}

Slider.prototype.checkAndSetLast = function(){
    Slider.replaceClass(this.imageContainer.children('img').last(), 'next-image',
    'previous-image');
}

Slider.prototype.prepareRandomMovement = function(){
    var imagesAvailable = this.imageContainer.children('img');
    $.each(imagesAvailable, function(index, imageObject){
        var img = document.createElement('img');
        var thumbs = document.getElementById('thumbs');
        img.setAttribute('class', 'thumb-images cursor-pointer');
        img.setAttribute('src', imageObject.src);
        $(img).on('click', function(){
            var distance = Slider.getDistance();
            imagesAvailable.filter('.previous-image').removeClass('previous-image');
            imagesAvailable.filter('.shown-image').removeClass('shown-image');

            imageObject = Slider.replaceClass($(imageObject).css({'left': '0px'}),
            ['next-image', 'previous-image'], 'shown-image');
```

```
            Slider.replaceClass(imageObject.nextAll('img').css({'left': distance[0]}),
            'previous-image', 'next-image');
            Slider.replaceClass(imageObject.prevAll('img').css({'left': distance[1]}),
            'next-image', 'previous-image');

            if(!$('.next-image').attr('src')){
                Slider.replaceClass(imagesAvailable.first().css({'left': distance[0]}),
                'previous-image', 'next-image');
            }

            if(!$('.previous-image').attr('src')){
                Slider.replaceClass(imagesAvailable.last().css({'left': distance[1]}),
                'next-image', 'previous-image');
            }

        });
        thumbs.appendChild(img);
    });
}

var slider = new Slider();
var next = $('div.next');
var previous = $('div.previous');

next.on('click', function(){
    slider.go('next');
});

previous.on('click', function(){
    slider.go('back');
});
```

Here, we will begin the explanation of the slider engine by taking up the elements in order of global elements, static members of the class, and other methods of the class, followed by the way these various components can be assembled to form a meaningful system. There are a few global elements: a slider object (Slider), an object representing the Next button, and an object representing the Previous button. We have defined these components toward the end of the functionality, to avoid allowing them hold a chunk of memory, even when these are not ready to be used.

There are the static methods getDistance() and replaceClass() to explain next. The getDistance() method returns an array of values that represent the magnitude by which the images will be slid to the left or the right. Upon passing an argument as next, the returned list represents the magnitude responsible for a left shift and a right shift (in order). Otherwise, the returned list represents the magnitude for a right shift and a left shift (in order).

The other static method, replaceClass(), serves a purpose that would otherwise be served by using two jQuery factory methods—removeClass() and addClass()—from one single window of operation. The method accepts three arguments: the target element, the list of CSS class names to be removed from the target element, and the new class attribute to be attached to the target element. So, if you happen to pass on an array, all of the classes specified in the array will be stripped from the element. If, however, a single element is passed on, the method will remove it from the target element. The returned value is the modified element.

The constructor of the class `Slider` is next on our list. This method performs the task of creating a jQuery object referring to the image container (`image-container`), calling two methods: `checkAndSetLast()` and `prepareRandomMovement()`.

The `checkAndSetLast` method does a rather simple task. It iterates over all the images available in the image container and replaces the CSS class attribute of the last image child of the image container by the previous image. On careful observation of the method call, you will see that the replacement is done without searching. This is particularly useful from an algorithmic point of view, because the method is called only once, and that, too, at the time of creation of the method object. Because the constructor is called once, and toward the end of the script, the success of the replacement operation is ensured.

The `prepareRandomMovement()` method ensures that a number of objectives will be met. It finds inside the image container all the `img` children to create the exact thumbnails matching the actual images. The method creates image elements and sets the CSS class attribute to the height and width of a thumbnail. For every image that is created, an action is assigned upon the `click` event. So, upon the `click` event on each of the thumb images, the previous and the next images inside the image container are stripped of their CSS attributes' `previous-image` and the `next-image`, respectively. On the image element that corresponds to the clicked thumb image, each of the existing CSS class, i.e., `previous-image` and the `next-image`, are replaced with `shown-image`, in addition to setting the left attribute to 0px. All of the next siblings of this (slide show) image are made next images by setting the CSS class attribute `next-image`, and all the previous siblings of the slide show images are made previous images by setting the CSS class attribute `previous-image`. The CSS left property of the next images is set to be located at the right adjacent end, and that of the previous images is set to be located at the left adjacent end. To make the movement smooth and regular, if there is no `next-image` available, the first image in the list of slide show images is made as the next image (by making the necessary CSS adjustments, as mentioned). The same is done for the previous image—by setting the last image as the previous image and making the other necessary CSS property adjustments. The created thumb image is appended to the thumb container—a `div` element (with ID attribute of `thumbs`) already created for the purpose of holding the slide show thumbnails. In short, this method creates the functionality to access any of the slide show images at random.

Next is this `getElement()` method. The purpose of this method is to return the desired element, based on the arguments that are passed to it. The `getElement()` method accepts three arguments: the current element, which is the reference point for the search; the target set, from which the search has to be performed; and the direction of the search. The direction of the search can be next or previous. The latter can be the default search, if no third argument is specified. The method returns the next element matched on the current element in the target set, if there is a next element. It returns the first element in the case of a no match found condition. Similarly, if there is no previous sibling in the DOM tree in reference to the current element, the last element in the specified target set of elements is returned from the method.

The main engine of the entire slide show animation is the `go()` method, which is the next on our list of components to be explained. This method performs a sequence of tasks, in the exact order specified as follows:

- It finds out the current element, the next element, and the next-to-next element from the list of images that are contained in the image container.

- The current element is animated to move to the left by a distance (in pixels), to hide it from view.

- Upon completion of the animation, the CSS class attributes are silently adjusted accordingly, as is done for the next element and the next-to-next element. This adjustment is made by animating the next legitimate element to the center stage, followed by setting the left attribute to 0px.

- Upon completion of the animation, the CSS class and left attributes are adjusted accordingly.

It is quite a lengthy script that we just demonstrated, so it took us a little time to explain the components that will be required to get this slider system running. Having knowledge of the various components, we can now discuss how to use the components. The object of the class Slider is created toward the end, for reasons previously explained (this mention was intended only as a refresher). Because the object is already created, we move ahead to the go( ) method, with the appropriate direction specified on the click events on the Next and Previous buttons.

No code is perfect. It submits to the churning of the code reviewers, quality assurance personnel, user feedback, and changes in the business requirements. The code we proposed is no exception. There are some limitations that have to be addressed in the script, which we list following:

- We have not considered the case for less than three images.

- Width should not be hard-coded, nor should height. In our calculations, we have specified the height as 570px.

- The thumbnails count should be allowed to accommodate more thumbnails once there are more than seven. This accommodation could take the form of sliding the thumbnails on the sliding of main images.

- Ours is a long code. We recommend using a separate JavaScript file for such codes. We dumped all code in one place for the sake of explanation. You can copy the JavaScript code into a separate file named Slider.js and include the same, using the script tag in the required web page.

We encourage you to make amendments to your code to address these issues and to go ahead and be an open source ninja warrior! We have created a fiddle, so that interested readers can view the code in action. The fiddle is located at http://jsfiddle.net/ankur6971/j1hyL4eh/.

Summary

In this chapter, we covered a lot of ground, making use of functions to attain maximum efficiency, thanks to a number of optional parameters. So, here's a quick recap of what you learned in this chapter. You discovered the importance of jQuery when it comes to animation. You explored the main animation method available in jQuery—animate( ). Through examples, you learned how to make use of the fading and the sliding functions provided by the jQuery library. Using the toggle( ) method, you were able to play with the visibility of some specific element. We showed you how to differentiate between the two versions of toggle( ), by describing the purpose of each. Using the information collected from the demonstrations, you were able to create a very basic form of light box. To familiarize you with the animation behavior, we described how to control it by turning it off globally and by adjusting the number of frames processed per second. To help you on your way to becoming a coding ninja, we encouraged you (via a demonstration) to create a basic image slider, using the information gathered throughout the chapter.

In the next chapter, we will guide you through the asynchronous world of AJAX, a technique that you may have used, but, this time, once you become familiar with it, you will not want to revert to the old ways of performing a task.

CHAPTER 8

■ ■ ■

Ajax with jQuery

Traditionally, the Web has relied on a synchronous HTTP request response model. While this has been widely used and still is, it prevents machine-to-machine background communication. Each HTTP request means reloading an entire web page, in order to display new information. This also has led to a difference in behavior between the desktop and browser-based applications. A new technology by the name of Ajax was introduced that soon began to be widely used as the HTTP request/response transporter. In this chapter, we will discuss Ajax and its related technologies, such as JSON. We will also consider Ajax using jQuery. In this chapter, you will find the following:

- An introduction to Ajax and JSON, the most popular and lightweight data interchange format

- How to use Ajax using the jQuery framework

- How to parse JSON using JavaScript

- Use of Ajax in some practical scenario

Introducing Ajax

The term *Ajax* is an acronym containing a reference to the technologies that are covered under it. We will describe the technologies in detail a bit later in this section, but for now, note that *Ajax* stands for *Asynchronous JavaScript and XML*. Although more than just JavaScript and XML are involved in Ajax, the name was coined to contain only the two technologies mentioned. Quoting Wikipedia,

> The term "Ajax" was publicly stated on 18 February 2005 by Jesse James Garrett in an article titled "Ajax: A New Approach to Web Applications," based on techniques used on Google pages.

Now, let's consider Ajax's functional origins and the technologies from which it is composed.

How Did Ajax Originate?

Ajax was not a completely new technology as such. It was a grouping of already-known technologies harnessed to attain some objective. When we say "already-known," we mean to say that none of the technologies in Ajax was new. They were already in use, to a rather considerable degree, in creating and maintaining web-based applications across the world. The engineers at Google were working tirelessly to create an e-mail system to be used in a web browser in which the end user would not have to reload an entire page to fetch a new e-mail. It was in 2004 that this hard work gave to the world Gmail, a fully cross-browser compliant application built using Ajax. Google extended its efforts and came up with another product that used Ajax—Google Maps—just about a year later, in 2005.

We would like to emphasize here that it was *not* Google that started using Ajax; it was Google that *popularized* it. There were attempts all around the world to attain something similar. Some approaches included writing some scripts inside the web page, so that even after the web page was downloaded, these scripts were able to pull more data from the server. This mechanism was available in Netscape, and this feature was known as LiveScript. The engineers at Netscape continued their hard work, and they enabled a feature to render some content written in XML, making it look like a regular web page. People at Microsoft were watching all this closely, and they added a method to the JavaScript implementation in their browser: the IE5. The name of the method was XMLHttpRequest. Using this method, the JavaScript rendered inside the web page could communicate to the web server and obtain data from the server. When Microsoft did this, Mozilla was the next to implement this method, in their JavaScript implementation in Firefox. It was after these giants moved ahead to secure this functionality that it began to garner attention, and Google made the maximum use of it. There was an e-commerce setup, with a web site located at www.kayak.com, which was another large-scale implementation of the phenomenon.

■ **Tip**   For an in-depth look into the history of Ajax, see www.aaronsw.com/weblog/ajaxhistory.

The Technologies That Make Up Ajax

As we already stated at the beginning of this chapter, Ajax is not a technology in itself; it is a group of already fully developed technologies. Speaking in very broad terms, the technologies used in Ajax are combined HTML/CSS and JavaScript. Let's look into the share each of the technologies mentioned possesses in Ajax.

Starting with the HTML/CSS combination, we would like to state that all web applications that are to be executed on the web browser need HTML to render the content to the end user. Thus, all the HTTP responses that are sent back to the web browser by the web server are interpreted by the web browser as HTML tags and codes. Because Ajax can be used to exchange data from the server, there needs to be HTML, and since the HTML needs to be presented in some useful format, CSS is used to decorate the (probably) ugly bits and pieces that are used to create the building blocks of the user interface (UI) related to the HTTP request sent and the HTTP response obtained thereby.

Another technology involved in Ajax is JavaScript, which plays a major role in Ajax. In the presentation component, JavaScript is used to provide the capability to perform DOM manipulation in order to "adjust" the data that has been received as a part of the Ajax response by the web server. At the data exchange layer, JavaScript makes provisions to have the data sent and received as JSON or plain text. In short, there is a method that we mentioned a while ago, XMLHttpRequest, which makes up for the *asynchronous* behavior in Ajax.

Considering it all together, you might want to ask a simple question: If it offers nothing new, why has the term *Ajax* become jargon? We will take pains to answer this simple question in a not-so-simple way. We suggest you pay careful attention to what we are about to say, because while the statements will answer your question, they will make an assertion regarding the advantages that are served by this jargon. The technologies were already there but were not used as a group, because no one in the industry bothered using them until someone found a use for them. Because a use was found, others began to look for ways to take advantage of this discovery. Thus, people started thinking of the possibility of eliminating the difference in the user experience between a desktop-based application and a web-based application.

The traditional user experience for a web-based application was such that for every requested change in the data, the entire page was reloaded. This is to say that the communication between the web browser and the web server was synchronous, in the sense that the server would resend all data synchronously to the web browser, which meant that the entire web page would be refreshed (by getting a fresh copy of the data on the server). With the use of Ajax, the communication could be asynchronous, because the same web page could make separate XMLHttpRequest communications to (the same or different) web server(s) without their interfering with each other.

Ajax Using jQuery

Having said enough about the technology, let us move ahead and carry out the task that pertains to the subject of this book. We covered what Ajax is and what is inside it, now it is time for us to establish the relationship between Ajax and jQuery. Most readers may wonder how the two entities are related to each other. For the sake of clarification, we will make an assertion and, later on, explain that assertion: Ajax is a concept encapsulating a number of well-known and already used technologies, and jQuery is a framework written in a scripting language—JavaScript. Simply stated, you can use an Ajax methodology or technique (whichever name you prefer) using a framework known as jQuery. How is discussed in the sections and the examples that follow.

The Nuts and Bolts of Ajax in JavaScript

Because it has been our approach to begin the discussion with the basics, and because we have already explained the basics of Ajax, we will take up the JavaScript approach to Ajax. While this might seem a topic off-topic, it is not. It will give you some insight into the working of the jQuery framework in the current context. Consider the following simple use case. There is a page containing some text, and there is a need to pull that data into some other section inside a web page. All this has to be done asynchronously. So, because we are front-end web developers, we will resort to using JavaScript as a first line of defense. We propose using its workhorse method—the XMLHttpRequest available with the JavaScript implementation of (new) browsers. We'll start by informing you about the essential details related to the XMLHttpRequest object.

The XMLHttpRequest encapsulates certain methods that are essential to complete the asynchronous functionality. Following, we list the necessary methods and members with a brief explanation related to what the methods/members are and what they do:

- **open()**: This method opens a new HTTP connection to the web server. In simple terms, this method initiates a new HTTP request.

- **send()**: This method sends the HTTP request to the web server on the open connection.

- **readyState**: The state of the HTTP request at any instant of time. The value starts from 0 when it is opened and has not been called. It turns to a 1 immediately after the connection has been opened (by calling the open() method). Then it attains a value of 2, when the server has presented the HTTP headers. The next value attained by the readyState is 3, which means that the data is being downloaded onto the client. The value which is attained after 3 is 4, which represents the state of the request when completed. You mostly would be interested in using this value to perform some desired action.

- **onreadystatechange**: You have to program the actual asynchronous functionality inside this function. That is to say that once you send an HTTP request to the server, the value of another property (readyState) encapsulated by the XMLHttpRequest changes. So, this onreadystatechange is defined as a function containing the activity to be performed once the readyState changes.

- **status**: The HTTP response code as returned from the server. The value that is of interest to us is 200. This value stands for *success*. You will most often look for an opportunity to have this status code returned from the server, to perform any action.

- **responseText**: This is the property exhibited by the XMLHttpRequest method (or class) to represent the text as returned from the server.

To sum up, we propose a way for you to look into the way JavaScript performs an asynchronous request. We begin with the HTML part, which is rather simple, as follows:

```
<!DOCTYPE html>
<html>
    <head>
        <title>:: Playing with Ajax ::</title>
    </head>
    <body>
        <span id="ajax-initiator" onclick="getData()">Click here to get data from an external
            source</span>
        <div id="ajax-data"></div>
    </body>
</html>
```

The corresponding JavaScript code will look as follows:

```
function getData(){
    var ajax = new XMLHttpRequest();
    ajax.open('GET', 'ajax-data.html');

    ajax.onreadystatechange = function(){
        if(ajax.readyState == 4 && ajax.status ==200){
            document.getElementById('ajax-data').innerHTML = ajax.responseText;
        }
    }

    ajax.send(null);
}
```

So, for a quick explanation, a new connection is set up to the HTML file (which is expected to contain some data), and once the server returns the value, this value is inserted into a div (which we had already put in with the ID ajax-data).

The jQuery Approach

We have been saying that jQuery is a framework written in JavaScript. The task of any framework is to ease the load of performing common tasks by providing methods/functions (whichever term you prefer) intended to solve common problems. Considering asynchronous requests as one such problem, the jQuery framework does not let you down. There are a number of ways in which the framework lets you work on asynchronous programming. Before we take up the methods provided in jQuery, we take this opportunity to state that there is a "mother" method, on the one hand, and there are wrapper methods that make available the functionality of this mother method to solve common problems. Trust us, most of the time, you will find the wrapper methods better than the mother method. This statement can be taken to be an extension of the objective of this book: JavaScript is the mother language, and jQuery is a wrapper to the jQuery methods, and people find jQuery more useful most of the time.

■ **Note**   The .ajax() method is also defined as a "low-level" Ajax interface.

Understanding the "Mother" ajax()

Let us begin with the mother method—ajax(). We call this the mother function because the jQuery implementation has been made in such a detailed way that in order to explain using this method by making use of all of the parameters, it would take another book, probably entitled *Learning Ajax Using jQuery*. But as we are in the middle of a book entitled *Practical jQuery*, we will take up the practical (and necessary) aspects of this method here. But we will also assure you that as the chapter progresses, we will take up those aspects that we find useful in light of the need of the hour. Allowing ourselves to reuse the same use case that we took up while explaining the way JavaScript relates to Ajax will keep the HTML code the same. To demonstrate how to make use of the ajax() method, we use the following jQuery code:

```
function getData(){
    $.ajax({
        url: "ajax-data.html",
        type: "GET",
        dataType : "text",
        success: function( text ) {
            $('#ajax-data').html(text);
        },
        error: function( xhr ) {
            alert( "The server has thrown an error. Please check console log for details!" );
            console.log( "Error: " + xhr.statusText );
            console.log( "Status: " + xhr.status );
        },
        complete: function( ) {
            alert( "The asynchronous task is done!" );
        }
    });
}
```

We will now explain the various elements used in this method call. The following list explains all of the elements in the current use case.

- **url**: This attribute specifies the location of the resource from which the data will be fetched.

- **type**: Using this attribute, you can set the type of request method you want to use. By request method, we mean one of the HTTP methods available, such as a GET or a POST.

- **dataType**: Because this is a world in which the server has the upper hand, we, the clients, have to know in advance the type of data the server will respond to. The possible values are text, html, or json, which you can specify according to type.

- **success**: This is a callback function that gets called once the server returns a status code of 200. We mentioned earlier that it is this status code that is of interest to you when you want to carry out some asynchronous task. You will find it useful to take another look into the JavaScript counterpart that we described in the section immediately preceding, which will allow you to gain some insight into the way this ajax() method is implemented.

- **error**: Servers are quite disciplined. They throw errors as soon as they detect something fishy in your input. So, using this attribute, you can specify a callback function that will be activated once the server returns an error. The server throws errors such as 403, for trying to execute an HTTP method that is not allowed on the server; 404, for a missing (not found) resource; 500, for some programming error at the server end; and so on. The callback function receives an object containing the response from the server, including the status code and the error text.

- **complete**: This is another callback function that gets activated once the request is complete. We would underline the fact that this completion takes place in all the cases, whether the server has returned an error or indicates a success. In other words, complete and success are completely disjointed and mutually independent. This callback function receives an object containing the response from the server, quite like the error counterpart in the ajax() method.

■ **Tip** We encourage you to do a console.log on this (response) object to discover more!

Commonly Used ajax() Functions

The ajax() method has the facility to offer fine-grained control over the functionality to be achieved. As noted previously, we do not intend to take up each and every element used in the ajax() method; however, we will take up the methods that are most commonly used for asynchronous tasks (and those that are quite similar in behavior to the "convenience functions" that we covered in Chapter 7 while discussing event handling) and compare their uses with those of the jQuery ajax() method to execute the same task. The commonly used functions we will take up are the load(), get(), and post() methods.

■ **Tip** The .load(), .get(), and .post() methods are known as *shorthand methods* for Ajax.

The load() Method

We start with the load() method, which performs the most basic asynchronous communication functionality, in that it cannot retrieve data from a location in the outside world. The URL to retrieve data has to be on the same server. To highlight the concept of Ajax functionality, we propose the following example of the load() method:

```
function getData(){
    $('#ajax-data').load('ajax-data.html', function(response, status, xhr){
        if(status == 'error'){
            alert( "The server has thrown an error. Please check console log for details" );
            console.log( "Error: " + xhr.statusText );
            console.log( "Status: " + xhr.status );
        }
    });
}
```

If you compare the preceding example with that of the ajax() method, you will find a striking similarity between the two. With the ajax() method, you had to specify each success as well as the error condition. But with load(), you just have to specify the error condition. The success condition (in which the server returns proper data and there is no error) is handled without your intervention.

You might ask us about using HTTP methods such as GET and POST in the load() method. If you do not pass on some data to the server, the HTTP method used by default is GET, and if you pass on some data to the server, the method is POST.

We, in turn, might ask whether using load() is not more convenient than its ajax() counterpart.

The get() Method

Moving on to the next commonly used convenience function to perform asynchronous tasks, we note that there is a method that simulates an asynchronous request using the HTTP GET method. Just like a usual GET request, you can pass on data to the server, if you wish to do so. There is no provision error notification with this method. This is probably what the jQuery developers took note of! Quickly moving to an example, let us take up the same use case that we took up at the beginning.

```
function getData(){
    $.get('ajax-data.html', function(response){
        $('#ajax-data').html(response);
    });
}
```

You have to specify the URL for the location of the resource from where you will get the required data, and you have to specify the callback method, in case you want some action to take place once the request is successfully responded to. In case you want to send some data to some URL, the get() method is there to help you as well. We propose the following usage of this method, in that case:

```
function getData(){
    $.get(
        '/some-url/on-webserver',
        {keyA: "valueA", keyB: "valueB"},
        function(result){
            $('some-id').html(result);
        },
        'json'
    );
}
```

You specify four options, each of which we will explain briefly (as they are used in the same context as the ajax() method). The URL specifies the location of the resource; the data that you pass is specified as a JSON object; the useful task you would want to perform is written inside the callback function; and the expected data type that the server will return is specified as the last option. Do not worry if you forget to specify the data type option, because the jQuery get() method is designed to perform an intelligent guess on the data type and proceed.

■ **Note** There also is a get() method available in jQuery that executes the task of finding the nth element in the DOM tree specified by a selector. We took up the treatment of that get() method in Chapter 0 and suggest that you not confuse the Ajax version and the one we discussed previously.

The post() Method

This method will be particularly favored by all those developers who are fans of the HTTP POST method and prefer using this method to change some data at the web server. The jQuery framework, understanding the need of such web developers, has made a provision to use a convenience method. As an example, let's consider the same use case that we have been employing. The proposed method usage in that case would be

```
$.post('ajax-data.html', function(response){
    $('#ajax-data').html(response);
});
```

There are options for you to use with this method as well. You can pass on data to the web server (just like we have been doing in all the examples for a while now). So, before attempting to explain the options available, why not have a look into the usage first? We propose a usage of the jQuery post method, employing all the options available, as shown (followed by an explanation of the options available).

```
$.post(
    '/some-url/on-webserver',
    {keyA: "valueA", keyB: "valueB"},
    function(result){
        $('some-id').html(result);
    },
    'json'
);
```

We move on to the explanation now. We restrict ourselves to a very short explanation, because, as the jQuery post() method is just a wrapper around the jQuery ajax() method, the options are more or less the same. So, the URL specifies a valid location to send the data to. The data that you have to pass on to the server is sent in the form of a JSON string (we will shed more light on this in the coming sections). There is a callback method that you have to specify once the server returns some information successfully. We will (again) like to underline the fact that it is this callback method by which you will write the useful code that you want to get executed asynchronously. The jQuery post() method provides you with an option to set the expected data type that the server will return, but at the same time, the method does not complain if you omit this option, because the method performs an intelligent guess regarding the data type and proceeds accordingly.

Introducing JSON

The term *JSON* stands for *JavaScript Object Notation*. JSON is a text-based data interchange format that humans as well as machines can understand. As with Ajax, JSON originated from JavaScript, and the intention of its developers was to facilitate the addition of statefulness to web applications, by using the built-in capabilities of the web browser. Because JavaScript gets interpreted inside browsers, the assumption was that even JSON would get executed, without having to add some other tool/software. JSON provides an alternate data interchange format over XML to developers trying to program intercommunication between machines. Although originally written and used with JavaScript, due to JSON being a data interchange format, there have been written libraries in various languages as well. But as our focus is JavaScript/jQuery, we will concentrate mainly on working with JSON using JS and jQuery. Let's have a quick introduction to what a typical JSON object looks like.

Understanding JSON

After reading this section, you should be able to connect a number of dots you have encountered previously in this book and come away with a meaningful picture. The following list explains the salient features related to what JSON looks like:

- The JSON object starts with a curly brace ({).

- JSON objects contain data for quick and easy access, so they are saved as a key value pair, with the key being a string and the value being any valid value that you desire. The value can be another JSON object, an array, a numeric value, a valid string value, or Boolean values such as `true` or `false`.

- A JSON array is quite like the array in JavaScript. It starts with an opening square brace ([) and contains a list of values separated by a comma (,). A JSON array ends with a closing square brace (]).

- Different JSON values stored in an object are separated by a comma (,).

- The JSON object ends with a curly brace (}).

■ **Note** In order to learn more about JSON, you can visit the official web site for JSON located at `http://json.org/`.

Now let's take a look at some typical valid JSON strings.
A simple JSON object is

```
{
    'bookName': 'Practical jQuery',
    'authors': 'Ankur & Mukund',
    'pertainsTo': 'Web Development'
}
```

A nested JSON object is

```
{
    'booksByAPress': {
        'name': 'Practical jQuery',
        'edition': 1,
        'chapters': 12
    },
    'fieldsCovered': {
        'technology': 'Web'
    }
}
```

A JSON object containing an array:

```
{
    'chapters': [
        'Chapter 1',
        'Chapter 2',
        'Chapter 3'
    ]
}
```

Parsing JSON with JavaScript

Because there is a format to be used with a programming language, there has to be some algorithm to obtain the correct and appropriate values from the format. We can call this phenomenon of extracting information from the JSON format *JSON parsing*. Parsing is a general process of analyzing some string to understand the structure of the relationship between its elements and employ the information contained within to attain some useful objective. You can parse JSON easily, using JavaScript; however, you do have to choose among a number of options available for parsing JSON. These options are as follows:

- Parsing without using library methods
- Parsing with the JavaScript library's parse() method
- Parsing with the JavaScript library's eval() method

Parsing Without Using Library Methods

Let's look at a sample JSON object (reusing the JSON example we took up a short while ago).

```
{
    'bookName': 'Practical jQuery',
    'authors': 'Ankur & Mukund',
    'pertainsTo': 'Web Development'
}
```

In order to use the individual elements of this JSON object, you just have to remember the methodology that you use to access the members of an object in some OOP language. A sample code is as follows:

```
var json = {
    'bookName': 'Practical jQuery',
    'authors': 'Ankur & Mukund',
    'pertainsTo': 'Web Development'
};

alert(json.bookName);
alert(json.authors);
alert(json.pertainsTo);
```

Now that we have provided an example to familiarize you with JSON, we encourage you to try out more combinations, rather than the simple alert we used in our demonstration, such as populating some HTML table with data or converting strings to sentence case, or even determining the length of each string, and so on.

Next, we move ahead to show you that the JavaScript library has methods available for these purposes. We will first discuss the parse() method and then the eval() method.

Parsing with the parse() Method

You can use the parse() method to achieve the same results that you were able to obtain in the example immediately preceding. There are actually two usages: one with a single argument and one with two arguments specified. We will show each usage, starting with the single argument. As far as the argument is concerned, you only have to remember (in both the cases we mentioned) that the method parse() accepts a JSON as a string.

Here is an example of the single-argument usage:

```
var json = '{"bookName": "Practical jQuery","authors": "Ankur & Mukund","pertainsTo": "Web
Development"}';
var result = JSON.parse(json);
alert(result.bookName);
alert(result.authors);
alert(result.pertainsTo);
```

Moving on to the next usage of the parse() method, you will make use of a function that the documentation terms as the *reviver* function, which we'll demonstrate in the next code example. What we have tried to demonstrate in this usage is that with the reviver method, you actually have the facility to iterate over every key value pair available in the JSON string specified as the first argument to parse(). Have a look at the code example.

```
var json = '{"bookName": "Practical jQuery","authors": "Ankur & Mukund","pertainsTo":
"Web Development"}';
var result = JSON.parse(json, function(key, value){
    if(typeof value === 'string')
        alert(JSON.stringify(key)+" : "+JSON.stringify(value));
});
```

So, in the code usage we proposed, we have made a sincere attempt to alert a message on the screen with the key value pair, provided the type of value is a string. We have used the comparison just as a means to have a simple demonstration. We again encourage you to try out more programming permutations and combinations.

Parsing with the eval() Method

There is a third method available for parsing a JSON input—the eval() method. Using the eval() method, you can very well parse a JSON string, but that is considered risky in all those use cases in which the (JSON) input is from some untrusted source. If you ask how, we would state that the eval() method available in the JavaScript library is a method to evaluate some valid JavaScript expression and execute it thereby. So, if the JSON input somehow contains some malicious code (for example, some string containing a database drop statement), the eval() could execute it as well. The result, you can easily imagine.

We now put before you an example of the use of the eval() method to evaluate JSON (more contextually, to parse JSON).

```
var json = '{"bookName": "Practical jQuery","authors": "Ankur & Mukund","pertainsTo":
"Web Development"}';

eval("var result = "+json);
alert(result.bookName);
alert(result.authors);
alert(result.pertainsTo);
```

What we have done here is ask JavaScript to evaluate a string for us. The trick we have played with the JavaScript interpreter is to make it think that the input is just a string. But because the eval() method evaluates and executes whatever you pass on to it, it evaluates the string to be a valid assignment statement, and then it executes the statement, giving us an object in the name of result. We have gone a step ahead to use this object to perform our task—getting the information contained in a JSON string successfully.

■ **Caution**   If you examine carefully, there could be a serious security issue with the usage of eval(). We could easily ask the eval() method to tell the JavaScript engine to generate an assignment statement. Bearing this possibility in mind, we warn you to use eval() with extreme care, because there are a number of people who take pleasure in destroying others' work. So, in case some such person happens to visit your web site, in which you might have used eval() to perform some task, be it parsing JSON or anything, this could result in extremely bad consequences for your site.

Using the jQuery Alternative to JavaScript

Yes, there is a functionality available in the jQuery framework that allows you to parse JSON and get the information contained within the object. The functionality is available to you in the form of a method—the parseJSON() method. Before we take this opportunity to explain the workings of parseJSON(), we would like to offer an example, so that you can connect the dots again. The code usage we suggest is

```
var json = '{"bookName": "Practical jQuery","authors": "Ankur & Mukund","pertainsTo": "Web
Development"}';
var result = $.parseJSON(json);
alert(result.bookName);
alert(result.authors);
alert(result.pertainsTo);
```

The result will be exactly the same as in all the previous cases we took up while explaining JSON parsing. There will be three message alerts on the screen: the name of the book, the name of the authors, and the technology the book pertains to.

Because jQuery is a framework written in JavaScript, the method parseJSON() makes use of the JavaScript method parse() (which you are now familiar with). So, under the hood, the framework checks if the parse() method is implemented in the browsers' implementation of JavaScript. If the method is available, the framework calls the parse() method by passing on the JSON string passed on to the parseJSON() method. If nothing is passed, nothing (a null) is returned!

Ajax and JSON Usage Example

No art is useful if it is not used. In order to be able to use some useful art, you need to be able to decide when to use that art and to be able to decide that, you need to use the useful art so that you can understand when to use the art.

Now, we would like to provide a simplified real-world usage that incorporates the knowledge you have obtained after going through all these lessons in jQuery.

Let us take up an extremely common problem (of performing user input validation) and try to solve it by using Ajax and jQuery (employing JSON as well). The entire use case is fabricated by us for this demonstration, but we can assure you that you will definitely be able to connect this demonstration to some common problem that you face in your day-to-day web development activity. So, let us list the points that will act as our roadmap for this demonstration.

- We will create a user input form.

- The form will collect some basic information, such as name, e-mail, and telephone number.

- There will be some validations to be applied on the input form, such as shown in the sublist that follows.

  - The name should not contain any non-alphabetic characters except for a period (.).

  - The e-mail should be a valid e-mail format.

  - The telephone number should contain a valid phone number format.

- The validations should be performed at the client side only.

- The data should be sent to some script running on some web server via Ajax.

- The success or failure message will be obtained from the server-side script and will be displayed onto the client side.

Following these points, we proceed to offer you an example. Assume there is an input form on an HTML page, as follows:

```
<form id="capture-data">
    <input type="text" name="name"/>
    <input type="text" name="email"/>
    <input type="text" name="phone"/>
    <input type="submit" value="Send" />
</form>
```

Given the requirements we have been provided with, we propose the following code solution:

```
$('#capture-data').submit(function (event) {
    if (!event)
        var event = window.event;
    event.preventDefault();
    try {
        var validation = new Validation();
        validation.check('name');
```

```
        validation.check('email');
        validation.check('phone');

        var data = '{"name": "' + validation.name + '", "email": "' + validation.email + '",
            "phone": "' + validation.phone + '"}';

        $.post('url-on-server',
            data,
            function () {
                alert("The server said 'OK mate!'")
            });

        } catch (exception) {
            alert('There was some issue, please check browser console');
            console.log(exception);
        }

    });

function Validation() {
    this.name = $('input[name="name"]').val();
    this.email = $('input[name="email"]').val();
    this.phone = $('input[name="phone"]').val();
}

    Validation.prototype.check = function (what) {
        switch (what) {
            case 'name':
                var validName = /^([a-z](\.)?(\ )?){3,}$/i;
                if (this.name.length > 0 && validName.test(this.name) === false) {
                    throw "Invalid characters in name";
                }
                break;

            case 'email':
                var validEmail = /^([a-z0-9]\.?\_?)+\@[a-z0-9]+\.?[a-z]{2,3}\.?[a-z]{2,3}$/i;
                if (this.email.length > 0 && validEmail.test(this.email) === false){
                    throw "Email format not proper.";
                }
                break;

            case 'phone':
                var validPhone = /^\+?[0-9]{6,15}$/i;
                if (this.phone.length > 0 && validPhone.test(this.phone) === false){
                    throw "Phone number needs to be worked upon";
                }
                break;
    }
}
```

Now comes the tougher part of the job—the explanation. We begin by explaining the bits and pieces that we put together to create this example. You will see big-time action here: jQuery selectors, JavaScript class, class members, regular expressions, exception handling, event handling, JSON, Ajax, and so on.

The code starts by assigning an event handler to the form element specified in the DOM. The action that is to be taken is tied to the submit event (which takes place when you hit the Send button in the form). So, once the event takes place, the event object is checked for a purpose. If it is not passed to the method as an argument, it is re-created from the window object. In light of the purpose we mentioned, our objective is to have the request as asynchronous, so we will have to prevent the default action of the form element (which is to send the data to the server in a synchronous way, by reloading the entire page). We achieve this objective by calling the preventDefault() method (in the window event context). By the way, we ask that you recall what you read about this method earlier in this book.

We move ahead to check the name, the e-mail, and the phone number to ensure that they are valid inputs. Our objective is achieved by the class Validation, which we have defined and the explanation for which we will provide shortly. Once we are sure that there is no issue in the user input, we convert the form data into a JSON string and pass it on to the post() method. So, this post() method performs the *asynchronous* data sending to the server and receives the response back from the server. You can use this response to perform some useful action.

■ **Note** You will note that we did not use any special tool to convert any existing data into a JSON string. This would be another example helping you to understand that the JSON is just a reuse of the technology.

So, once there is some issue in the input, there is an alert message shown to the user, the error message is logged to the browser console, and the script execution ends. If there is no issue in the input, there is no exception thrown, the data is sent asynchronously to the server, and the useful task associated with the response is carried out in the callback method.

Moving on to the Validation class that we defined, we believed that the validation logic had to be kept separate from the other logics, and this drove us to write a JavaScript class for the same. This class contains a total of four (4) members in all—three member variables representing the *name*, *phone*, and the *e-mail* inputs provided by the *input* form, and the fourth being the method as the only member method to this class. We have used the attribute selector (which we treated in detail in Chapter 3) to select the appropriate inputs. The method check accepts a name representing the element that is to be validated as the only argument to it, and that, too, is mandatory. Our code makes a decision based on this argument and validates the three inputs according to the corresponding criteria. With regard to the criteria, have a look at the following list:

- A valid name is that which can contain any alphabetic character (lowercase or uppercase), a period (.), and a space in between. There must be at least three alphabetic characters in the name to allow it to qualify as valid.

- A valid e-mail is one that contains a mixture of alphanumeric characters, a period or an underscore, followed by an @ symbol. Following this should be all alphabetic characters, with only a period allowed in between.

- A valid phone number is one that contains an optional + (plus) sign at the beginning, followed by 6 to 15 digits.

We made use of regular expressions. For all of you who shudder at the mere sight of a regular expression, we would console you by acknowledging that regular expressions evoke the same degree of trepidation in most developers. So, all we can do is encourage you to practice using regular expressions more frequently. To the end, the following might prompt you to use regular expressions. String searches can be extremely complex. If you use strings to search, you might have to specify a number of them to specify a match. But if you resort to using regular expressions for the same search, you might end up simplifying your code, because you would cut down on the number of strings you would have to specify. So, taking another look at the regular expression part of the example we offered, if you had to specify all the e-mails that would be valid, you would end up having a *huge* list. Instead, you used a pattern, and your code was cleaner and shorter and, most important, it worked!

■ **Note**   We should state that ours is not a production code. It is our intention only to demonstrate how things work. So, ours may not be the best code, as the best programmer could be you and not us. Nonetheless, we encourage you to go ahead and use the code we suggest and to optimize and convert it to better and more useful code.

Summary

With this we come to the end of a topic that was concise yet extremely useful as far as web development is concerned. We hope that you found the information contained in this chapter interesting and that you will benefit from using Ajax in your web development routine. Summarizing this chapter, you learned what Ajax is and about the context that led people to think about Ajax. We also covered JSON and the utility that it provides when it comes to transporting data between the client and the server. We ended the chapter with a glimpse into how Ajax looks in practical use. In the next chapter, you will discover the utility of a plug-in, after you learn how to write one. We will continue where we left off in the current chapter by teaching you about creating plug-ins related to the same tasks that we outlined in this chapter.

■ ■ ■

CHAPTER 9

Creating Plug-ins with jQuery

Web developers often tend to deviate from the path of software engineering. This chapter will bridge the gap by explaining and demonstrating a very essential principle of software engineering—reusability. In this chapter, we will familiarize you with plug-ins in a jQuery context. You will learn that (jQuery) plug-ins are often handy in regard to functionalities that span multiple projects. By the end of this chapter, you will become familiar with

- Why you would need a plug-in

- The basic features of a plug-in

- How to write a good plug-in

- Creating a form validation plug-in

- Creating an accordion plug-in

What Is a Plug-in?

The most concise answer to this question is "A plug-in is a piece of software written to add some functionality to an existing software system." In simple terms, plug-ins are programs written in some language that have the intention of adding certain functionality to the language itself. To provide a better and deeper understanding of what a plug-in is, let us consider a specific scenario. Suppose there is a language X and that you are an expert developer in that language—call yourself a ninja programmer. If some task were to be programmed by you, you would go ahead and write classes (if X follows OOP) and member methods to complete the task. So far, so good. But suppose that same piece of functionality was required by a fellow developer (assuming a non-ninja), and that other developer had to rewrite the entire functionality. This is one of the many occasions necessitating code reusability, and we will explain this in more detail in this chapter.

Having said that, it is quite natural for you to ask why you would need a plug-in. From the beginning of this book, we have emphasized the DRY (don't repeat yourself) principle. You may remember that in Chapter 1, we recommended using jQuery for this very reason. Applying that criteria in the current context, if you solve problems by writing code, you are doing work. But if you solve problems by writing reusable code, you are doing *good* work. Of the number of ways to ensure good work, use of plug-ins is only one approach. Why we selected this one is owing to the context in which this chapter is proceeding. If you want to use a plug-in, it will be you who will have to develop it. It is you who creates one, and it is you who uses one.

Let us consider an HTML input form-validation use case, formulated by us to better demonstrate the need for a plug-in. Almost every business requirement that you are asked to fulfill involves validating user input in some form or other. Because it is the age of client-side programming, validating user input on the client side (inside a web page) is the need of the hour. So, just imagine that you have to perform validation across some five web pages. Will you be able to repeat the same code for all five of them? If somehow you had managed to, we guarantee that the warranty of that web page would be questionable. You definitely need a plug-in, to reduce the number of lines of code written, to keep the source code modular, to implement code reusability, and to stick to the principle of software engineering.

You should also be aware of the benefits of plug-ins in software development. Following is a list of some such benefits:

Code modularity: A plug-in enhances code modularity. We already discussed this in brief in the preceding section, but we should state the reason behind this effect of code modularity. Whenever a plug-in is created, it is with the intention of solving some particular problem. You can draw some sort of analogy to a library function—let's say sort. The implementation of a sort method would always be in such a way that you can use it to solve a number of sorting problems—sorting lists, arrays, and whatever data structure is available in the particular language. So, if we apply the term *modular*, we would not be incorrect, because whenever we feel like making changes to a plug-in, we will only have to modify the code inside the plug-in. Doing this will not affect the source code written to use that plug-in! What else would you want from a software source code?

Ease of use: A plug-in enables ease of use. We say this because a change in the usage of a plug-in will merely mean a change in the options or configurations that will be present with the plug-in. In other words, if your software requires a change in functionality, all you have to do is adjust the usage of the plug-in by the adjustment factors available.

Focus on business requirements: A plug-in lets you think about the bigger picture. You can make use of the time provided by the solution the plug-in offers to focus on larger problems. For example, for the problem of form validation that we mentioned previously, you would only have to call the appropriate method to be assured of the functionality of the input validation (provided the plug-in developer was trustworthy). Having a plug-in to solve a problem frees you of worry regarding implementation. Someone has already worked hard to solve that particular problem.

With the preceding, we have laid the groundwork for another discussion—using plug-ins that you will create using what you will learn from this chapter.

In keeping with the name of the chapter, we will increase our field of coverage by including jQuery in the picture. You will be glad to know that there is a jQuery plug-in directory, which you can refer to whenever you need a plug-in. (We will cover this plug-in directory in detail in the next chapter.) Because jQuery is an open source framework on which the world is going nuts, the development of plug-ins to extend the already diverse functionality is a nice way to become popular. Imagine the notoriety you will gain in the world of web development once you have created a plug-in that solves a problem nobody else in the world was able to solve! The last statement also underlines a fact that we have been alluding to throughout this book: all we can do is give you knowledge related to creating a plug-in, but it is left to you to do the actual work of identifying a persistent problem affecting that and writing a piece of software will not only be useful to you but also to others.

Now that we have provided you some information about the advantages of a plug-in, we can assume you have gained sufficient momentum to move ahead in the learning process. We will address the difficulties of writing a plug-in, so that, in the end, you will be able to successfully write your own. In the next chapter, you will further understand the utility of a plug-in, when we guide you in using the same plug-in in some other web page.

Plug-in Best Practices

There are nuts and bolts to every piece of machinery. Then there are some settings too. These settings enable the smooth functioning of the machinery, so that in case the usage changes somehow, the machine does not break down. The same can be said of software as well. The same is true of a plug-in. After all, a plug-in is like software in some regards. So, if one has to create some machinery, certain principles are to be followed. Having stated that, let's now consider the essential components of a plug-in.

A plug-in in jQuery has a striking resemblance to a member function in JavaScript. This makes sense, because, by the definition, a plug-in is written to enhance the functionality of some existing software application. Here, the software application is jQuery itself, which, in turn, is a collection of a large number of methods. If we were to call it a jQuery class, we would not be incorrect. So, once we consider jQuery a class, we find it comfortable to add more methods or even subclasses to this class itself. Once we look at a plug-in that way, there are a number of points that pop up that resemble the property of a class. We consider this aspect of a plug-in as an essential component of a jQuery plug-in. You will not be able to write a good plug-in without having these components. A list of components follows, with some brief explanation related to them.

- Private variables
- Public variables
- Parameters

Private Variables

Trust us, you will end up using a number of private variables inside your plug-in. Private variables inside a plug-in are variables that are required to provide temporary storage for calculations or similar operations. Let us quickly consider what a private variable looks like in a named function. By this time, you have had a fair amount of exposure to programming, so we can easily declare a function and show how a private variable would look inside the function.

```
var namedFunction = function(){
    var privateVar = "I am safe in my home";
    ...//Some logic
}
```

Because we have not exposed you to a plug-in until now, all we can do is suggest what a private variable would be like inside a plug-in. You can assume that when you write a plug-in, you are basically writing a method for the jQuery class. So, allowing ourselves the freedom to connect chords between topics, if there is need of a method inside a plug-in as namedFunction, a private variable will take the same shape as privateVar. Continuing with the importance of private variables inside a plug-in, suppose there is an object that has obtained some value by some calculation performed in some other part of the code doing some entirely different task. If you have to gain some advantage of the value, the best possible way (in most of situations) would be to make a copy of that object and perform calculations on this local/private copy of the object and later discard/return this locally modified value. This would also add the advantage of having the name privateVar prevail for the method you write.

Public Variables

You need a public variable inside of a plug-in as much as you need muscles in your body. Without muscles, your body would be stiff and would not function (as well as not look nice). So it is in the case of public variables. Public variables serve to add flexibility to a plug-in. This is quite obvious. The use of a plug-in can vary, and it varies considerably, as in the case of processing some user input. Sometimes your target is to achieve some substring out of a numeric input provided by the end user (probably to have the first few digits), and sometimes you might be required to perform an arithmetic calculation on the same input. Because a public member can be accessed outside of the class by the object reference (in most of the OOP-based programming languages and JavaScript alike), you can set some value before performing the expected calculations. Again, the solution will require a great deal of imagination on your part, because we have yet to provide you with a plug-in, but you can trust us that a plug-in will look similar to our demonstration. Consider that a sample plug-in (method) with a public variable could be as follows:

```
var namedFunction = function(){
    var privateVar = "I am safe in my home";
    this.publicVar = "This is for public use";
    ...//Some logic
}
```

Without the usage, the declaration does nothing. So, the usage of the public variable `publicVar` would be

```
var anObject = new namedFunction();
alert(anObject.publicVar); // Do something with the publicVar
```

Another important aspect of the public variable in a plug-in is that it makes your plug-in more social (in the existing source code ecosystem). A public variable is some attribute that is meant to be accessed publicly. So, another piece of code can use this attribute if the business requirement for the plug-in demands it.

■ **Caution** Using public variables in excess increases the chances of having side effects as a result of accidental change, so the ideal software engineering practice advises using getter and setter methods for the purpose of accessing public attributes.

We admit that our consideration of the public variable as an essential component of a plug-in is not complete. We will provide a more complete demonstration later, but until then, we ask that you try to follow the basics, so that you acquire a higher comfort level while writing your first plug-in.

Parameters

This component is quite important in regard to an aspect of plug-ins that we have already discussed. Adding parameters to plug-ins helps to control their behavior a great extent. We understand that our statements are generating more questions than answers, but trust us, this is the last such aspect of plug-ins that we will take up before actually writing one. You can consider this the curtain raiser to writing a plug-in! Moving the discussion forward, parameters in a plug-in increase the usability of the plug-in: parameters make the plug-in functionality depend on the input provided. This is quite normal, considering the usage of any machine, because the machine should behave in accordance with the input you provide it. In essence, a plug-in should adjust according to your input. You might ask what the difference is between a public variable inside a plug-in and a parameter passed to a plug-in. A parameter and a public variable *can* be related, if you want, but there is no explicit relationship between the two. The two move along different paths but achieve the same goal for a plug-in—flexibility. Let us move on to a demonstration. Consider an imaginary plug-in method, as follows:

```
var doIt = function(thisWay){
    var privateVar = "I am safe in my home";
    this.publicVar = "This is for public use";
    if(thisWay === 'this-way'){
        ...//DO THIS
    } else {
        ...//DO THAT
    }

    ...//Some more logic here
}
```

The usage of the method would be as follows:

```
var someAction = new doIt('some-way');
someAction.publicVar = "This can also depend on external factors";
```

Another usage can be the following:

```
var someOtherAction = new doIt('this-way');
someOtherAction.publicVar = "We will write a plugin soon";
```

Again, we would underline the fact that the examples provided are merely representative and only for the purpose of getting a feel for how the components would look inside a real plug-in. Having said that, and assuming the time is ripe to introduce a plug-in, we will offer you the essential tips that you should keep in mind when writing a plug-in.

Plug-in Writing Guidelines

So, there you are, in the trenches with all those delicate components that you have to assemble or create in order to come up with a shining (and, obviously, working) solution for a business that requires it. In this section, we provide the information that will not only help you gain knowledge but also give you the confidence to a write plug-in yourself.

Do You Really Need the Plug-in?

At the beginning of any new task, there is a question we must ask ourselves: "Is what we are about to start building really necessary?" While this question might seem ridiculous to you, in reality, it is not. Just think, if you spent a number of hours developing something that was not needed at all (due to reasons that we will mention), what would be the utility of that product or that of the time that you spent on developing it. You could easily have spent your time more fruitfully on other things. As to the uselessness of a product, there can be a number of reasons. There might be another plug-in performing exactly the same task as yours. You might have miscalculated the requirement of the business, and so on. Of the two reasons, the latter can occur less often, but the chances of the former are quite high. If you write a plug-in when there is another already available, you will be violating the very basic principle that we mentioned at the start of this chapter—the DRY principle.

Reuse What Already Exists

When we talk about the DRY principle, we allude to reusability. This reusability aspect covers all sorts of reusability, be they in the form of reusing a variable, an object, a method, or any form of written code. Considering a plug-in as a written piece of code (albeit a large one at times), you can reuse some existing plug-in in such ways as stated. The jQuery framework was intended to make things easier for you while programming, and thus, there have been a number of methods that you only have to call with some proper parameters, to get the work done. So, while sitting down to write a plug-in, if you happen to require some functionality, it we advise you to use jQuery's built-in methods as small chunks in the functionality, instead of writing everything on your own. This will serve a number of purposes, two of which we mention here. The jQuery framework itself is worked on by developers who are adding new features to the framework while improving old functionalities and features that have already been provided. So, once you have used the methods and components provided by the jQuery library, you are in the safe zone, because the updates and enhancements that the jQuery team add to the framework will automatically be reflected in your plug-in. Because your plug-in will enhance the functionality of jQuery, another purpose of reusing jQuery methods and properties is that the jQuery framework code ensures that you do not start from scratch. We will offer an example toward the end of this section, after we first provide some additional useful information.

■ **Caution** You have to stay apace of plug-in development, lest there be changes at the plug-in end (either in the functionality of certain library methods or in deprecating some existing methods) that might break the functionality of your code, which depends on the plug-ins. This is not to cause anxiety; we just want to advise you to be careful.

Preserve the Reference to jQuery

The most commonly used reference to the jQuery object is the dollar symbol ($). While creating a plug-in, you should ensure that you do not create some other reference to jQuery but continue with the same reference. This is particularly useful and important too, because by a reference, the jQuery object containing the methods and the attributes is used. The jQuery object contains the representation of the current DOM tree, for example. So, if there is more than one reference to the same jQuery framework, the changes done in one object will create problems with changes done in the other objects, and hence, there will be code conflicts.

From another perspective, which we already discussed in Chapter 2, you must preserve the reference to jQuery to prevent conflicts with other frameworks (if there are any other frameworks in your code base). Restating the essential part of the explanation, if you have to use another framework inside your web page, and that other framework uses the same dollar symbol ($) for its operations, your jQuery plug-in will not function properly. As we explain in Chapter 2, you have to use the noConflict() method to avoid conflicts.

Do Not Unnecessarily Modify Objects

Humans are social. They coexist with other humans. So should your plug-in be; it should coexist with other code written in the surrounding ecosystem. This is to say that the code you write in the form of a plug-in should not disturb other objects or properties already prevalent in the code. For example, if you wish to perform some operation on some object already present in another part of the source code responsible for driving your web page, we advise you to make a copy and then modify that copy. The reason is simple: you might not know the intention of the other developer who created or maintained that copy, and so you would not know what side effect modifying an object would cause. As another aspect of working on a copy of some object, you must be able to perform operations to the object atomically. Once there is an error, the copy of the object that you created can be easily discarded, and the entire operation restarted or aborted, in accordance with the business requirement.

Ensure Chainability

We mentioned chaining in Chapters 1 and 2 when we were covering the basic topics of jQuery. For a quick refresher, chaining in jQuery is that property by virtue of which a sequence of operations can be performed in one single statement that comprises the operations in the desired order of execution. We remember mentioning this as one of the factors that would drive you toward using jQuery. Over the course of this book, the benefits of this have no doubt become clearer—and will continue to become clearer still in this chapter.

Whenever you sit down to write a plug-in, you have to make sure that the method you write for should not break the jQuery system of chaining. So, suppose there are *n* independent tasks to be done by the plug-in. Using chainability, you must ensure that the user of the plug-in can employ the *n* tasks by chaining. We suggest one possible way of doing this. The methods you create inside your plug-in should return the modified object that was operated upon. This will ensure that the next operation to be chained is performed on the returned object itself. In short, we recommend that your plug-in be able to do the following:

```
someObject.doThis().doThisToo().pleaseDoThisToo();
```

Here, doThis makes some changes to someObject and makes it available for other methods/operations on it. doThisToo takes the torch from here and passes it to the pleaseDoThisToo method. Hence, once this statement has finished executing, the someObject must have the modifications made by both of the operations.

Having given you the guidelines, we have fulfilled our promise to usher you through the world of plug-in development, by suggesting a few use cases for which to write a plug-in. In the next section, you will note that all the cumbersome theory we provided in the preceding text will be put to use to write a plug-in.

Creating a Form Validation Plug-in

At the beginning of this chapter, we stated that we would offer some common-use cases, in order to provide specific examples and explanation regarding the use of plug-ins. We will now provide you with some information as to how to write a basic form validation plug-in, while ensuring that the plug-in adheres to the guidelines provided previously in this chapter.

The expected functionality that the form validation is to provide is as listed.

- The text box containing the name should not include any nonalphabetic characters. This should be checked while providing input to the input box, as well as at the time of submitting the form.

- E-mail should have a particular format, which should be checked at the time of submitting the form.

- The phone number should contain a valid phone number format.

To ensure that we do not go off the track, we will make use of the validation rules that we took up in Chapter 8.

Starting from scratch, the plug-in should be given a name. We name it according to the action it will take—validate. You should always remember that a jQuery plug-in is just a regular JavaScript method, so it has to follow the law of the land—the rules that are used to write methods in JavaScript. Thus, considering the jQuery object as the parent class, you will have to add a new method to it. In JavaScript, you add

`ClassName.prototype.methodName = function(){ }` and write the method body. In jQuery, this is `jQuery.prototype.validate = function(){ }`. Because jQuery is a framework meant to increase usability, there are a number of utility methods/properties available. So, you have the `jQuery.fn` as the alternative to `jQuery.prototype`. You also have the additional freedom to write `$.fn`, which is the same as `jQuery.prototype`.

When we talked about public variables and their utility in a plug-in, we mentioned that the most common usage of the public member is specifying the default settings required for the plug-in to work. The default settings make the plug-in work when no settings are passed on while calling the plug-in. Here, too, you will observe a similarity between the way you write jQuery and the way you write JavaScript. Public members in JavaScript are written as `ClassName.prototype.memberName` when they are outside of the class. When written inside the class, `this.memberName` is used as the syntax. Here, you will note that because the plug-in method is added to the class, when you write this, it will point to the jQuery object. So, you can write `this.defaultOptions`. You can also write `jQuery.fn.defaultOptions`, to achieve the same effect.

■ **Tip** Specifying default settings as the public variable has value from the point of view of plug-in user experience, so we recommend that you take this approach.

We also mentioned that there are members private to the plug-in, and you should find it extremely easy to write a private member (method or variable). So, back on track, private methods in plug-ins are needed to encapsulate those actions inside a plug-in that you do not want to spill out into the global namespace. This is in accordance with the philosophy of using private members! As a simple word of advice, write as many private members as you can, as long as the code remains clean and readable (and functional as well). Now, we move ahead and put before you the plug-in, as proposed by us, which will perform a simple form validation, similar to what we did when we demonstrated the use of Ajax in sending some data to the server. Here we have considered only the client-side programming and left the server-side part up to your imagination and the business requirement.

Our proposed plug-in code is as shown, followed by a line-by-line explanation of the nuts and bolts that drive the machinery.

```
jQuery.fn.validate = function (inputOptions) { // inputOptions is the configuration as well
as the parameter

    jQuery.fn.validate.defaultOptions = { // Public Variable
        name: {
            regExp: /^([a-z](\.)?(\ )?){3,}$/i,
            errorMessage: "Invalid characters in name"
        },
        email: {
            regExp: /^([a-z0-9]\.?\_?)+\@[a-z0-9]+\.?[a-z]{2,3}\.?[a-z]{2,3}$/i,
            errorMessage: "Invalid characters in email"
        },
        phone: {
            regExp: /^\+?[0-9]{6,15}$/i,
            errorMessage: "Invalid characters in phone"
        }
    };

    jQuery.extend(jQuery.fn.validate.defaultOptions, inputOptions);
```

```
function check(targetElement) { //Private method
    var value = targetElement.val();
    var type = targetElement.attr('name');
    if (value.length > 0 &&
        jQuery.fn.validate.defaultOptions[type].regExp.test(value) === false
    ) {
        throw jQuery.fn.validate.defaultOptions[type].errorMessage;
    }
}


try {
    jQuery.each(this.find('input[type="text"]'), function () {
        check(jQuery(this));
    });
} catch (exception) {
    console.log(exception);
    return false;
}

return this;
}
```

We suggest that you read the code again. Before moving on, we include some comments for a first-hand explanation of what is going on inside.

We began by naming the method. We created the plug-in as a public member of the jQuery class. We ensured that there would be a parameter accepted by the plug-in. In order to achieve the three objectives, we wrote

```
jQuery.fn.validate = function (inputOptions);
```

We included a public variable—to be used by the plug-in internally as well as externally by other parts of the code—that will call the plug-in by writing jQuery.fn.validate.defaultOptions =...In this way, we also ensured that the name defaultOption does not create conflict when some other plug-in uses it.

We had to ensure that the plug-in is flexible enough to accept user input and adjust it accordingly. We ensured that the validation criteria can be specified by the user, and we also ensured that the plug-in will not stop when the user does not pass any validation criteria, by writing jQuery.extend(jQuery. fn.validate.defaultOptions, inputOptions). This ensured that in case the user provides some input, the existing criteria should not be forgotten by the plug-in.

■ **Tip** The jQuery.extend method merges the second and onward objects to the first object. Thus, after the execution of the statement mentioned previously, defaultOptions will now contain the inputOptions as well.

Next, we have a method that acts according to the input provided to it. Here is the actual validation logic written to check the input provided on the HTML input form. By this method, the code decides if the text contained in the specified input box is valid or not. The validation criteria is, as mentioned, regExp, in the public object, and defaultOptions, for each of the three default cases (name, e-mail, and phone number). Based on the name attribute of the input element, the code decides the type of validation it has to perform. The input value is checked against the pattern specified for the particular element in defaultOptions. If the

219

validation fails (the regular expression match fails), there is an exception thrown to the code, which will call this check method.

The final action of actually calling the check method with the jQuery context is done in a try-catch, by looping through the DOM and finding all those inputs that are of the type text. The check method, which is a method privately accessible to the plug-in, is called as a result of the selector operation. This is done as

```
try {
    jQuery.each(this.find('input[type="text"]'), function () {
        check(jQuery(this));
    });
} catch //...
```

Here, you should take care of the way the this keyword is used inside the each loop. So, when we write this.find('input[type="text"]'), we are pointing to the context in which the plug-in will be called. The action we take is in accordance with the one-line theory that the this keyword points to the current object being treated. Inside the each method, the usage of this can be better understood by the way the each method works. The each method iterates over each component of the element specified as the first argument to it. The planned usage of the plug-in is to validate the form elements by calling the plug-in on a form element. So, iterating over the input elements found inside the form element would provide you a reference to one input element. When we write check(jQuery(this)), we are actually referencing the input element (which happens to be the current object being treated, hence the one-line theory again stands true!).

If you would prefer an example of how to use the plug-in to test the functionality, we have one ready for you. The HTML part will be as simple as writing an HTML form, as shown.

```
<form id="capture-data">
    <input type="text" name="name" />
    <input type="text" name="email" />
    <input type="text" name="phone" />
    <input type="submit" value="Send" />
</form>
```

Considering that you have the plug-in available (probably by writing the code inside the same HTML file, or including the external JavaScript file in which the plug-in is written), the usage of the plug-in will be as follows:

```
$('#capture-data').submit(function (event) {
    if (!event)
        event = window.event;
    event.preventDefault();
    if ($(this).validate() === false) {
        alert('There was an error, Please check browser console for details');
        return false;
    }
    var data = $(this).serialize();
    alert(data); // This can be replaced by some other and useful activity

});
```

Here, we have followed the same habit that has informed all the event handling code written in this book. We have attached the functionality of validating the form input on the submit event of the form element. Because the form is to be submitted on pressing the Submit button, we have prevented the default action from occurring, by calling the `preventDefault` method on the event (or `window.event`) object. Once the plug-in method `validate` returns some value, we check whether it is false. If the returned value is false, we provide an alert message to the browser and exit from the function. In the other case, i.e., when the condition fails, we gather the form data into a single query string, by using the `serialize` method, available in the jQuery framework. Some useful activity can be performed on the collected data, such as sending it to some URL, depending on the business requirement.

Note We used `jQuery` instead of the usual symbol $ to write the plug-in. We did that to avoid possible conflict of the jQuery reference with other (and probable) frameworks that use the $ symbol. We explained this in Chapter 2, under conflict resolution. An alternative way to preserve the reference is to use the self-executing anonymous function, as follows:

```
(function( $ ){
  $.fn.validate = function(inputOption) {
    // The plugin logic
  };
})( jQuery );
```

Creating an Accordion Plug-in

Before starting our accordion plug-in, we'll begin by discussing what an accordion is and how it works. An accordion is a collapsible content panel for presenting information in an inadequate amount of space. When you click the panel, it expands/collapses. Accordion is very helpful in situations in which you have to show a lot of information in little space. For example, you might have an F.A.Q. page on which you have lots of questions and answers that are not possible to show on one page, and if you do manage to show them somehow, it is very difficult for users to get around. Accordion gives you a better experience, in terms of what the users require in order to navigate. They can click the title, to see the details, and other sections remain hidden.

Tip You may recall accordion from when you attempted to create it in Chapter 6.

Accordion is easy to create, but you must take care of few points, as listed following:

- You have to check if the panel is expanded or not. If it is expanded, then you must write code to collapse it, and if it is collapsed, you have to expand it.

- If any of the siblings is expanded, it has to be collapsed.

- On collapse, you can offer effects, such as slide down/slide up, fade in/fade out, animation, or you can also use a simple show-and-hide function.

Now it's time to bake another plug-in, this time a new accordion plug-in. You already know the basics of creating a plug-in, as we have made a form validation plug-in under a previous section. So, moving ahead, we will create a basic HTML page that includes the jQuery library from Google Server, an accordion script, and a CSS style sheet.

Here's the HTML code on which we will be working:

```html
<html>
    <head>
        <title>Accordion Plugin Example - Chapter 9 | Practical jQuery </title>

        <script type="text/javascript" src="https://ajax.googleapis.com/ajax/libs/
jquery/1.5/jquery.min.js"></script>
        <script type="text/javascript" src="jquery.accordion.js"></script>

        <link rel="stylesheet" type="text/css" href="accordion.css" />
        <script type="text/javascript">
            $(document).ready(function() {
                $(".accordion").accordion();
            });
        </script>
    </head>

    <body>

        <ul class="accordion">
            <li><a href="#" class="accordionTitle">ICC Cricket World Cup 2015 Teams</a>
                <div class="wc15content">
                    <ul>
                        <li><a href="#">INDIA</a></li>
                        <li><a href="#">SOUTH AFRICA</a></li>
                        <li><a href="#">SRI LANKA</a></li>
                        <li><a href="#">ENGLAND</a></li>
                        <li><a href="#">NEW ZEALAND</a></li>
                        <li><a href="#">PAKISTAN</a></li>
                        <li><a href="#">WEST INDIES</a></li>
                        <li><a href="#">BANGLADESH</a></li>
                        <li><a href="#">ZIMBABWE</a></li>
                        <li><a href="#">AFGHANISTAN</a></li>
                        <li><a href="#">IRELAND</a></li>
                    </ul>
                </div>
            </li>
            <li><a href="#" class="accordionTitle">Pool A Teams</a>
                <div class="wc15content">
                    <ul>
                        <li><a href="#">New Zealand</a></li>
                        <li><a href="#">Australia</a></li>
                        <li><a href="#">Bangladesh</a></li>
                        <li><a href="#">Sri Lanka</a></li>
                        <li><a href="#">England     </a></li>
                        <li><a href="#">Afghanistan</a></li>
                        <li><a href="#">Scotland</a></li>
                    </ul>
                </div>
            </li>
```

```
            <li><a href="#" class="accordionTitle">Pool B Teams</a>
                <div class="wc15content">
                    <ul>
                        <li><a href="#">India</a></li>
                        <li><a href="#">South Africa</a></li>
                        <li><a href="#">Pakistan</a></li>
                        <li><a href="#">Ireland    </a></li>
                        <li><a href="#">West Indies</a></li>
                        <li><a href="#">Zimbabwe</a></li>
                        <li><a href="#">United Arab Emirates</a></li>
                    </ul>
                </div>
            </li>
        </ul>
    </body>
</html>
```

Next is the CSS code that we will work on. We have put the CSS in a file named accordion.css and kept it in the same directory.

```
body { font-family: Arial, verdana, tahoma; font-size: 13px; }
.accordion,.accordion ul {
    list-style:none;
    margin:0;
    padding:0;
}

.accordion li {
    background:#cc9900;
    float:left;
    width:100%;
    margin-bottom:4px;
}
.accordion li a {
    display:block;
    font-weight:bold;
    color:#fff;
    padding:10px 10px 9px;
    text-decoration: none;
}

.accordion li .content { display: none; }
.accordion li li {
    background:#222 ;
    border-bottom:1px solid #cc9900;
    margin:0;
    float:none;
    width:auto;
    color: #fff;
}
```

223

```
.accordion li li a {
    color:#cc9900;
    font-weight:normal;
    height: 15px;
    line-height: 15px;
    margin-left: 10px;
    text-decoration: none;
}
.accordion li li.active,
.accordion li li:hover {
    background:#e6ac00;
}
.accordion li li.active a,
.accordion li li:hover a {
    font-weight:800;
    color:#fff;
}
```

Finally, we come to our plug-in code. We have created a file with the same name as the plug-in, but it's not mandatory to keep the same name. Following the standard, we have created a file jquery.accordion.js, which will be the main file of our plug-in work.

To start with the plug-in, we have used the following code:

```
(function($){
    $.fn.accordion = function(options) {
        // plugin code will go here
    };
})(jQuery);
```

If you noticed, we have given a function name, which will be used to call the plug-in. We have also set function(options), this will allow us to specify some options for the plug-in.

Now we use the code to set up options. This works by specifying some defaults and then using jQuery's extend function to merge any passed options into the default array.

```
var defaults = {
    aTlt: 'accordionTitle',
    aCnt: 'wc15content',
    active: 'opened'
};

// Merging the content using extend method

var settings = $.extend({}, defaults, options);
```

We have used the jQuery extend method, which is used to merge the content of an object onto the jQuery prototype, to provide new jQuery instance methods.

The next piece of code will hide all the content panels, if they are not already hidden.

```
$(document).ready(function() {
    // hide all the content panels
    $('.'+settings.aCnt).hide();
```

```
$('.'+settings.aTlt).each(function() {
    if($(this).hasClass(settings.active))
    {
        $(this).siblings('.'+settings.aCnt)
            .addClass(settings.active)
            .slideDown();
    }
});
});
```

Moving to the next piece of code that will run on load, this sets up the list so that it is ready for being made into an accordion, by hiding all the content. One thing to note is how we reference the settings variable from the preceding section of code. This allows the plug-in to run either the default values or the passed parameters.

```
$('.'+settings.aTlt).click(function() {
    // object for the button that has been clicked
    var obj = $(this);
    //console.log(obj);
    // Here we are checking if we have clicked the currently active tab

    var slide = true;
    if(obj.hasClass('opened'))
    {
        slide = false;
    }

    // Here we are closing all the current elements
    $('.'+settings.aCnt).slideUp().removeClass(settings.active);
    $('.'+settings.aTlt).removeClass(settings.active);

    // checking if we should still slide
    if(slide)
    {
        // Here we make the clicked button active and opened
        obj.addClass(settings.active);
        obj.siblings('.'+settings.aCnt).addClass(settings.active).slideDown();
    }

    return false;
});
```

Yes, you have written all and know that you can pass in the options. For example, start the plug-in with something like this:

```
$('.accordion').accordion({
    'aTlt' : 'accordion_button',
    'aCnt' : 'accordion_content',
    'active' : 'accordion_active'
});
```

By doing this, you can change all references to 'aTlt' to 'accordion_button', 'aCnt' to 'accordion_content', and 'opened' to 'accordion_active'.

If you present the whole code at once, it will look like the following:

```
(function($){
    // Here we gave function name
    $.fn.accordion = function(options) {
    // Here we set some defaults
        var defaults = {
            aTlt: 'accordionTitle',
            aCnt: 'wc15content',
            active: 'opened'
        };

        // Merging the content using extend method
        var settings = $.extend({}, defaults, options);

        $(document).ready(function() {
            // hide all the content panels
            $('.'+settings.aCnt).hide();
            $('.'+settings.aTlt).each(function() {
                if($(this).hasClass(settings.active))
                {
                    $(this).siblings('.'+settings.aCnt)
                        .addClass(settings.active)
                        .slideDown();
                }
            });
        });

        // Here we check for clicks
        $('.'+settings.aTlt).click(function() {
            // object for the button that has been clicked
            var obj = $(this);
            //console.log(obj);
            // Here we are checking if we have clicked the currently active tab

            var slide = true;
            if(obj.hasClass('opened'))
            {
                slide = false;
            }

            // Here we are closing all the current elements
            $('.'+settings.aCnt).slideUp().removeClass(settings.active);
            $('.'+settings.aTlt).removeClass(settings.active);
```

```
        // checking if we should still slide
        if(slide)
        {
            // Here we make the clicked button active and opened
            obj.addClass(settings.active);
            obj.siblings('.'+settings.aCnt).addClass(settings.active).slideDown();
        }

        return false;
    });
};
})(jQuery);
```

Figure 9-1 shows the accordion in action.

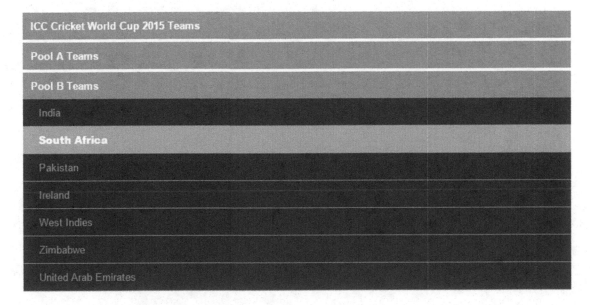

Figure 9-1. *Accordion in action*

You can also get the plug-in code from GitHub at `https://github.com/mukund/accordion-plugin`.

Summary

This chapter led you along the path of software engineering known as reusability. You learned what a plug-in is. You also learned how to write a plug-in, by reading about the essential components that make up a plug-in. This chapter gave you information about the various aspects that you should consider during the plug-in development life cycle. You came to know how a plug-in works firsthand, by looking at two plug-ins that are both basic and useful on a daily basis. In the next chapter, we will walk you through the use of plug-ins, by providing examples of some of the commonly used plug-ins that also demonstrate the extent to which jQuery is useful in solving web development problems.

CHAPTER 10

■ ■ ■

Integrating Plug-ins with jQuery

Good software code is that which can be easily reused. An instance of easily reusable code is a plug-in. Having discussed developing reusable pieces of code previously, this chapter will guide you in reusing such a piece of code in your existing web application, to yield an enhancement in functionality. This chapter will also deal with the nuts and bolts of customizing an existing plug-in written in jQuery. By the end of this chapter, we will have covered

- How to find a plug-in for use

- Integrating plug-in(s) to enhance functionality

- Making a plug-in behave according to requirement

- Making a plug-in production-ready by compressing

Plug-in Repositories

The use of search engines plays a pivotal role in achieving an important principle of software engineering—not reinventing the wheel or, more precisely, the DRY (don't repeat yourself) principle. In the previous chapter, when we were discussing creating plug-ins, we hinted that instead of jumping off to write a plug-in to meet a business requirement, you should try and search for some existing plug-in to save time and effort. Assuming that the previous statement would trigger a number of questions regarding the location of the search engine to find the right plug-in, we have the answer at the ready. There are a number of search facilities available for you in this wide world. But to arrive at the best one for your needs, you must take a mixed approach. None of the facilities will provide a completely correct result by itself. Let us talk about the choices available, taking one at a time.

The jQuery Registry

We stated that the jQuery framework follows the philosophy of free and open source software, and it is maintained by the jQuery developer community. So, the feature enhancements that are done, or some new functionality that is being added, is carried out on the part of the jQuery community. The add-ons and plug-ins developed for jQuery in the form of plug-ins are available under an official repository located at `http://plugins.jquery.com/`. On that portal, you will be able to search for a plug-in, by using some appropriate keywords that you think will identify your expected plug-in. Because searching is the most frequent operation to be done on the repository, the web site UI designers have made it quite prominent on the home page. You will easily be able to make out the search box, once you visit the repository via a web browser. Here, you might be interested to know that the keyword(s) that you would specify for the search is matched for an occurrence against two criteria: the name of the plug-in and the small description of the plug-in. The dual search is helpful in cases in which your search term does not appear in the name of the plug-in you are looking for but does occur in the description. In such cases, your search will find the plug-in via its description.

For ease of use, some of the popular plug-ins that are already searched for in quite handsome numbers have been grouped as tags. A tag is an indicative entity that is attached to something to serve the purpose of quick reference. In our context, tags are just categories under which the pertaining plug-ins have been grouped. A few of the tags are *animation, slider, Ajax,* etc. A grouping tag with the name *animation* contains plug-ins that perform some action related to animation, such as having some exciting effects, or the like. A tag with the name *Ajax,* similarly, contains plug-ins that carry out some task related to loading of contents using Ajax. Here, we would like to make an important statement regarding the plug-in repository ecosystem: a single plug-in can appear under multiple tags.

■ **Note** A single plug-in can have more than one tag attached to it, and hence, once you select a certain tag, chances are you will find some of the plug-ins in some other tags as well. This is possible, because a single plug-in can do more than one thing (albeit related), and, therefore, it can be tagged more than once.

At this point, you should know that the official jQuery plug-in registry is in read-only mode. This means that you will not be able to receive any updates from the registry. It also means that you will not be able to find and use some new plug-in that some other jQuery developer has contributed. But at the same time, the registry provides information as to where to find new releases of plug-ins: the Node Package Manager (NPM) open source package repository.

■ **Note** You can find out the reason for making the jQuery plug-in registry read-only and move toward the NPM repository at `https://github.com/jquery/plugins.jquery.com/issues/161`.

The NPM Open Source Package Repository

The Node Package Manager (NPM) site provides a repository that includes a collection of jQuery plug-ins. The following URL takes you to that collection, where you will be able to find newer jQuery plug-ins: `https://www.npmjs.com/browse/keyword/jquery-plugin`.

NPM, as indicated by its name, is a package manager for another JavaScript framework—Node.js, as it is named by the community. Using Node.js, you can program server-side and network-based applications. In the words of nodejs.org, the official web site for Node.js, "Node.js uses an event-driven, non-blocking I/O model that makes it lightweight and efficient, perfect for data-intensive real-time applications that run across distributed devices." Interested readers are encouraged to learn more about this technology at the official web site at `https://nodejs.org/`.

The GitHub Repository

In Chapter 2, we mentioned cloning the jQuery repository and building a copy for your usage, when we discussed setting up jQuery for development. Here, we take it up again and state that the GitHub repository is a version control system that provides code hosting solutions to the world for free (codes that are available for public use are the FOSS, or *free and open source software*, source codes). Because jQuery follows the FOSS philosophy, the codes are hosted at GitHub, so that developers across the world can have access to the code and provide their valuable efforts to the community in return. If you have had previous exposure to a version control system, you will be able to understand this usage. If not, we are here to make you understand. GitHub is a code-hosting service that provides version control to the code that is hosted. So, if you feel like something is terribly out of place in some FOSS software (read jQuery), you can download a copy (read pull, to adhere to GitHub terminology), make changes in the code to address the issue, and upload the changed code back to GitHub (read push, to adhere to the GitHub terminology).

■ **Note** Pushing and pulling is not as easy as we may have implied, because you need a certain amount of experience to handle both GitHub and the target source code. You can learn more about using GitHub through the official tutorial available at `https://guides.github.com/`.

Getting back to explaining the use of the repository, you can look up a possible occurrence of the plug-in that you are planning to create. The GitHub web site provides a search functionality for the purpose, which can be accessed at `https://github.com/search`, by typing in the search keyword in the prominent text box visible on the search page. The results of the search will include a list of items that have matched your keyword or keywords. For a better user experience, the words that match the searched keyword(s) are highlighted in the name of the resulting plug-in(s), as well as in the description of the resulting plug-in(s), and presented to you in the form of a list. You will have to expend some effort to find out which is the right plug-in for you, by reading the plug-in description. The plug-in description is available on the page, which, in turn, is available when you click the name of the plug-in. If the plug-in search has not succeeded, you might want to repeat the same cycle again.

The GitHub repository keeps up with the popularity it has gained over the years by providing excellent service to end users. If you want to perform an advanced search, you can do so via the web interface at `https://github.com/search/advanced`. If you happen to visit the URL, you will notice that there are a number of options available for you. Using the advanced search, you can customize your search to find a plug-in better matching your needs. Suppose you have some information about the plug-in that you want to download. You can put in information ranging from the author of the plug-in to the date of creation to the extension of the code contained in the plug-in, even the last modified date of the plug-in. The advanced search option is intended for those who have already tried their luck with the basic search.

■ **Note** You can also perform a basic search from the advanced search page, by using the topmost search box available on the advanced search page.

```
┌─────────────────────────────────────────────────────────────────────────┐
│                  THE GOOGLE CODE-HOSTING SERVICE                          │
└─────────────────────────────────────────────────────────────────────────┘
```

Although the code-hosting service Google Code began as much as two years prior to the start of GitHub, the growing popularity of the latter caused the former to shut down the service. Yes, it has been officially declared that Google Code service has been turned to read only at the time of writing, and the service will officially shut down in January 2016. We do not intend to dive into the reasons why Google Code did not succeed. Instead, our intention is to inform you that until such time as this service is up, you can find some plug-ins on your own, by searching through the repository, because it is quite possible that some of the plug-ins you require are still available on Google Code. Some of the popular searches on the web site have been grouped as labels project-wise. Some of the labels on the web site are jQuery, JavaScript, Plugin, etc. The code-hosting service is accessible at `https://code.google.com/`, and there is a search button dedicated to the purpose of putting in search keywords, on the basis of which you may find the plug-in. The result returned by the search engine contains the name of the project (which can be the name of the plug-in, in case your search keyword is accurate), some description related to the project, and, most important, the labels under which the project is grouped.

■ **Caution**   You have to be cautious while keying in the search phrase; otherwise, you may end up with a number of results pertaining to some other technology/language.

You still need not to worry if a search misfires on the aforementioned repositories. There may well be other plug-ins out there that have not been hosted on any of those sites. So, the question of how to find those plug-ins is answered by Google or another search engine.

Integrating Plug-ins

You will have to be alert throughout this section, because we will list some tips that you will find quite useful when writing code for some business objective. In the previous chapter, we guided you as to how to write reusable code in the form of plug-ins. It is now time to show you how to include such pieces of reusable code in some of your existing code. This will serve two purposes. It gives you an idea as to how plug-ins are integrated into some existing source code, and it will also give you some idea as to how a reusable piece of plug-in code should be written. We believe that the testing of a code is done undertaken when the same person who has developed it actually uses it. So, you would be wise to visit Chapter 9 and review the best practices for writing a plug-in.

■ **Tip**   We recommend that you read this chapter only after you have read and understood Chapter 9, because in this chapter, we make some modifications in the same code that we wrote in the previous chapter, thereby eliminating the possible shortcomings in the plug-in code that we provided, and making it more reusable.

Downloading and Saving

The first step involved in attaining code reusability is to find and download the appropriate plug-in. In order to download the desired plug-in, you have to search for it over the Internet, using the search facilities that we outlined in the previous section. One of the ideal practices for writing reusable software is to accompany the software with proper documentation. In the current scenario, the documentation can exist in the form of a read me file. So, the read me, as the name suggests, is a mandatory document to read, in order to understand the plug-in, and it contains the instructions to coexist with the software that you have already written.

Do a Test Run on Some Simple Elements

When you learned to drive, did you head straightaway to the highway, to cover a hundred-mile distance? The most probable answer to this question is no. You would not have risked your own life or others' by doing that. You must first have had at least a number of days of driving experience on less traveled streets to acquaint yourself with your vehicle and gain hands-on experience with the way traffic moves. This real-life example has an analogy with the current context. When you download a plug-in, you can obviously not afford to move on to the implementation of the plug-in, to achieve a large amount of functionality. You must first have a test run related to some smaller section of the problem. So, whenever you start off with downloading a plug-in from whichever source, we recommend that you try a test run. Let us assume you downloaded some plug-in from the jQuery plug-in repository concerned with performing some special animation. Assuming the usage of the plug-in `$('selector-expression').specialAnimation();`, instead of specifying a selector to some complex structure, we recommend that you have a simple structure such as a `div`, or a `span`, to check the integration. Here we would also like to state that the test run is quite dependent on the read me file, because the choice of the test element will depend on the way the plug-in is intended to behave.

Include the Plug-in File in the script Tag

We have been saying that jQuery code is JavaScript code under the hood. This is quite simply because jQuery is a framework written using JavaScript. So, just as all external JavaScript resources have to be included in the `script` tag, you must do the same for the plug-in. Assuming the name of the plug-in file is `jQuery.specialAnimation.js`, you have to write the following code:

```
<script type="text/javascript" src="/path/to/jQuery.specialAnimation.js"></script>
```

Be aware that there can be a number of files inside a plug-in, and here again, the read me file comes into the picture, in order for you to know which files are to be included.

The Dilemma—in the Head or at the End of the Body

Time and again, there have been a number of arguments as to where exactly an external script should be included. Some arguments favor including the external script in the `script` tag, so that the functionality is available even before the page is loaded. But, this approach has a serious shortcoming: most of the functionality provided by some external script is to perform some modification or calculation based on the DOM tree and its nodes, and if the calculation is present, even before the operands, the entire functionality will not be fully functional until such time as the DOM has loaded completely and is ready for your interaction. The web page in which you would include the external resource (the script) will keep on throwing errors, because it will not be able to find the target operand(s).

Another argument supports the inclusion of the scripts immediately after the body finishes. The support statement for this step is that the functionality provided by the script will be able to enjoy the entire DOM, because by the time the body tag finished loading, all of the visible elements on the web page will have been loaded, and the script will be able to function normally. This approach has a drawback too. Because you are delaying the loading of the plug-in to take place after the body tag, other functionality that will depend on the plug-in will have to be strictly included after the plug-in, or else the dependency will be broken and there might be errors on your web page. But, despite all arguments, your common sense prevails! If you wish to have some plug-in that you believe will have to be active before the visible elements (such as some resource-checking or preloading functionality, etc.), you can include the plug-in script in the head tag. If you believe that the functionality that you wish to include requires DOM to be completely present on the web page (such as for animations, etc.), you can include the plug-in script after the body tag.

■ **Note**   You can refer to Chapter 2, in which we provide a solution to this problem.

Keep the Code Clean

Having included the plug-in at the appropriate position in your web page, now comes the trickier part of the job—using the plug-in. In order to use the plug-in, you might need to put some wrapper method around the plug-in method as well. It might be the case that you have to filter the data before passing on to the plug-in method. Our recommendation in this case would be to keep such implementation details away from the main web page. Instead, include the implementation as another external resource. By doing that, you will not only keep the web page code cleaner but also make the code more modular. Whatever change you would need to make in the filtering method, you can do so without disturbing the plug-in method. Essentially, you will be adding a layer of abstraction when you do this.

We take up a short demonstration here for the purpose of making this concept clear. Let us assume you have a plug-in with the name jQuery.validation.js, in which there is a method named check(), and you have to filter out the strings and let only the numbers pass to this check() method. For the purpose, if you create a method with the name filter(), the recommended way for you to keep the code clean is as follows:

```
// jQuery.validation.js

function check(someValue){
    // do some checks on someValue ...
}

// myFilter.js
// this would be a file containing the wrapper code

function filter(aValue){
    // if aValue is a string
    check(aValue);
}
```

So, now, you will have to include the file myFilter.js as well, and call the filter() method, instead of calling the check() method, to attain the added functionality.

Plug-in Customization

More often than not, you will have to work on some plug-in to fulfill the business requirement quickly. But, if you talk to people about using jQuery plug-ins to attain some objective, you discover that merely including a plug-in does not necessarily solve the problem at hand. You have to do some more work to fine tune the plug-in, so that the business requirement is addressed with the maximum accuracy. Here is where customizing a plug-in comes into the picture. To put it simply, customizing a plug-in is equivalent to making a plug-in behave according to a requirement. If we consider the idea behind plug-in customization, what was stated is the only idea. This idea will be better understood with an example, so let us move on to one.

We will take up the same form validation plug-in as part of the demonstration, so that while we learn how to use a plug-in, we will actually test the plug-in's usability and, thus, ensure software quality! For a quick recap, in Chapter 9, we developed a plug-in that performed a basic form validation for an HTML input form containing a name field, an e-mail field, and a phone number field in the input, as provided by the end user over the web interface (the web page). We assume that the plug-in was saved in a file named jQuery.validation.js. This makes the name quite descriptive as well. You will observe that this step will be used later in this chapter, for the purpose of making the plug-in that we wrote more useful.

In the following example, we will make the form validation plug-in validate input elements according to the regular expressions that we provide. You can assume the regular expressions to be business-driven. In the previous chapter, we validated name, e-mail, and phone number. This time, we will take up validating a credit card number, the CVV (Card Verification Value) number (found on the back of Visa credit cards, for example), and the time from which the credit card is valid (let's not argue over start date vs. end date; we are merely providing an example, after all). For our purposes, we will have an HTML form, as follows:

```
<form id="capture-data">
    <input type="text" name="ccnumber" />
    <input type="text" name="validfrom"/>
    <input type="text" name="cvv"/>
    <input type="submit" value="Send" />
</form>
```

The HTML form needs no special explanation. We have put in just the name attributes, so that the selection can be made while validating the individual input elements inside the form. To select the form, we have kept the same ID attribute with the form element. Here, because we must have the DOM loaded completely so that we can process the form, we have included the plug-in script after the closing of the body tag. Also, our plug-in makes use of the jQuery library, so we have ensured that the inclusion of the plug-in script is done after the inclusion of the jQuery library. Thus, the included script will look like

```
<script src="jquery-1.10.2.js"></script>
<script src="jQuery.validation.js"></script>
```

Now comes the jQuery part, and here we require your full attention to see how to use the same plug-in under various conditions. The jQuery code to customize (and use) the plug-in is as follows:

```
var patterns = {
    ccnumber: {
        regExp: /^((\d){4}-){3}(\d{4})$/i,
        errorMessage: 'Invalid Credit Card number supplied'
    },
```

```
    validfrom:{
        regExp: /^((0(\d)?)|(1[0-2]?))\/(\d){2}$/i,
        errorMessage: 'Input not in MM/YY format.'
    },
    cvv:{
        regExp: /^(\d){3}$/i,
        errorMessage: 'CVV format not proper'
    }
};

$('#capture-data').submit(function (event) {
    if (!event)
        var event = window.event;
    event.preventDefault();
    if ($(this).validate(patterns) === false) {
        alert('There was an error, Please check browser console for details');
        return false;
    }
    var data = $(this).serialize();
    alert(data);

});
```

Now to explain what is taking place in the current plug-in usage. We begin the regular expression. For a valid credit card, we look for the following pattern:

- A group of characters repeating three times, with exactly four digits and a hyphen (-) following the fourth digit

- The above mentioned group followed by a mandatory sequence of exactly four digits

Thus, a valid credit card number will look as follows: ABCD-EFGH-IJKL-MNOP, where the letters *A* to *P* are placeholders for the digits 0 to 9.

Next, we move ahead to verify the validity date of the credit card. So, a valid date will take the form of MM/YY, and, hence, the pattern to be tested against will be a valid month, which can range from 01 to 12, and a year, which can range from 00 to 99 (indicating the years 2000 to 2099—quite a long span of time to consider for a credit card's validity!). As far as the regular expression is concerned, we have created a pattern that contains the three groups, in the order in which they are written.

- Either the digit 0 followed by a single digit between 1 and 9, or the digit 1 followed by the digits 0, 1, or 2

- A forward slash (/) following the preceding expression

- Exactly two digits following the slash

The CVV pattern is relatively simple, but we will explain that as well. Here, the pattern to check a valid CVV number is a sequence that contains exactly three digits. Having explained the patterns, let us move ahead to the usage of the plug-in.

As with the usage illustrated in the previous chapter, we have used the plug-in here. We call the plug-in validation method on the submit event of the form element. So, when a submit event is fired for the target form element, the input elements inside the form element are validated using the validate method. Here, you will notice a difference in the usage, however. The difference is due to the use of an argument with the plug-in method. Here is where the customization of the plug-in enters the picture.

What we have done here is created a few new rules for the user input validation and passed it on to the plug-in method, so that the new rules are digested by the validation system. At this point in time, you might want to revisit the plug-in code in the previous chapter, to review the structure of the validation rules. For a quick recap, we provide the rules to you again, as follows:

```
jQuery.fn.validate.defaultOptions = {
    name: {
        regExp: /^([a-z](\.)?(\ )?){3,}$/i,
        errorMessage: "Invalid characters in name"
    },
    email: {
        regExp: /^([a-z0-9]\.?\_?)+\@[a-z0-9]+\.?[a-z]{2,3}\.?[a-z]{2,3}$/i,
        errorMessage: "Invalid characters in email"
    },
    phone: {
        regExp: /^\+?[0-9]{6,15}$/i,
        errorMessage: "Invalid characters in phone"
    }
};
```

It would be quite natural for you to wonder why we did not use the public variable inside the plug-in script when we had the freedom to do so. We would answer that had we done that, the plug-in would not have been customized but changed entirely. This is the essence of customization: you are able to get some extra work done with the plug-in, without disturbing the existing functionality. So, the plug-in code that used to function without specifying the argument (by accepting the default settings) works equally fine by accepting the argument, and this argument in the current scenario happens to be the value of the variable patterns. The humble plug-in just wants you to stick to the syntax of the pattern rule and nothing else. Here, you should also notice an interesting phenomenon related to the plug-in. In the current usage, if you happen to merge the input elements specified in the previous chapter, the plug-in will still work fine. This is another advantage of customization.

The only principle that we have followed here is to encapsulate wherever possible, and we were able to achieve this by using JSON. We covered JSON in some detail when we discussed Ajax. You will see that grouping elements together to form one JSON object is a task that requires a fair amount of knowledge. If you happen to nest too deep, the JSON object will take quite a lot of complex loopings, thus increasing the script processing time. On the other hand, if you happen to make the JSON object quite shallow, you might end up with a longer list of elements, which would render your code unreadable. So, there has to be an optimum balance between the depth and length of the JSON object.

Minifying Code for Distribution

Despite having made the plug-in behave according to the business requirement, our task is not over. Readers may argue that we should have covered distribution in the previous chapter, when we were creating plug-ins. The reason we didn't cover it then is that we firmly believe this chapter and the previous chapter go hand-in-hand. If you do not know how to create a plug-in, you will not be able to realize the advantages of using a plug-in, because you will not be able to understand the engineering that goes behind it. Similarly, if you know only how to use a plug-in, you will not be able to make full use of it, because you will not be able to employ the plug-in under various conditions (customizing a plug-in). In the same way, if you do not know how to distribute a plug-in to other fellow developers who are in need of it, there is no advantage to learning this much about plug-ins.

Compression vs. Minification

When considering distributing code, our intention is to inform you about techniques that help minimize the amount of data one has to spend in order to obtain a fully functional version of the code. So, whenever we intend to distribute some code, we usually tend to compress it, so that it occupies the least storage space. But if we compress it, it becomes unusable, until it is uncompressed back to the original form. This happens because compressing, in general terms, means changing the contents in such a way that the representation changes. There are two types of compression techniques. With these techniques, the changes made to the target content can be either reversible or irreversible, depending on which of the techniques is chosen. In the language of computation, this is termed *lossless* compression—nothing is lost in the process. With the other technique, there are certain less important data removed from the original data while compressing, such that the effect of the loss is negligible, and, while uncompressing, some data is lost, hence the name *lossy* compression.

In our current scenario, the technique of compression ceases to work completely. The reason behind this failure is that JavaScript is an interpreted language, and, hence, it requires the code at the time of execution. So, if we compress some JavaScript code and present it to the JavaScript interpreter, we will have to have an additional (proxy) system to uncompress the code and then pass it on to the JavaScript engine. Instead of compression, we resort to a technique that is termed *minification*.

More often than not, it happens that the name explains a part of the story. If you observe the name *minification*, you will understand the idea behind the relevant phenomenon, to some extent. The phenomenon of minification makes the target file/script "mini"-er than the original script, hence the name. Minification works in a rather tricky way, and we will attempt to unlock its tricks, to make you understand it better. Let's have a look at something we have made a practice while writing code.

When in school you were learning how to write code to attain some objective, you were always taught to use spaces liberally. The spaces were added to make the code that you write more readable, so that the examiner could understand what was written. We used indents to demarcate blocks of code; we used spaces before and after variables declaration, method declaration, and definition. We used comments, so that our code became descriptive. In essence, we did everything to make the code more readable. While this approach had no or negligible effect on the code we wrote at school and for languages that get compiled to become executables, those languages that get interpreted took a performance hit: the interpreters took longer time to process all those extra (and probably unwanted by the interpreter) characters.

In the current context, the JavaScript code has to be transported over the network, from the web server right to the end user, onto the web browser. If we consider the effect of adding the extra characters that contribute to the beauty of the code, we observe that a larger file will consume higher bandwidth while being transmitted over the network. Because the interpreter has nothing to do with the readability quotient of the code that you write, we can exploit this behavior to remove the unwanted spaces, tab characters, and comment blocks from the code, to have a compact and precise code for the interpreter.

You will be able to understand the difference between compression and minification by having a look at Figure 10-1.

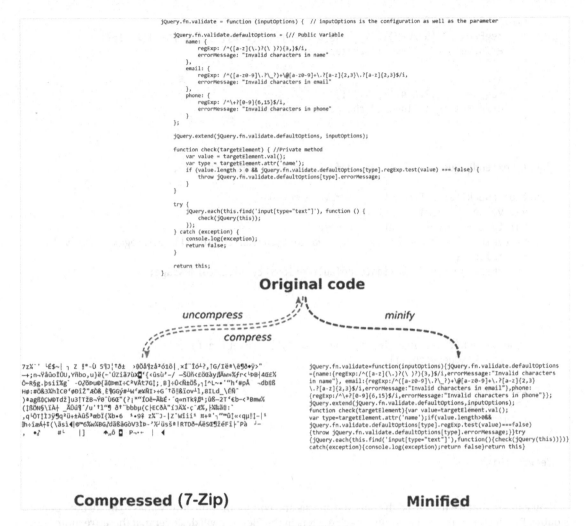

Figure 10-1. *The difference between compression and minification*

What Does Minified Code Look Like?

After having dry discussions about the phenomenon of minification, we firmly believe that you will have a better understanding once you see the effect of minification. Here, we would like to offer an example, to further explain minification. We will use the same plug-in that we created in the previous chapter, so that you can understand the effect of minification more clearly. So, the plug-in code is

```
jQuery.fn.validate = function (inputOptions) {  // inputOptions is the configuration as well
as the parameter

    jQuery.fn.validate.defaultOptions = {// Public Variable
        name: {
            regExp: /^([a z](\.)?(\ )?){3,}$/i,
            errorMessage: "Invalid characters in name"
        },
```

```
        email: {
            regExp: /^([a-z0-9]\.?\_?)+\@[a-z0-9]+\.?[a-z]{2,3}\.?[a-z]{2,3}$/i,
            errorMessage: "Invalid characters in email"
        },
        phone: {
            regExp: /^\+?[0-9]{6,15}$/i,
            errorMessage: "Invalid characters in phone"
        }
    };

    jQuery.extend(jQuery.fn.validate.defaultOptions, inputOptions);

    function check(targetElement) { //Private method
        var value = targetElement.val();
        var type = targetElement.attr('name');
        if (value.length > 0 && jQuery.fn.validate.defaultOptions[type].regExp.test(value)
=== false) {
            throw jQuery.fn.validate.defaultOptions[type].errorMessage;
        }
    }

    try {
        jQuery.each(this.find('input[type="text"]'), function () {
            check(jQuery(this));
        });
    } catch (exception) {
        console.log(exception);
        return false;
    }

    return this;
}
```

You can see that we have used the tabs and spaces and comments and empty lines to make our code readable. But, if you consider the number of characters in the file, you will discover that there are more than 1000 characters in the file (1162, to be exact). If you assume the encoding of the character to be UTF-8, a single character will consume 1 byte, and so the code will consume more than 1162 bytes of bandwidth when you send this file over the network. Does this seem excessive to you? Let us have a quick look at the minified version of the same code.

```
jQuery.fn.validate=function(inputOptions){jQuery.fn.validate.defaultOptions={name:
{regExp:/^([a-z](\.)?(\ )?){3,}$/i,errorMessage:"Invalid characters in name"},
email:{regExp:/^([a-z0-9]\.?\_?)+\@[a-z0-9]+\.?[a-z]{2,3}\.?[a-z]{2,3}$/i,errorMessage:
"Invalid characters in email"},phone:{regExp:/^\+?[0-9]{6,15}$/i,errorMessage:"Invalid
characters in phone"}};jQuery.extend(jQuery.fn.validate.defaultOptions,inputOptions);
function check(targetElement){var value=targetElement.val();var type=targetElement.
attr('name');if(value.length>0&&jQuery.fn.validate.defaultOptions[type].regExp.
test(value)===false){throw jQuery.fn.validate.defaultOptions[type].errorMessage;}}
try{jQuery.each(this.find('input[type="text"]'),function(){check(jQuery(this))})}
catch(exception){console.log(exception);return false}return this}
```

No, we are not pulling a prank on you by including false lines. What may appear to be gibberish or confusing makes perfect sense to the JavaScript engine. Let's review the facts quickly. The number of characters in the file has been reduced to about 600, although the intent is still clear to the interpreter. So, while the original code would have consumed 1162 bytes of network bandwidth, the minified code consumes nearly one-third of that. We were able to cut more than 60% of the characters, in the case of a simple and humble plug-in, and this figure will definitely go up as we increase the size of the file, by adding more and more functionality. The best part of minification is that you only have to change the name of the file while including it to your web page, as follows:

```
<script type="text/javascript" src="/path/to/jQuery.validation.min.js"></script>
```

It is important to note that the name of the minified file is conventionally written with the suffix .min. We mentioned this back in Chapter 2, when we discussed setting up the jQuery library.

■ **Note** We used the term *UTF-8*, which is actually an acronym. It stands for the Universal Coded Character Set (U) plus Transformation Format—8-bit (TF-8). For details about UTF-8, you can visit the Wikipedia page located at http://en.wikipedia.org/wiki/UTF-8.

There Is More: Uglification and Beautification

You need look into the minified code once more. If you take a closer look, you would see that what we stated in the explanation was executed to perfection in the sample code. All the comments were removed; all the new lines were removed; and the extra spaces were removed. You may be amused to know that besides minifying a code, you can uglify the code as well, when you have to take another approach to distribute your code, by changing the names of the methods and variables in it. When you do that, you are preventing a normal human being from reading the code with ease. Even if the code could be read by a human somehow, it would be really very hard to make sense of the method. Let's look at an illustrative example. Considering the same plug-in for this operation as well, the uglified code would look like

```
jQuery.fn.validate=function(a){function b(a){var b=a.val(),c=a.attr("name");if(b.length>
0&&jQuery.fn.validate.defaultOptions[c].regExp.test(b)===!1)throw jQuery.fn.validate.default
Options[c].errorMessage}jQuery.fn.validate.defaultOptions={name:{regExp:/^([a-z](\.)?(\ )?)
{3,}$/i,errorMessage:"Invalid characters in name"},email:{regExp:/^([a-z0-9]\.?\_?)
+\@[a-z0-9]+\.?[a-z]{2,3}\.?[a-z]{2,3}$/i,errorMessage:"Invalid characters in email"},
phone:{regExp:/^\+?[0-9]{6,15}$/i,errorMessage:"Invalid characters in phone"}},jQuery.extend
(jQuery.fn.validate.defaultOptions,a);try{jQuery.each(this.find('input[type="text"]'),
function(){b(jQuery(this))})}catch(c){return console.log(c),!1}return this};
```

The character count is almost the same in this case, but you have to take a closer look to see what has happened. If you remember the original plug-in (do not worry, you can always revisit the example), there was a private method with the name check(), which has disappeared, and there are strange, rather ugly, names, such as a, b, and c for the methods in the plug-in.

If you can make something ugly, you can also make the same thing beautiful. So, when you beautify a code, you introduce proper spacing, indents, and formatting, so that the code can be read with ease by human beings. This is what is meant by *beautification*. In order to demonstrate beautification, we will consider the uglified version of the same plug-in code that we have been using throughout this chapter. So, let us develop a deeper understanding, by having a look into the beautified version of the uglified code.

```
jQuery.fn.validate = function(a) {
    function b(a) {
        var b = a.val(),
            c = a.attr("name");
        if (b.length > 0 && jQuery.fn.validate.defaultOptions[c].regExp.test(b) === !1) throw
        jQuery.fn.validate.defaultOptions[c].errorMessage
    }
    jQuery.fn.validate.defaultOptions = {
        name: {
            regExp: /^([a-z](\.)?(\ )?){3,}$/i,
            errorMessage: "Invalid characters in name"
        },
        email: {
            regExp: /^([a-z0-9]\.?\_?)+\@[a-z0-9]+\.?[a-z]{2,3}\.?[a-z]{2,3}$/i,
            errorMessage: "Invalid characters in email"
        },
        phone: {
            regExp: /^\+?[0-9]{6,15}$/i,
            errorMessage: "Invalid characters in phone"
        }
    }, jQuery.extend(jQuery.fn.validate.defaultOptions, a);
    try {
        jQuery.each(this.find('input[type="text"]'), function() {
            b(jQuery(this))
        })
    } catch (c) {
        return console.log(c), !1
    }
    return this
};
```

Here, the uglification procedure has rearranged the entire plug-in code. It has put the private methods ahead of all other elements, and the name of the method has been changed. Not only that, the process of uglification has changed all the elements that were private to the plug-in. We again state that while this may not seem significant to you in the current scenario, in real-world scenarios in which the code spans thousands of lines, uglification and minification together can make your effort safe from copycats, besides saving network bandwidth. You may be surprised to learn that uglification is used by Google. If you try to view the source of a Google search page, you will not be able to make any sense of the code that is visible to you.

■ **Note** We used an online service, located at `http://javascriptcompressor.com/`, to minify the code. We used the online uglification service located at `https://marijnhaverbeke.nl/uglifyjs`, and we used the online beautification service located at `http://jsbeautifier.org/`.

Having achieved minification, you must save the minified (and/or uglified) plug-in code with the name `jQuery.your-plugin-name.min.js`, and your plug-in will be ready to be distributed. We recommend adding some additional documentation with the plug-in to be distributed, so that the next person who uses it will not have to take pains to contact you to learn how the plug-in works.

Summary

In this brief chapter, you learned to integrate a plug-in and use it with your code. You now understand the concepts that are behind customizing a plug-in, through examples related to the plug-in that you wrote in the previous chapter. This chapter also explained the tasks that you have to carry out prior to distributing your plug-in. In the process, you were introduced to the concepts of minification, uglification, and beautification. In the next chapter, you will delve further into the world of code reusability, by discovering some popular frameworks written with jQuery and gathering information on how to use those frameworks in order to solve common programming problems.

CHAPTER 11

■ ■ ■

Using jQuery Frameworks

The jQuery framework helps you to make your web page with ease. We have discussed how developing reusable pieces of code and frameworks are the best example of code reusability. Each framework has its own way of implementing a solution, and in this chapter, we will explore multiple frameworks, and you will learn about some popular ones built using jQuery and be provided information about some commonly used and popular methods. By the end of this chapter, you will be familiar with

- Some popular frameworks

- Components in jQuery

- jQuery user interface (UI) and features

- jQuery mobiles and features

JavaScript and jQuery Frameworks

A framework is a set of reusable components, libraries, or set of classes in a software system. In general terms, a framework is something that forces you to implement a solution by using a specific sets of rules. For example, different frameworks may have different ways of selecting a database or executing queries. As you know, jQuery is a set of JavaScript libraries that is designed to simplify the client-side scripting of HTML. jQuery is one of the most frequently used libraries. A framework can do several things, such as the following:

- It makes it easier, even for beginners, to work with complex technology, as you don't have to know the full details of a framework to begin with.

- It forces the development team to adhere to the software engineering principles, so that it is consistent, has fewer bugs, and more flexible applications, assuming you have chosen the correct framework.

- It also allows users to test and debug with only little information.

There are a few good frameworks available on the market, but we will focus on a few built on top of jQuery or JavaScript. The first we will discuss is Bootstrap.

Bootstrap

Bootstrap is the most popular HTML, CSS, and JavaScript framework for developing responsive, mobile first projects on the Web. Bootstrap comes with three different suites, and you can use them according to your business requirement. You can download and set up Bootstrap easily with the clear steps outlined in the Bootstrap documentation, available at `http://getbootstrap.com/getting-started/#download`.

Bootstrap helps you to create a web page with less effort. Bootstrap is a sleek, intuitive, and powerful front-end framework for web development. It is one of the best frameworks built on the top of jQuery, and, therefore, we decided to provide an overview of it. Bootstrap is equipped with HTML, CSS, and JavaScript for various web and user interface components.

Before we discuss some of the important methods of Bootstrap, let us review some of its biggest advantages. The first and most important is that it comes with a free set of tools for creating flexible and responsive web layout. Another advantage is that by using the Bootstrap data API, you can create advance interface components without writing a single line of JavaScript.

Some other advantages include

- Time-saving in web development

- Responsive layout

- Ease of use

- Consistent design

- Supports major browsers

- Is open source

Some Important Methods

In this section, we will demonstrate a few important methods used in Bootstrap. First, we will include Bootstrap CSS and JavaScript, as follows:

```
<!-- Latest compiled and minified CSS -->

<link rel="stylesheet" href="https://maxcdn.bootstrapcdn.com/bootstrap/3.3.4/css/bootstrap.
min.css">

<!-- Latest compiled and minified JavaScript -->
<script src="https://maxcdn.bootstrapcdn.com/bootstrap/3.3.4/js/bootstrap.min.js"></script>
```

Using Bootstrap Grid

Bootstrap allows you to create a grid, by adding up to 12 columns across the page. The grid system in Bootstrap is responsive in nature, and columns can be rearranged depending on the screen size, so you don't have to worry how they look on a mobile device, tablet, or on a big screen.

The grid system in Bootstrap adheres to the following rules:

- Rows should be placed within a `.container` for a *fixed-width* layout, or if the *full width* is used, it must be placed within `.container-fluid`.

- All the content must be placed within columns, and only columns can be immediate children of rows.

- Bootstrap has some predefined classes, such as `.row` and `.col-sm-4`, for making grid layouts.

- Grid columns are created by using a total of 12 available columns. For example, if you needed two equal columns, you would use `.col-sm-6` and, for three equal columns, `.col-sm-4`.

■ **Note** There are some additional rules that are not mentioned here. You can see them at
`http://getbootstrap.com/examples/grid/`.

The Bootstrap grid system has four classes

- xs (for phones)
- sm (for tablets)
- md (for desktops)
- lg (for larger desktops)

■ **Note** Adding more than 12 columns to a row makes no difference to the viewport. Also, when considering a grid class such as sm or xs, note that if you want to provide the same scale view on all devices, you must use xs.

The following example shows two unequal column layout grids:

```
<!DOCTYPE html>
<html lang="en">
<head>
    <title>Bootstrap Example</title>
    <meta charset="utf-8">
    <meta name="viewport" content="width=device-width, initial-scale=1">
    <link rel="stylesheet"
        href="http://maxcdn.bootstrapcdn.com/bootstrap/3.3.4/css/bootstrap.min.css">
    <script src="https://ajax.googleapis.com/ajax/libs/jquery/1.11.1/jquery.min.js"></script>
    <script src="http://maxcdn.bootstrapcdn.com/bootstrap/3.3.4/js/bootstrap.min.js"></script>
</head>
<body>

<div class="container-fluid">
    <h1>Welcome to Bootstrap Grid System!</h1>
    <p>Resize the browser window to see the effect.</p>
    <div class="row">
        <div class="col-sm-4" style="background-color:orange;">Showing .col-sm-4</div>
        <div class="col-sm-8" style="background-color:lightblue;">Showing .col-sm-8</div>
    </div>
</div>

</body>
</html>
```

In Figure 11-1, you can see that we have used a layout with two unequal column widths—one 25% and the other 75%—by using class="col-sm-4" and class="col-sm-8", respectively.

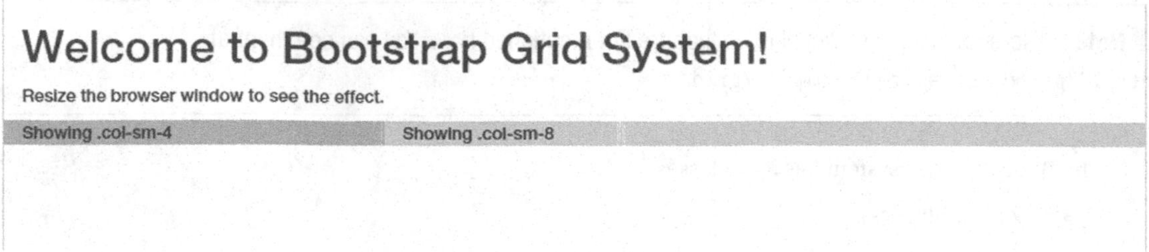

Welcome to Bootstrap Grid System!

Resize the browser window to see the effect.

Showing .col-sm-4	Showing .col-sm-8

Figure 11-1. *Output of our sample grid, with unequal column widths*

Adding Buttons and Icons

Adding buttons and icons is very easy in Bootstrap. You can use button classes with `<a>`, `<button>`, or `<input>` elements. If you want to have a large light blue button, you have to use `.btn-lg` and `.btn-info`. If you want to have a small green button, use `.btn-sm` and `.btn-success`.

For example,

- for a large button with light blue shade:

```
<input type="button" class="btn btn-info btn-lg">Submit</a>
```

- for a small button with green shade:

```
<input type="button" class="btn btn-success btn-sm">Submit</a>
```

For adding an icon, Bootstrap has glyphicons, and you can choose from among 260 icons, according to your need. To get the list of all Bootstrap glyphicons, go to `http://getbootstrap.com/components/#glyphicons-glyphs`.

■ **Note**　In Bootstrap, particular buttons are associated with specific colors by default. For example, `btn-suceess` is green, `btn-info` is light blue, `btn-danger` is red, and so on. The default colors can be changed if you choose to do so. For more information, see `http://getbootstrap.com/components/#alerts`. It explains about alert colors.

For example, if you wanted to add an icon for search, you would use `class="glyphicon glyphicon-search"` under the `<span>` element, as in the following:

```
<span class="glyphicon glyphicon-search"></span>
```

To use a print icon you have to write

```
<span class="glyphicon glyphicon-print"></span>
```

Adding a Navigation Bar with Bootstrap

A navigation bar is common to any web page. It's a navigational header at the top of the page. In Bootstrap, you can extend or collapse the navigation according to the screen size or your specific requirement. For creating a navigation bar, you have to write `<nav class="navbar navbar-default">`. If you want to create a *fixed navigation* bar that will stay in a fixed position, you have to use `<nav class="navbar navbar-inverse navbar-fixed-top">`.

The following example shows a basic navigation bar in Bootstrap with `container`.

```html
<!DOCTYPE html>
<html lang="en">
<head>
    <title>Bootstrap Case</title>
    <meta charset="utf-8">
    <meta name="viewport" content="width=device-width, initial-scale=1">
    <link rel="stylesheet"
        href="http://maxcdn.bootstrapcdn.com/bootstrap/3.3.4/css/bootstrap.min.css">
    <script src="https://ajax.googleapis.com/ajax/libs/jquery/1.11.1/jquery.min.js"></script>
    <script src="http://maxcdn.bootstrapcdn.com/bootstrap/3.3.4/js/bootstrap.min.js"></script>
</head>
<body>

<nav class="navbar navbar-default">
    <div class="container-fluid">
        <div class="navbar-header">
            <a class="navbar-brand" href="#">Practical jQuery</a>
        </div>
        <div>
            <ul class="nav navbar-nav">
                <li class="active"><a href="#">Home</a></li>
                <li><a href="#">Apress</a></li>
                <li><a href="#">Springer</a></li>
            </ul>
        </div>
    </div>
</nav>

<div class="container">
    <div class="jumbotron">
        <h1>Practical jQuery!</h1>
        <p>Some text may go here...</p>
        <a href="#" class="btn btn-info btn-lg"><span class="glyphicon glyphicon-search"></span> Search</a>
    </div>

        <div class="clearfix visible-lg"></div>
    </div>
</div>

</body>
</html>
```

AngularJS

Before moving to the basics of AngularJS, you should understand that it is not related to jQuery. AngularJs is a JavaScript framework, and it is included for those readers interested in knowing about the basics of that framework. All others can skip this topic, which has no connection to any other covered in this book.

AngularJS is a JavaScript framework written in JavaScript. It is a structural framework useful for making dynamic web apps and SPAs (Single Page Applications). AngularJs extends HTML attributes with directives, sometimes also called ng-directives, and binds data to HTML with the use of expressions.

To use AngularJS, you must have a basic knowledge of HTML, CSS, and JavaScript. AngularJS is supported by Google, and it was developed in 2009 and released in 2010. It is easy and fun to learn.

To get started with AngularJS, you have to add the file to a web page with `script` tag

```
<script src="http://ajax.googleapis.com/ajax/libs/angularjs/1.3.14/angular.min.js"></script>
```

There are a few concepts that you must understand, although they are not limited to those explained below.

- **Directive:** This extends HTML with custom attributes and elements. Directives are markers on a DOM element, such as an attribute, element name, or CSS class, that tell AngularJS's HTML compiler to attach a specified behavior to that DOM or to its children. There are a set of directives in AngularJS, including `ngBind`, `ngModel`, and `ngClass`.

- **Expression:** It accesses variables and functions from the scope. An expression in a template is similar to a JavaScript code snippet that allows to read and write variables. Just like JavaScript, AngularJS also provides a scope for variables accessible to expressions.

■ **Note** The variable in an expression is not global. It has a scope.

- **Data Binding:** It syncs data between the model and the view. For example, if we use an `ng-bind` directive in the title, it keeps the title of the page in sync with our model, before including CSS files in the `<head>`, and JavaScript files before closing of `<body>` tag.

There are additional concepts, and we recommend that you learn more about them from `https://docs.angularjs.org/guide/concepts`.

Now you have some idea about AngularJS. Don't worry; you will learn more as you get your hands dirty with the code. So, here is our first example of AngularJS:

```
<script type="text/javascript" src="http://ajax.googleapis.com/ajax/libs/angularjs/1.0.7/
angular.min.js"></script>
<div ng-app>

    Write your name in the box:
    <input type="text" ng-model="sometext" />

    <h1>Hello {{ sometext }}!</h1>

</div>
```

If you run it and write some text in the box, you will see how the value after `Hello` changes. We didn't write a single line of JavaScript, and the code works perfectly! You may have noticed that there are some tags that we put in our HTML document. Let's discuss the code step-by-step.

The first thing that you see is an attribute ng-app within the tag that tells AngularJS to be active in that page. So whenever you want to enable AngularJS at a specific location in your web page, it is mandatory for you to define the ng-app attribute to the <div> element or other tag.

We then define ng-model in a text box as ng-model="somevalue"; ng-model binds the state of the text box with a model value; and we define a model somevalue. The model value is bound to the value of the text box, and AngularJS automatically displays the text.

Following is another example, showing an application in AngularJS from scratch:

```
<!DOCTYPE html>
<html>
<head>
    <script
        src="https://ajax.googleapis.com/ajax/libs/angularjs/1.2.5/angular.min.js"></script>
</head>
<body ng-app="apressApp">
    <div ng-controller="MyController" >

        <h2>Hello {{welcome.title}}</h2>

    </div>

        <script>
var app = angular.module("apressApp", [])
        app.controller("MyController", function($scope) {
        $scope.welcome = {};
        $scope.welcome.title = "Welcome, Readers!";
        });
    </script>·
</body>
</html>
```

Time to look at the example in detail. First, we have to include the AngularJS file in the HTML page, in order to use AngularJS. After that, we have to tell which part of the page contains the AngularJS app, which can be done by adding ng-app to the root element. In the preceding example, we have added it to the body element ng-app="apressApp". This tells AngularJS that all controller functions must be added to the apressApp module. After the body section, we have the div element containing the ng-controller attribute with the value MyController. This means that the controller function used by view is named MyController.

The HTML part of the view is

```
<h2>Hello {{welcome.title}}</h2>
```

If you notice, this is a normal HTML, except for the expression part {{welcome.title}}. This tells AngularJS to insert the model value named welcome.title into the HTML at that location.

Finally, we have a controller that takes a single parameter. We call it $scope parameter. The $scope parameter is the model object to be used by the controller function and its view. The controller function can insert data and functions into the model object.

Moving on to the script section, we have called a function angular.module(). Also, we have passed the parameter apressApp, which matches the name specified in the ng-app attribute in the root element. Thus, AngularJS knows which controller function is registered to apressApp module.

■ **Note** The `angular` object is a global object created by the AngularJS JavaScript, which is included at the beginning of the page.

There is a lot to learn in AngularJS, and we recommend that you go through the official documentation at `https://docs.angularjs.org/tutorial` for further information.

Components in jQuery

Everything in the world exists for some purpose and so do components. Citing the Object Management Group UML specification,[1] the Wikipedia "Component (UML)" article (`http://en.wikipedia.org/wiki/Component_(UML)`) states that

> *A component in the Unified Modeling Language "represents a modular part of a system, that encapsulates its content and whose manifestation is replaceable within its environment. A component defines its behavior in terms of provided and required interfaces."*

jQuery is rich in UI components, and there are many good ones that you can explore. We are highlighting one simple component that selects color in same way as Adobe Photoshop.

To use this *color picker* component, you first have to download the source. It can be downloaded from `www.eyecon.ro/colorpicker/#download`.

Additional to this, you have to attach JavaScript and CSS files to your document, by editing its path as follows:

```
<link rel="stylesheet" media="screen" type="text/css" href="css/colorpicker.css" />
<script type="text/javascript" src="js/colorpicker.js"></script>
```

That's all. You are now ready to invoke the code. All you have to do is select the elements in a jQuery way and call the plug-in, as follows:

```
$('input').ColorPicker(options);
```

Now let us see the possible options value.

- **eventName**: The type will be string, and you can provide any event name that you want to trigger the color picker. The default event is click.

- **Color**: It can take a string or hash. The default color is ff0000.

- Some other option values may be **flat, livePreview, onShow, onBefore Show, onHide, onChange, onSubmit.**

For example, you can use the following, if you want to set a new color:

```
$('input').ColorPickerSetColor(colorname);
```

Figure 11-2 shows the color picker.

---

[1]Object Management Group, "OMG Unified Modeling Language (OMG UML), Superstructure, V2.1.2," `www.omg.org/spec/UML/2.1.2/Superstructure/PDF`, 2007.

Figure 11-2. *The color picker in default mode*

■ **Note**   All parameters shown in the preceding are optional.

---

jQuery UI

Before we dive into the depth of jQuery UI features, we need to know what jQuery UI is. JQuery UI is a great tool for UI developers and designers and is an organized set composed of user interface interaction, effects, widgets, and themes that is built on top of the jQuery JavaScript library. jQuery UI provides a powerful theming engine, and here *UI* stands for *user interface*, and the jQuery library provides lots of UI enhancements to your web site.

There are two options available for theming: you can download a theme that is already available and customize it, or, as the experts suggest, you can create a theme from scratch. Creating a theme from scratch has no waste or unused function, as you create it by yourself for some specific purpose. Those who are more interested in reading about theming are requested to check the jQuery UI ThemeRoller at http://jqueryui.com/themeroller/. It allows you to select different colors, fonts, drop shadows, etc., to suit your web page. You can select the theme from the ThemeRoller gallery and customize it per your requirements.

Before you can create a theme from scratch, you have to know the structure of a jQuery UI theme. Download a theme from jQuery resources to familiarize yourself with the structure of the folders. They contain CSS, JS, and a development bundle. The development bundle contains a folder named themes, which is where jQuery UI themes resides. You can rename the theme folder and have it contain a CSS file that incorporates the CSS markup for all of the components or widgets. Now you can start customizing in accordance with your requirements.

In addition to its theming capabilities, jQuery UI is a rich source of a variety of pre-baked functions that are easy to use. These are categorized into user interaction, widgets, and effects. We will select a few examples from each category and explore them in detail.

Drag and Drop Using jQuery UI

jQuery UI provides drag-and-drop functionality for any DOM element. Let's see examples of making elements draggable and droppable.

Making an element *draggable* allows it to be moved using the mouse. By enabling the draggable functionality on any DOM element, we can move the object by clicking it, using a mouse.

■ **Note**   The draggable widget has three dependencies: UI core, Widget Factory, and Mouse Interaction.

Following is a code example:

//HTML
```
<script src="http://code.jquery.com/jquery-1.10.2.js"></script>
    <script src="http://code.jquery.com/ui/1.11.4/jquery-ui.js"></script>
<div id="apress-drag">
    <p>Drag me using mouse.</p>
</div>
```

//CSS
```
<style>
#apress-drag p {width: 200px;padding: 0.5em; background-color:rgba(0,0,0,.5); border-
radius:50%; padding:18% 0;text-align:center; color:#fff;}
</style>
```

//jQuery
```
<script>
$(function() {
    $( "#apress-drag" ).draggable();
});
</script>
```

■ **Note**   You can see the results at `http://jsfiddle.net/mukund002/7ojoy3eh/`.

You make an element *droppable* to create a target for a draggable element. The drop function can enable any DOM element to be droppable.

Here is another sample code:

//HTML
```
<script src="http://code.jquery.com/jquery-1.10.2.js"></script>
    <script src="http://code.jquery.com/ui/1.11.4/jquery-ui.js"></script>
<div id="apress-drag">
    <p>Drag me to my target</p>
</div>

<div id="apress-drop">
    <p>Drop here</p>
</div>
```

//CSS
```
<style>
#apress-drag p {width: 150px;padding: 0.5em; background-color:rgba(0,0,0,.5); padding:10%
0;text-align:center; color:#fff;}

#apress-drop p {width: 300px;padding: 0.5em; background-color:rgba(0,0,0,.5); padding:15%
0;text-align:center; color:#fff;}
</style>
```

```
//jQuery
<script>
$(function() {
    $( "#apress-drag" ).draggable();
    $( "#apress-drop" ).droppable({
        drop: function( event, ui ) {
            $( this )
                .addClass( "ui-state-highlight" )
                .find( "p" )
                    .html( " You Dropped me !" );
        }
    });
});
</script>
```

Figure 11-3 shows the HTML output before the element is dragged and dropped.

Figure 11-3. *Showing the HTML before dropping the element*

Once you drag the element to another div, it will trigger the drop function, which is triggered when an acceptable draggable is dropped on the droppable.

In the preceding code, we can see that we have initialized the droppable with the drop callback specified.

```
$( "#apress-drop" ).droppable({
    drop: function( event, ui ) {

// code goes here...

}};
```

CHAPTER 11 ■ USING JQUERY FRAMEWORKS

Figure 11-4 shows the result of the drop.

Figure 11-4. *Execution of the drop*

■ **Note**   You can see the output at `http://jsfiddle.net/mukund002/for1eax7/`.

Moving to the next segment of UI widgets, we have Accordion, Autocomplete, and Datepicker. Because we have already covered Accordion in previous chapters, we will discuss Autocomplete and Datepicker here.

Autocomplete

Autocomplete enables users to quickly find and select results from a pre-populated list of values as they type and enhances the user experience. It offers suggestions, such as if you type in JA, it will offer you such suggestions as Java, JavaScript, and so on.

Any field that can receive input can be converted into Autocomplete as either an `<input>` element, `<select>` element, or `<textarea>` element.

Let's take up a sample code.

//HTML
```
<div class="ui-widget">
    <label for="name">Search Name: </label>
    <input id="name">
</div>
```

//jQuery
```
$(function() {
    var availableNames = [
        "Aalia", "Arun","Ankur","Brandon","Celia",
        "Citu","Durien","Enthony","Fummi","Gary",
        "Hamir","Javed","Jahid","Priyansh","Priyanshu",
        "Rohit","Sambit","Sameer"
    ];
    $( "#name" ).autocomplete({
        source: availableNames
    });
});
```

Figure 11-5 shows Autocomplete in action.

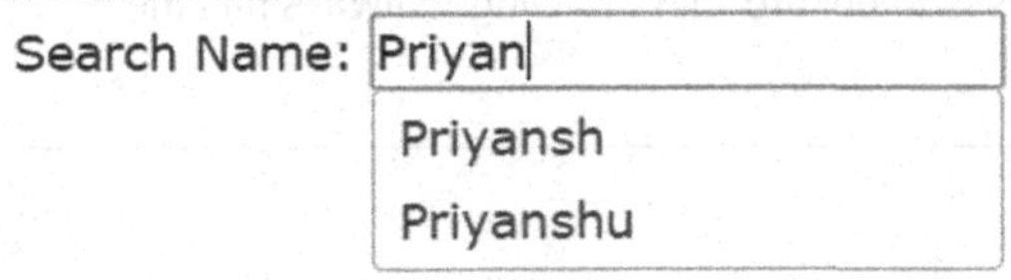

Search Name: Priyan
> Priyansh
> Priyanshu

Figure 11-5. Output of Autocomplete

■ **Note**   You can also see the result at `http://jsfiddle.net/mukund002/3wc5atcr/`.

Have you noticed how it works? It is simple, although it requires a bit of explanation. We passed `selector.autocomplete`, and inside that we mentioned `source`. In our case we have a simple source as an array, but you can use a different source.

`source` can be of three types, namely, *array, string,* or *function (object request, function response [object data])*.

- **Array**: An array is a special variable that can hold more than one value at a time. For example, if you have a list of books, storing the books in a single variable looks like the following:

  ```
  var books = new Array("Practical jQuery", "PHPStorm Cookbook", "Guide to PMP");
  ```

  It can be used for local data and for when we have less data to search. There are two formats of array that are supported:

  - An array containing a string, such as `["Ankur","Mukund"]`

  - An array of objects with label and value properties, such as `[ { label: "Enter Name", value: "Madhav" }, ... ]`

- **String**: A string is an immutable object that contains none, one, or many characters. When you use a string in a source, the Autocomplete plug-in expects that string to point to a URL resource that will return JSON data. The Autocomplete plug-in adds a query string with a term field, which the server-side script should use for filtering the results.

  For example, if the source option is set to `"http://apress.com"`, and the user types jQuery, a GET request will be made to `http://apress.com?term=jquery`.

- **Function**: The last source, a callback, can be used to connect any data source to Autocomplete. The callback gets two arguments:

- A request object, with a single term property, which refers to the value currently in the text input. For example, if the user enters `"Del"` in a city field, the Autocomplete term will equal `"Del"`.

- A response callback, which expects a single argument: the data to suggest to the user. This data should be filtered, based on the provided term, and can be in any of the formats described previously for simple local data.

When filtering data locally, you can make use of the built-in `$.ui.autocomplete.escapeRegex` function. It'll take a single string argument and escape all regex characters, making the result safe to pass to a new `RegExp()`.

■ **Caution** When providing a custom source callback to handle errors during the request, you must always call the response callback, even if you encounter an error. This is to ensure that the widget always has the correct state.

Datepicker

Datepicker is used to select a date from a calendar. The jQuery UI Datepicker is one of the highly configurable plug-ins that can be customized for almost any kind of business requirements. You can customize the date format or language and put restrictions on date ranges and add icons.

Here is a code example:

```
//HTML
<script src="http://code.jquery.com/jquery-1.10.2.js"></script>
    <script src="http://code.jquery.com/ui/1.11.4/jquery-ui.js"></script>

<p>Select Date: <input type="text" id="datepicker"></p>
```

```
//jQuery
<script>
$(function() {
    $( "#datepicker" ).datepicker();
});
</script>
```

Figure 11-6 shows the datepicker.

Figure 11-6. Output of the datepicker

By default, the datepicker calendar opens in a small overlay. For an inline calendar, simply attach it within a `<div>` or `<span>` element.

To change the default options for all the datepickers, you have to use

```
$.datepicker.setDefaults( options )
```

Here, `options` is used to change options for instances. To format a date into a string value with a specified format, you have to write:

```
$.datepicker.formatDate( format, date, options )
```

■ **Note**   For further details about Datepicker, go to `http://api.jqueryui.com/datepicker/`.

---

jQuery Mobile

With the increase of smartphones, tablets, and other handheld devices, your business faces an urgent need to build a touch-friendly, responsive web site, and that's where jQuery Mobile comes in. jQuery Mobile is an HTML5-based user interface system designed to make responsive web sites and apps that are accessible on smartphones, tablets, and desktop devices. It sticks to the jQuery principle of "Write less, do more."

The jQuery Mobile framework uses progressive enhancements to improve user experience, such as touch-friendly input forms and easy and efficient page loading. Before going through the features of jQuery Mobile, let's explore some reasons to use it.

- **Widely supported platform**: jQuery Mobile supports all major devices, such as desktops, tablets, and smartphones or other handheld devices. Most of these devices have enhanced and Ajax-animated page transition, and this is due to progressive enhancement.

- **Touch-friendly form input and UI widgets**: jQuery Mobile helps you to offer a complete user experience. It has big, chunky tap targets that are easy for your fingers to manipulate. They support finger-friendly form input and UI widgets.

- **Responsive web design**: You are able to develop responsive web sites on top of jQuery Mobile, because it's a mobile-first framework. And in the 1.3 version of jQuery Mobile, a lot more focus is given to responsive web design features. With the increased use of handheld devices, it is mandatory to have web sites that are responsive in nature.

Some Cool Features of jQuery Mobile

jQuery Mobile is rich in features and is a mobile-first framework, although not exclusive to mobile. The key features of jQuery Mobile are

- Responsive web design (RWD)
- Ajax-powered navigation system
- Powerful and unified UI widgets

- Wider browser and OS support

- Modular architecture for creating custom builds

- Minimal size

There are many more features other than those listed, but let's walk through these points one-by-one.

Responsive Web Design

Responsive web design begins with a media queries class. A media query consists of a media type and at least one expression that limits the style sheet's scope, by using media features such as width, height, color, and font. Media queries, added in CSS3, are helpful in tailoring the presentation of content in various devices. They are useful when working on responsive web design. You have to define the min/max width breakpoint, as, for example, min-width:40rem and max-width:60rem.

The following sample code shows the basic media query class:

```
@media screen and (max-width:40em) {
    h1{
    font-size:2.44444rem;
    }
 }

@media screen and (min-width: 40.063em) and (max-width: 64em) {
    h1{
        font-size:2.05556rem;
    }
}

@media screen and (min-width: 64.063em) and (max-width: 120em) {
    h1{
        font-size:1.5rem;
    }
}

@media screen and (min-width: 120.063em) {
    h1{
        font-size:1.27778rem;
    }
}

/ Landscape Orientation /
@media screen and (orientation: landscape) {
    h1{
        font-size:1.1rem;
    }
}

/ Portrait Orientation /
@media screen and (orientation: portrait) {
    h1{
        font-size:1rem;
    }
 }
```

Width breakpoints in jQuery Mobile are added using the `$.mobile.addResolutionBreakpoints` function, which accepts either a single number or an array of numbers that will be added to the min/max breakpoints whenever they apply. For example

```
//adding a min/max class for 800 pixel widths
$.mobile.addResolutionBreakpoints(800);
```

```
//adding min/max classes for 800, and 1200 pixel widths
$.mobile.addResolutionBreakpoints([800, 1200]);
```

You can also test whether a CSS media query applies or not. You have to call `$.mobile.media()` and pass a media type or query. If the browser supports it, the function returns `true`; otherwise, it returns `false`.

```
//Testing for screen media type
$.mobile.media("screen");
```

```
//Testing a max-width media query
$.mobile.media("screen and (max-width: 1200px)")
```

■ **Tip**   We recommend using CSS3 for writing media queries and also that you use em or rem instead of px while breaking the min/max width.

Ajax Navigation System

We'll start our discussion with jQuery Mobile's navigation model. A page in jQuery Mobile is usually composed of a `<div>` element, with a `data-role` attribute set to a page containing `<div>` elements assuming the role of header, content, and footer, each containing common *markup, forms,* and *customized jQuery Mobile widgets.*

While loading a page, an HTTP request is made first, then the subsequent pages are requested and inserted into the page's DOM. Hence, the DOM may have a number of "pages" at a time, and these can be revisited by using the `data-url` attribute. The main advantage of using jQuery Mobile navigation is that it allows you to pre-fetch static pages that are likely to be visited.

Ajax and Hash Driven Page Navigation

Hash values created by jQuery Mobile are full-path, relative to the URL. If you want to retrieve a non-hashed URL, you have to remove # from the URL. For example, if you have #about.html on your address bar, the page will be refreshed by removing #. All the navigation within jQuery Mobile is based on changes and updates to `location.hash`, whether the page is already in DOM or is automatically loaded via Ajax.

When a page is loaded, the hashchange event handler sends the `location.hash` to the `$mobile.changePage()` function, which in turn loads or reveals the referenced page. Once the reference page enters the DOM, `$mobile.changePage()` applies the transition between the current active page and the new page. When it comes to a new page, the active class (any class that makes it active) gets added, and the previous one is removed.

For example, the following enasbles a transition to the "contact us" page with a slideup transition:

```
$.mobile.changePage( "contact/us.html", { transition: "slideup"} );
```

Here, the transition is to the search results page, using data from a form with an ID of apress:

```
$.mobile.changePage( "searchresults.php", {
    type: "post",
    data: $("form#apress").serialize()
});
```

■ **Note**   The `$.mobile.changePage()` function contains all of the logic required for finding pages to transition to and from and how to handle various response conditions, such as a page not found, by searching a record based on ID using URL, type (get or post).

Pop-ups in jQuery Mobile

Pop-up boxes are very useful when you want to display some text, photos, a menu, or other content. They look similar to dialog boxes. Because dialogs are deprecated in jQuery Mobile's version 1.4, and may be removed in the next version, this book will not cover dialogs.

Creating a pop-up is very easy. You have to add the data-role="popup" to the <div> element within the pop-up. After that, you must create a link with href and set the ID of the div. Now, insert the content that you want to show inside the div.

Let's look at an example.

```
<!DOCTYPE html>
<html>
<head>
<meta name="viewport" content="width=device-width, initial-scale=1">
<link rel="stylesheet" href="http://code.jquery.com/mobile/1.4.5/jquery.mobile-1.4.5.min.css">
<script src="http://code.jquery.com/jquery-1.11.2.min.js"></script>
<script src="http://code.jquery.com/mobile/1.4.5/jquery.mobile-1.4.5.min.js"></script>
</head>
<body>

<div data-role="page">
    <div data-role="header">
        <h1>Welcome To PopUp</h1>
</div>

    <div data-role="main" class="ui-content">
        <a href="#Popup" data-rel="popup" data-transition="slideup" data-overlay-theme="a"
class="ui-btn ui-btn-inline ui-corner-all">Click to open Popup</a>

        <div data-role="popup" id="Popup">
            <p>Popups are similar to dialogs, in that they both overlay a part of a page.
A popup box can be useful when you want to display small text, photos, maps or other
content.</p>
        </div>
    </div>
```

```
    <div data-role="footer">
        <h1>@2015. All right reserved with Apress</h1>
    </div>
</div>

</body>
</html>
```

In the preceding code, you can see that we have used data-rel="popup", which asks to reveal the pop-up. To find the pop-up, we use id="Popup". By defualt, pop-ups don't have any transition effects, so if you want a transition, you must tell data-transition="*somevalue*". In the preceding example, we have used data-transition="slideup", but you can use any value, such as fade or slidedown.

Also, you can see that to add a header and footer section to a pop-up dialog, we have used data-role="header" and data-role="footer".

Here's a sample code showing menu navigation:

```
<a href="#menu" data-rel="popup" data-role="button">Apress Menu</a>
<div data-role="popup" id="menu" data-theme="a">
    <ul data-role="listview" data-theme="c" data-inset="true">
        <li data-role="divider" data-theme="a">Home</li>
        <li><a href="#">Apress Access</a></li>
        <li><a href="#">Access Library</a><span class="ui-li-count">12</span></a></li>
    </ul>
</div>
```

In the preceding code, we have not included the jQuery library. You have to include it to run the code. Figure 11-7 shows the result.

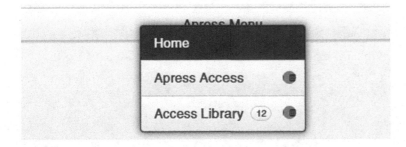

Figure 11-7. *Code execution*

Summary

In this chapter, you were introduced to the basics of Bootstrap and AngularJS and the power of code reusability and maintainability. You also discovered the power of jQuery UI and widgets. This chapter also focused on jQuery Mobile. In the next chapter, we will explore some interesting topics, including QUnit, testing your jQuery code with QUnit, refactoring code, and testability.

■ ■ ■

CHAPTER 12

Testing jQuery with QUnit

Software engineering is not only about development. The developed software product has to be checked for quality at all times, even while it is being written. So, having spent a substantial amount of time learning the ways and means of writing quality software using jQuery, this last chapter will provide ample information regarding testing the same, using QUnit, a framework written in JavaScript. Because developers often find testing to be a tedious task, and although they know the importance of testing from the knowledge they've obtained at school, they tend to shy away from this process.

   This chapter will prove that just like working with jQuery is fun, testing can be too. By the time you finish this chapter, you will have learned

- What QUnit is

- What unit testing is

- Getting ready with QUnit

- How to test DOM manipulation using QUnit

- Refactoring code to enhance testability

QUnit as a JavaScript Framework

Looking at things from a broad perspective, you will notice that QUnit is a framework written in JavaScript, just as jQuery is. But, while jQuery is a framework mainly intended to provide ease of development, QUnit is a framework intended to provide ease of automating the testing procedure of the code that you write in jQuery (or JavaScript). The purpose of writing QUnit is to attain the goal of ensuring quality assurance for the code that you write. This quality assurance comes from automating a task that you would otherwise find quite tedious and, hence, refrain from carrying out. It is a very common (and unhealthy) practice among front-end developers to assume that JavaScript or jQuery code cannot be tested. The major reason for this is that browsers behave differently, and, hence, the JavaScript code that developers write has to cover a lot of functionality. Keeping track of all such functionality is an extremely tedious task.

   The two frameworks did not exist as separate entities at the inception of QUnit. John Resig, the creator of jQuery, did a great job of writing QUnit too. Originally, QUnit was written as a part of jQuery itself, as that part of the code used to test the functionality provided by jQuery. Later on (in 2008), QUnit evolved as a separate project from the jQuery source code. In the initial stage of QUnit, the usage of QUnit depended on using jQuery to obtain the correct functionality, but just about a year later (in 2009), QUnit was rewritten in such a way that the dependency on jQuery was removed completely, and QUnit became a standalone project. QUnit is used quite heavily with jQuery and its related frameworks, such as jQuery UI and jQuery Mobile, but you should know that QUnit doesn't differentiate between any kind of JavaScript code, and you can use it to test generic JavaScript code as well.

■ **Note** The term *QUnit* was coined by taking the *Q* from *jQuery* and *Unit* from *jUnit*. For the record, jUnit is a testing framework written in and for testing the code written in Java, another programming language that revolutionized the Internet ever since its launch in 1995.

The idea behind using QUnit is to automate the software code-testing process. When we say *automate*, we mean that the automation is achieved by writing code. Yes, you are understanding correctly. You have to write some additional code to test some target code. While the very idea may seem insane to you, we assure you that you will find it fun to write the code that will do the testing. By the way, we will refer to such code as the *test case* for the remainder of this chapter. We chose this elusive term to pique your interest in the remaining sections, where we will explain in detail unit testing and related concepts.

Introduction to Unit Testing

Let us be straightforward and state that QUnit is a framework written to ease unit testing. So, whenever we do unit testing, we actually test the functionality of the smallest possible functional chunk of the target code. You may wonder why the term *unit* is used. To this, we would answer that since an ideal code is written modularly, a unit in such modular code is the most basic piece of code that is used by other parts of the code to provide added functionality. We understand that grasping this concept is not easy, so we are ready with a small example that explains what a unit code looks like.

Suppose there is a method do() and a method check. Both methods accept a parameter denoting what to do and what to check. The JavaScript style of writing the two methods would be as follows::check method

```
function do(thisThing){
...// carry out a task named "thisThing"
}

function check(thisThing){
...// check if a task named "thisThing" is OK to be carried out
}
```

Now suppose there is a functionality that is meant to take a task, check it, and then execute it. The JavaScript implementation for this functionality would be as follows:

```
function carryOut(someThing){
    var thisThing = someThing;
    if(check(thisThing)){
        do(thisThing);
    } else {
        ...// show appropriate error
    }
}
```

Here, the method carryOut is dependent on the methods check and do. Thus, in order to test whether the method carryOut functions properly, you must ensure that the methods check and execute each function properly. This is to say that check, carryOut, and do are the smallest chunks of code that function independently, and the output of the three methods will not change for the same input, irrespective of the number of times they are called. Hence, they are the units in the entire code ecosystem that includes check, do, and carryOut methods. So when it comes to testing the functionality of these units, the principle of unit testing comes into play.

■ **Note**   A unit is the smallest testable part of an application.

We wish to cover as much as possible on unit testing, so that you are ready to shift gears to begin working on QUnit. So, there is an important concept with the name *test case* that you have to master. It will not only help you in working with QUnit in particular but also with any other unit-testing framework. Speaking in the most general terms, a test case is an algorithm that makes an attempt to find out if some target application is working well or not. Here, you may want to revisit the example that we provided, to get a feel for how a test case might look. Thus, in terms of an algorithm, the very procedure that you would write to check the methods in the target code will be the test case. So, if you write a method named testCarryOut to check if the method carryOut produces the correct output on passing the correct input, congratulations, you have created a test case. Creating a test case is a topic that we will deal with very soon in the coming sections.

The Need for Unit Testing

The very purpose of mentioning testing in a book containing information related to writing code is to make you believe that the process of testing can be carried out by writing code, i.e., testing can be automated. With information on how to write some code to test some existing piece of code, you can easily go ahead and implement more and more functionality, without having to worry about the changes producing unwanted side effects on the existing code. We provide an example that will show you why and when you have to have a unit test in place.

We firmly believe that using the same example to demonstrate various dimensions of a problem is more beneficial to you, the reader; therefore, throughout this book, we have adhered to our belief. Here, too, in order to demonstrate why and when you might require unit testing, we take up an example that we took up in Chapter 8. In that chapter, we wrote a class named Validation when we were discussing form validation using Ajax. If you are asked to check the functionality of the class, a very common way for you to do so would be to write some HTML form, attach the Validation functionality to it, and pass on some random values to check the output. While this may seem appropriate in the simple case of the Validation class, for a more complex functionality, you could end up missing out on a number of possible error-producing inputs.

Here is where testing the unit part of your code by writing test cases comes into action. In the class named Validation, we can identify a unit as the method check. We remind you that the check method in the Validation class accepts a name argument and basis that it uses to check if the HTML form element, as identified by the selector, contains some invalid elements. As soon as the method used encounters any invalid element, an exception is thrown. So, if you wish to test the functionality of the check method, you will have to write some code for the purpose. Let's see how the tester code would look.

```
Validation.prototype.testCheckName = function(value, expected){
    this.name = value;
    var result = 'Passed';
    try{
        this.check('name');
    } catch(exception){
        result = "Failed";
    }
```

```
    if(result != expected){
        return "Failed";
    } else {
        return "Passed";
    }
}

var validate = new Validation();
console.log(validate.testCheckName("Practical jQuery", "Pass"));
```

Please note that we have added this testing functionality to the Validate class itself. This will give you insight into the origin of QUnit as well. We will cover that shortly. Getting back on track, in the method testCheckName, we have made an attempt to check if the functionality to validate a name works correctly. We have done that by passing a value to the tester method, along with an expected outcome. If the value we have provided is valid, the method will return "Passed". It will return "Failed", if the value is not valid. The implementation is also quite straightforward: if the provided input is not valid, the check method will throw an exception, and we will have made good use of this feature. By default, the tester method assumes that the input will pass the test. If there is an exception, it is due to the invalid input, and the method returns a message "Failed". If there is no exception, the method returns "Passed". Similarly, there can be a number of such methods, including testCheckEmail, testCheckPhone, and so on, depending on the types of values the method is processing.

■ **Note** Just as we have added a new method to the Validate class to perform testing of the functionality of a particular method, you can very well imagine the origin of the QUnit framework. Later on, realizing the need for a proper testing framework to be in place, the methods were separated, for use with generic JavaScript code.

Why QUnit?

A very natural question that could enter your mind once you get into writing code for testing is why do I need a framework when I can write code myself? This question is quite understandable, considering certain factors, such as the learning curve, intensity of the business requirement, and so on. But, again, a framework helps you to prevent repetition of coding intended to execute some common tasks. Here, the common task is unit testing, and the QUnit framework provides you a number of methods that can assist you in doing that. So, you will not have to worry about, let's say, the UI of how to display the results of executing the test cases once you use QUnit.

If you wrote a test case in order to check the functionality of the check method, you would have to implement the entire process of testing, which is not standardized. Another person doing the same thing would have to implement the same algorithm all over again. It would not be a wise and efficient use of programming resources. Using a framework (contextually QUnit) prevents this inefficiency. You can have a number of methods wherein you have the ease to test multiple methods (taken one at a time), using the method provided by the framework. We assure you that we will present all such methods that QUnit provides. We are just waiting until we have imparted in you sufficient knowledge on the fundamentals of QUnit.

While the reason(s) to use QUnit that we cited may not appear significant—you may be easily tempted to believe that you can create your own user interface to view the test results—the difference created in using a framework for the purpose is substantial. The difference is quantifiable in terms of the effort you will exert in creating the UI, plus the effort you would put into making the UI browser compatible. It is okay that by now you have the expertise and the information to write a browser-compatible user interface, but when someone

(Mr./Ms. QUnit, personified) is doing the task for you at no extra cost (QUnit is free and open source), availing oneself of a helping hand is not an unwise decision! A less apparent but significant effect of using QUnit is that you can write test cases (the scenarios under which you want the application to be tested) for the target code. While the methods provided by the QUnit framework are properly documented, you are essentially making the task easier for a new developer who will start working on the target code base. The reason is quite straightforward, if you think of it. You are writing down the various scenarios in which the code will function, so that the new developer will be able to have a flatter learning curve! The test case(s) written by you will ease the task for testing the JavaScript or jQuery code across browsers. You will only have to execute the test cases, or your code-testing program, whichever you name it. Once you are done with the execution, you can easily compare the results, to see which code fails on which browser, and, hence, you can move ahead to find the fix for the issue.

Getting Started with QUnit

The very first step in getting started with any framework is to download it to the development system. The same applies for QUnit. You have to get a copy of the framework from the official QUnit web site at `http://qunitjs.com`. The QUnit web site makes available the latest version of the framework. At the time of writing, the latest version is 1.18.0 and is available as `qunit-1.18.0.js`. At this point in time, you should know that the functionality provided by QUnit is to be used inside a web page, so that the results of executing the tests can be seen in a visually appealing format. For the purpose, you must download a style sheet with the name `qunit-1.18.0.css`.

■ **Tip** Having had a fair amount of exposure to the jQuery framework, it is quite natural for you to wonder about browser compatibility for any application that must be executed on a web browser. QUnit clears this confusion by stating that QUnit 1.x supports all those browsers that the jQuery 1.x framework supports.

QUnit Syntax

Let us have a quick look into the syntax of the QUnit framework. We intentionally mentioned the word *quick*, because the syntax of the QUnit framework is not very hard to understand. It is just a JavaScript-derived framework, so the syntax will be quite familiar to you. If we say that the syntax will remind you of the jQuery syntax, you will readily agree with us, because you may recall from earlier in this chapter that QUnit originated from jQuery itself. In order to familiarize you with the syntax of QUnit, let us have a glimpse into a function that you will need to write test cases. The method is intuitively known as `test`. All it does is test some functionality. The method is written as `QUnit.test`. This `test` method has to have two inputs as parameters: the first parameter being the title of the test case and the other being the callback function that will actually test the code. So, the entire `test` method syntax would be as follows:

```
QUnit.test('Test case title', function(assert){
    ...// Testing code here
});
```

■ **Note** We will explain the `test` method in detail shortly, so you need not worry about such aspects as the functionality and usage of the method.

This is the *only* syntax you need to consider. All the methods available in the entire QUnit framework use this syntax. If you take a closer look into the syntax of the test method, you will notice just from the way the jQuery methods are called, either as jQuery.*methodName* or $.*methodName* (depending on the alias), that QUnit methods are called in exactly same manner. Here, you should know that QUnit is the name of the class in which the testing methods are written, and, hence, the method has to be called with the name of the class.

Styling the Test Result

We mentioned earlier that QUnit provides a *styled* way in which to put up the result of the test case that you execute using QUnit. For the purpose of styling the results, QUnit requires that you add some elements, so that it can inject the styling into the web page for which you want the result of the test case execution to be done. So, you have to add two HTML div elements with IDs qunit and qunit-fixture, respectively. You must also add the following div elements:

```
<div id="qunit"></div>
<div id="qunit-fixture">
```

■ **Tip** When downloading the framework, you may recall that we asked you to download a CSS file in addition to the JavaScript file. The styling that we mentioned comes from this style sheet exclusively.

In order for the CSS styling to be available for the entire web page containing the test result, you have to add the script tag inside the head section of the document. As far as including the JavaScript file (the QUnit framework itself), you must decide where to place it. You might have to refer to Chapter 2, wherein we recommended that you include some of the JavaScript library inside your web page.

Writing the First Test Case

You can now move ahead with the methods available in the QUnit framework that will help you write your first-ever test case using QUnit. We will put before you a test case considering the same Validation functionality that you wrote in Chapter 8, so that you are able to relate topics and understand how things work. To make things even simpler, we will write the JavaScript code and the test code side-by-side, so that you have a better view of the two. Later, when you are sufficiently confident, you can easily separate the two types of code. Here, we should also state that we have made subtle changes in the Validation class, so that it fits properly into the testing. At the same time, however, we assure you that the changes will not alter the way you wrote the Validation class. We provide you the code, as follows:

```
<html>
    <head>
        <link rel="stylesheet" href=" http://code.jquery.com/qunit/qunit-1.18.0.css" />
        <script type="text/javascript" src=" http://code.jquery.com/jquery-1.10.2.js" >
        </script>
        <script type="text/javascript" src=" http://code.jquery.com/qunit/qunit-1.18.0.js" >
        </script>
```

```
<script type="text/javascript" >
    function Validation() {
        this.name = !$('input[name="name"]').val() ? '' :
        $('input[name="name"]').val();
        this.email = !$('input[name="email"]').val() ? '':
        $('input[name="email"]').val();
        this.phone = !$('input[name="phone"]').val() ? '':
        $('input[name="phone"]').val();
    }

    Validation.prototype.check = function (what) {
        switch (what) {
            case 'name':
                var validName = /^([a-z](\.)?(\ )?){3,}$/i;
                if (this.name.length > 0 && validName.test(this.name) === false) {
                    throw "Invalid characters in name";
                }
                break;
            case 'email':
                var validEmail = /^([a-z0-9]\.?\_?)+\@[a-z0-9]+\.?[a-z]{2,3}\.?[a-z]
                {2,3}$/i;
                if (this.email.length > 0 && validEmail.test(this.email) === false) {
                    throw "Email format not proper.";
                }
                break;
            case 'phone':
                var validPhone = /^\+?[0-9]{6,15}$/i;
                if (this.phone.length > 0 && validPhone.test(this.phone) === false) {
                    throw "Phone number needs to be worked upon";
                }
                break;
        }
    }

    QUnit.test("Checking Valid Name", function(assert){
        var validate = new Validation();
        validate.name = 'Practical jQuery ED1';
        assert.throws(
            function () {
                validate.check('name');
            },
            /Invalid characters in name/,
            "Input String Not Proper"
        );
    });

</script>
</head>
```

```
    <body>
        <div id="qunit"></div>
        <div id="qunit-fixture"></div>
    </body>
</html>
```

Looking at the code provided, you realize that we have just reused the check method. The new piece of code you will notice here is the test case that we have written using one of the methods provided by the QUnit framework: the test method. So, the test method, as provided by the QUnit framework, is a way of executing a test case. You may recall from the previous parts of this chapter, when you had a glimpse of this method, that it accepts a string as the first argument and a function to be executed as callback as the second parameter. The callback function specified as the second argument to the test method is actually an object defined inside the QUnit framework, and this framework contains the methods that perform assertions.

Assertion in unit testing is a process that attempts to make some statement and then checks whether that statement executes successfully. In simpler terms, if there is a functionality, an assertion makes an assumption about the function giving correct output and then checks whether the output is really correct. For this purpose, the QUnit framework provides an object with the name assert. This object is a child object of the parent object QUnit and contains the methods that provide the functionality of making assertions. It is this assert object that is passed as the only argument to the callback method, which is to be executed by the test method. We will take up the most commonly used assertion methods in later parts of this chapter, but for now, in order to make you understand how to write a test case, you have to understand the throws method, which is an assertion method, in order to check the check method provided by the Validation class.

Getting back to explaining the code we provided, we have executed a test that checks if the target method (the check method) is able to identify an invalid string. In order to make the test case function properly, we have made a subtle change in the constructor of the Validation class. If you remember the older version of the Validation class, you will recall that there was no check for non-empty value inside the constructor; we have added such checks for each of the member variables—the name, the e-mail, and the phone number. While this adds a checkpoint to prevent uninitialized variables, the less apparent difference it serves is that we can now set some value to each of the member variables from outside the class.

Speaking of the test case, inside it, we have declared a new object of the Validation class. Using that object, we set the value to be tested in the member variable name. Having prepared the object to check the input, we call the throws method to test if the method check is working properly for the given input. We use three arguments to the throws method. The first argument is a function that makes a call to a method (specifically the check method), which is presumed to throw an exception. The second argument to the throws method is a regular expression pattern that we want to compare the thrown exception message to. The third argument (which happens to be the last argument) is a message that will be shown to the web browser in case the test passes. Here, you will note the output to the browser. You are passing an invalid input, and you are expecting that the invalid input will throw an exception. Once the exception is thrown, the throws method matches the message shown upon the exception being thrown. In short, you will see the message "Input String Not Proper" when the test passes, i.e., the input message itself is an invalid string.

Upon executing the test, you will see a page such as that shown in Figure 12-1.

Figure 12-1. *Execution of the test*

Commonly Used QUnit Methods

You can now have a look into the other assertion methods that are provided by the QUnit framework. We feel confident that the demonstration we provided was sufficient to allow you to explore the various methods available with QUnit. These will also help you to write test cases for various conditions.

The QUnit API contains a number of methods for making assertions while testing some target code. We list some of the commonly used methods in this chapter, with demonstrations of their use, wherever possible. The following discussion will help you a great deal in understanding how to write test cases using QUnit.

equal

Programmers know the importance to comparison of the equality operator. It is one of the most commonly used operations when it comes to comparison. In QUnit, a provision exists to check for equality using the equal method. The equal method is actually an assertion. It accepts three arguments: the first argument is an object that represents what it is that you want to test; the second argument is an object representing the expected value; and the third argument (which happens to be the last argument for this assertion method) represents the message to be output to the browser, once the assertion is successful. Let us see an example to understand the usage better. Consider a function that returns some value depending on a type argument to it. We will demonstrate how you can check the output of the function using the equal assertion method.

```
function returnValue(type){
    switch(type){
        case "number":
            return 987654321;
        case "string":
            return "I return string";
        case "boolean":
            return true;
    }
}
```

```
QUnit.test("Checking equal()", function(assert){
    assert.equal(
        returnValue('number'),
        "987654321",
        "Match Pass"
    );
});
```

The output of executing the test case is shown in Figure 12-2.

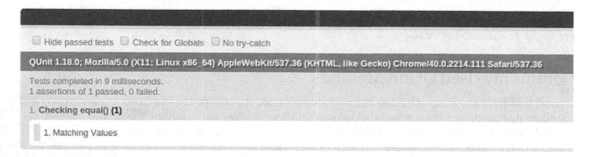

Figure 12-2. *Output of the equal assertion*

strictEqual

Careful developers like you are acutely observant. You can easily see that even though the value returned from the method returnValue is a number, the equal method simply checks for the value and ignores the type. The strictEqual assertion overcomes this and checks for the type, besides checking for the value. Considering the same method returnValue, the usage of the strictEqual assertion will be sufficient to make you understand its workings. The code to make this assertion is as follows, and Figure 12-3 shows its output.

```
QUnit.test("Checking equal()", function(assert){
    assert.strictEqual(
        returnValue('number'),
        "987654321",
        "Matching Values"
    );
});
```

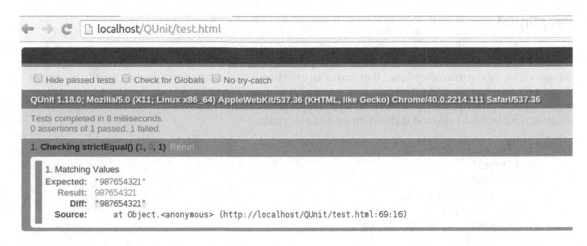

Figure 12-3. *Output of strictEqual*

notEqual

When there is an equal assertion, there must be a notEqual assertion as well. Quite obviously, it does just the opposite task of equal; it asserts for inequality without considering the type of the value to be matched. Considering the same returnValue method, the code to supplement the explanation of the notEqual assertion is as follows:

```
QUnit.test("Checking notEqual()", function(assert){
    assert.notEqual(
        returnValue('number'),
        "987654321",
        "Matching Values"
    );
});
```

The output of the assertion is as shown in Figure 12-4.

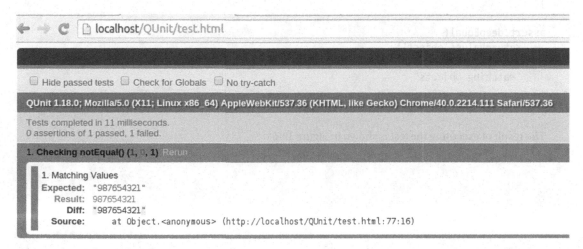

Figure 12-4. *The notEqual assertion output*

deepEqual

You were able to match values when the target values were primitive, such as string, numeric, Boolean, but what would you do if you had to compare two non-primitive values (the objects)? For this purpose, QUnit provides a method named deepEqual that makes an assertion while comparing two objects and checks that the assertion is true. Considering the same returnValue method, we add a new case to it to demonstrate returning of objects upon request (via passing the appropriate value as argument to it). The code and the usage of the deepEqual method is shown in the following code:

```
function returnValue(type){
    switch(type){
        case "number":
            return 987654321;
        case "string":
            return "I return string";
        case "boolean":
            return true;
        case "object":
            var returnObject = {
                name: "Practical jQuery",
                authors: "By Kumar and Chaudhary",
                isbn: 9781484207888
            }
            return returnObject;

    }
}

QUnit.test("Checking deepEqual()", function(assert){

    var checkObject = {
        name: "Practical jQuery",
        authors: "By Kumar and Chaudhary",
        isbn: "9781484207888"
    };

    assert.deepEqual(
        returnValue('object'),
        checkObject,
        "Matching Objects"
    );
});
```

The result of executing the test is shown in Figure 12-5.

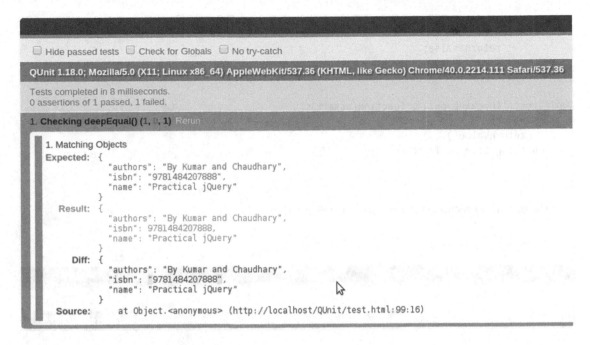

Figure 12-5. *Execution of deepEqual*

ok

This is the most easy-to-use assertion method and is quite useful in those scenarios in which you have to check Boolean values (`true` or `false`), and this assertion succeeds when a `true` value is encountered. This method accepts two arguments: the first being the value or the expression to be checked, and the second is the description of the assertion (in the form of a string). Let us have a look into the usage of this assertion method. We have again made some modifications to the `returnValue` method, to add a default case. Adding this will enable the method to return a Boolean `false` if no argument is passed to this `returnValue` method. Putting it all together, the code and the test case is as follows:

```
function returnValue(type){
    switch(type){
        case "number":
            return 987654321;
        case "string":
            return "I return string";
        case "boolean":
            return true;
        case "object":
            var returnObject = {
                name: "Practical jQuery",
                authors: "By Kumar and Chaudhary",
                isbn: 9781484207888
            }
```

```
            return returnObject;
        default:
            return false;
    }
}

QUnit.test('Checking ok()', function(assert){
    assert.ok(
        returnValue(),
    "Checking true or false"
    );
});
```

The output of executing the test is shown in Figure 12-6.

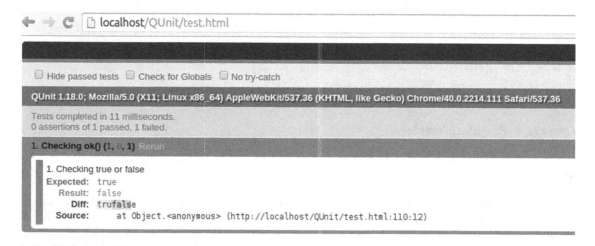

Figure 12-6. *Execution of ok assertion*

notOk

The notOk assertion provided by the QUnit framework functions in just the opposite way as the ok assertion. Quite similar to the ok assertion, notOk also accepts two arguments: the first is the value or the expression to be checked for true or false (i.e., Boolean values), and the second argument is a string that denotes the description of the assertion. The difference between notOk and ok comes from the fact that the notOk assertion succeeds when the value or the expression to be evaluated gets evaluated to false (in contrast to the true value in the ok assertion). You will get the idea clearly by having a look at the code that follows:

```
QUnit.test('Checking notOk()', function(assert){
    assert.notOk(
        returnValue(),
    "Checking true or false"
    );
});
```

In this example, we changed nothing and made use of the same functionality provided by the returnValue method. When nothing is passed as the argument to the returnValue method, it returns a Boolean false. Thus, when the value returned from the returnValue method was false, the notOk assertion succeeded.

The output of executing the test case is shown in Figure 12-7.

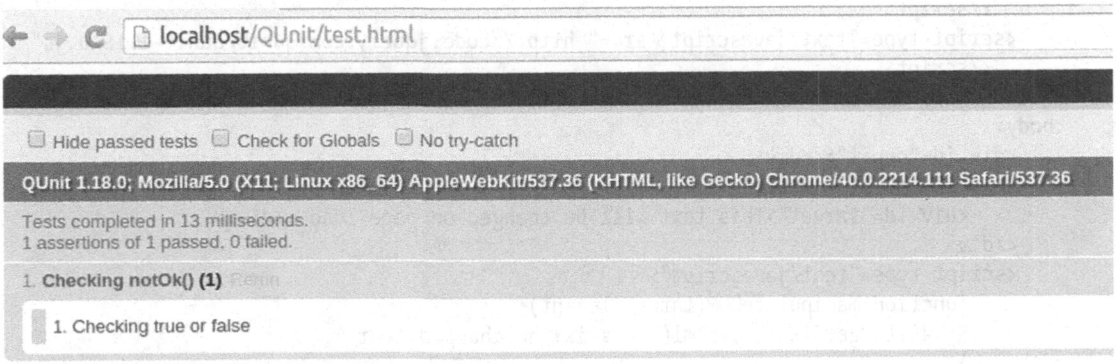

← → C 🗋 localhost/QUnit/test.html

☐ Hide passed tests ☐ Check for Globals ☐ No try-catch

QUnit 1.18.0; Mozilla/5.0 (X11; Linux x86_64) AppleWebKit/537.36 (KHTML, like Gecko) Chrome/40.0.2214.111 Safari/537.36

Tests completed in 13 milliseconds.
1 assertions of 1 passed, 0 failed.

1. **Checking notOk() (1)**

  1. Checking true or false

Figure 12-7. *Output of test execution notOk*

■ **Tip** As we stated that the QUnit is a framework meant to automate unit testing, it provides you a rich set of methods via the QUnit API to assist you in testing the target application. We just took some of the methods that we felt would enable you to start. The complete set of API documentation is available at the official QUnit web site, which is located at http://api.qunitjs.com/.

Testing DOM Manipulation

By the time you read this, you will have gained sufficient information about writing test cases to test the unit part of your code. Also, it will be quite natural for you to start thinking about the possibility of implementing this knowledge to test the usage of jQuery with the more frequently used feature: DOM (Document Object Model) manipulation. You will recall that the jQuery framework is a DOM manipulation library, because it provides facilities to manipulate the DOM with ease. Hence, we take this opportunity to relate the current chapter to the rest of the book, by discussing how you can use QUnit to test if the changes made by jQuery code are valid.

You will recall that the DOM represents the HTML rendered on the web browser, and in order to manipulate the web page, you have to make changes in the DOM (using jQuery). The type of manipulation to the DOM that you have performed throughout this book was either changing (by adding or replacing) some text value to some DOM node or changing some CSS property. This type of DOM manipulation is the most common when it comes to use of jQuery. Let us focus on writing a test case for some such DOM manipulations, so that you will learn how to write test cases for the other DOM manipulations that you may encounter in your daily web-development activity.

Assuming you are already familiar with DOM manipulation, let us have a look at a code sample that will help you understand how to write test cases for testing valid DOM manipulation. Assume that you have a very simple HTML, such as

```
<!DOCTYPE HTML>
<html>
    <head>
        <title>--::Testing DOM manipulation using QUnit::--</title>
        <link rel="stylesheet" href=" http://code.jquery.com/qunit/qunit-1.18.0.css" />
        <script type="text/javascript" src=" http://code.jquery.com/jquery-1.10.2.js" >
            </script>
        <script type="text/javascript" src=" http://code.jquery.com/qunit/qunit-1.18.0.js" >
            </script>
    </head>
    <body>
        <div id="qunit"></div>
        <div id="qunit-fixture">
            <div id="target">This text will be changed on page load </div>
        </div>
        <script type="text/javascript">
            function manipulateDOM(targetElement){
            $('#'+targetElement).html('This is the changed text');
            }

            QUnit.test('Testing simple DOM manipulation', function(assert){
                manipulateDOM('target'),
                assert.equal(
                $('#target').html(),
                'This is the changed text',
                'Checking DOM manipulation'

                );
            });
        </script>
    </body>
</html>
```

■ **Note**   This HTML provided to you contains a very interesting property of the QUnit framework that you should know. In the HTML we provided, we have made use of the div with the id qunit-fixture, which we previously left empty. Whatever the code to be tested, this code lets you know that it is there and that the correct location in the DOM will be inside this qunit-fixture div.

Let us explain the DOM manipulation test case. The DOM manipulation that we are testing here is with the div with id target. When the test case executes, it first makes the change in the div element with the id as target and then makes an assertion regarding the changed value (by obtaining the text contained inside the target div using jQuery html() method). Since the assertion made by the test case is correct, the test passes.

The output of executing the test is shown in Figure 12-8.

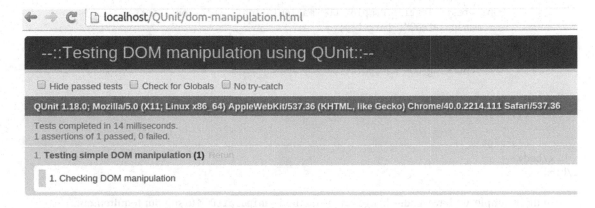

Figure 12-8. Output of our DOM manipulation test

■ **Tip** If you take a close look at the way we tested the DOM manipulation, you will observe that we are treating the changes done to the DOM in textual format. Hence, the same set of functions work fine here as well, just as they worked for the regular strings discussed earlier this chapter.

The example that we took up is of a very simple DOM manipulation. We only made changes to the text contained inside a div element. In order to make you more comfortable with writing test cases to check a wide range of DOM manipulations, let us consider a more complex example of DOM manipulation. In this example, we will add a node to the existing DOM, and then we will check whether or not the node has been added properly. The code will be as follows:

```
<!DOCTYPE HTML>
<html>
    <head>
        <title>--::Testing DOM manipulation using QUnit::--</title>
        <link rel="stylesheet" href=" http://code.jquery.com/qunit/qunit-1.18.0.css" />
        <script type="text/javascript" src=" http://code.jquery.com/jquery-1.10.2.js" ></script>
        <script type="text/javascript" src=" http://code.jquery.com/qunit/qunit-1.18.0.js" >
        </script>
    </head>
    <body>
        <div id="qunit"></div>
        <div id="qunit-fixture">
            <div id="target">This node will be changed on page load </div>
        </div>
        <script type="text/javascript">
            function manipulateDOM(targetElement){
                var span = document.createElement('span');
                span.innerHTML = 'This is the inserted node';
                $('#'+targetElement).empty().append(span)
            }
```

```
QUnit.test('Testing complex DOM manipulation', function(assert){
    manipulateDOM('target');
    assert.ok(
        ($('#target').find('span').html() ? true : false),
    'Checking DOM manipulation'

    );
});

</script>
</body>
</html>
```

In this example, we have made changes in the method manipulateDOM to suit our requirement. The change that we have made is to create a new span element, add some text to it, and then to append it to the div element with the id attribute as target. In the process, we ensure that we remove whatever is already contained inside the div element, by making a call to the jQuery empty() method, which simply deletes all child elements from the selected element. Inside the test case, we have made a call to this manipulateDOM method. The test case makes an assertion regarding the presence of a span inside the target div. If found, the assertion gets evaluated to true and the test succeeds; if not found, the assertion gets evaluated to false, and the test fails.

The output of executing the test is shown in Figure 12-9.

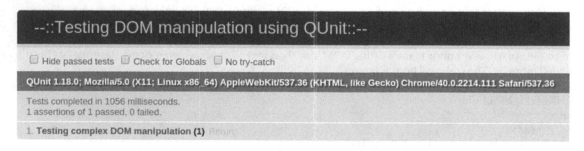

Figure 12-9. *Output of DOM manipulation using QUnit*

Refactoring Code

Once you have learned how to write test cases, you have fought half the battle. The other half is obviously the more difficult to fight. Most of the JavaScript or jQuery code is written intermingled with the HTML code. Writing test cases to check code in which the jQuery/JavaScript and HTML are mixed is not an easy task. When you are not able to identify the units in the code itself, how can you move ahead to unit test it? But where there is a problem, there is a solution.

You will need to reorganize such code in such a way that the unit parts in the code are identifiable and you can spend time in designing the test cases for those units. This is where refactoring the code comes into the picture. In simple terms, when you reorganize some code in such a way that the form of the code changes but the functionality provided by it remains the same, you are essentially refactoring the code. The refactoring of code requires a great deal of care, because once you make an attempt to change the form of the code, you are running the risk of introducing some side effects or even missing out on some functionality. To be able to proceed in refactoring, you will have to have test cases in place, but to have test cases in place, you will have to identify the unit parts of the code, and you are unable to identify the unit parts, because the code to be tested is mingled with the HTML code. This is a vicious cycle that has to be broken.

A Simple Refactoring

In order to break this vicious cycle, you must go one step further, and we recommend that you move ahead to separate the JavaScript or jQuery code to be tested from the HTML code, so that once you must test, you do not have to include the entire HTML in the test case itself. Let us take up an example for this that happens to use the same HTML we used to demonstrate how to test DOM manipulation. What we are refactoring here is the JavaScript code that manipulated the DOM, by moving it into a separate script with the name manipulation.js. In order to use it inside the web page, we just include the JavaScript file, and the function becomes available. The code is

```html
<!DOCTYPE HTML>
<html>
    <head>
        <title>--::Testing DOM manipulation using QUnit::--</title>
        <link rel="stylesheet" href=" http://code.jquery.com/qunit/qunit-1.18.0.css" />
        <script type="text/javascript" src=" http://code.jquery.com/jquery-1.10.2.js" ></script>
        <script type="text/javascript" src=" http://code.jquery.com/qunit/qunit-1.18.0.js" >
            </script>
        <script type="text/javascript" src="manipulation.js" ></script>
    </head>
    <body>
        <div id="qunit"></div>
        <div id="qunit-fixture">
            <div id="target">This node will be changed on page load </div>
        </div>
        <script type="text/javascript">

        QUnit.test('Testing complex DOM manipulation', function(assert){
            manipulateDOM('target');
            assert.ok(
            ($('#target').find('span').html() ? true : false),
                'Checking DOM manipulation'

            );
        });

        </script>
    </body>
</html>
```

The advantage of this refactoring is that the script manipulation.js can be included in any test, wherever needed. Although here, there is just one single function, manipulateDOM, but in practical use cases, you will enjoy the advantage of moving the JavaScript to an external file. Once you move the JavaScript methods to an external file, you have the unit parts of the code ready for consideration to be tested.

■ **Note** According to the official QUnit web site, "The process of extracting code and putting it into a different form without modifying its current behavior is called refactoring."

Moving Ahead in Refactoring

The task of refactoring is not over yet. The example that we took up was rather simple, and taking that into account, we will provide you with a more complex example, so that you will be able to understand better how refactoring assists in writing unit test cases. Let us revisit the Validation class example, because in our opinion, it is quite useful for qualifying a number of explanations. The code that we use as the starting point for refactoring is as follows:

```html
<!DOCTYPE html>
<html>
    <head>
        <title>:: Refactoring the Ajax Stuff ::</title>
    </head>
    <body>
        <div>
            <form id="capture-data">
                <input type="text" name="name"/>
                <input type="text" name="email"/>
                <input type="text" name="phone"/>
                <input type="submit" value="Send" />
            </form>
        </div>
    </body>
<script type="text/javascript" src=" http://code.jquery.com/jquery-1.10.2.js" ></script>
<script type="text/javascript">

        $('#capture-data').submit(function (event) {
            if (!event)
                var event = window.event;
            event.preventDefault();
            try {
                var validation = new Validation();
                validation.check('name');
                validation.check('email');
                validation.check('phone');

                var data = '{"name": "' + validation.name + '", "email": "' + validation.email
                    + '", "phone": "' + validation.phone + '"}';

                $.post('url',
                    $(this).serialize(),
                    function () {
                        alert("The server said 'OK mate!'")
                    });

            } catch (exception) {
                alert('There was some issue, please check browser console');
                console.log(exception);
            }

        });
```

```
function Validation() {
    this.name = !$('input[name="name"]').val() ? '' : $('input[name="name"]').val();
    this.email = !$('input[name="email"]').val() ? '': $('input[name="email"]').val();
    this.phone = !$('input[name="phone"]').val() ? '': $('input[name="phone"]').val();
}

Validation.prototype.check = function (what) {
    switch (what) {
        case 'name':
            var validName = /^([a-z](\.)?(\ )?){3,}$/i;
            if (this.name.length > 0 && validName.test(this.name) === false) {
            throw "Invalid characters in name";
            }
            break;
        case 'email':
            var validEmail = /^([a-z0-9]\.?\_?)+\@[a-z0-9]+\.?[a-z]{2,3}\.?[a-z]
            {2,3}$/i;
            if (this.email.length > 0 && validEmail.test(this.email) === false) {
                throw "Email format not proper.";
            }
            break;
        case 'phone':
            var validPhone = /^\+?[0-9]{6,15}$/i;
            if (this.phone.length > 0 && validPhone.test(this.phone) === false) {
            throw "Phone number needs to be worked upon";
            }
            break;
    }
}
</script>

</html>
```

You can easily perform the first type of refactoring, based on the previous example we provided. This will entail including the JavaScript code in an external file. On saving the JavaScript code in an external file validation.js, the HTML will now look as follows:

```
<!DOCTYPE html>
<html>
    <head>
        <title>:: Refactoring the Ajax Stuff ::</title>
    </head>
    <body>
        <div>
            <form id="capture-data">
                <input type="text" name="name"/>
                <input type="text" name="email"/>
                <input type="text" name="phone"/>
                <input type="submit" value="Send" />
            </form>
        </div>
    </body>
```

```
<script type="text/javascript" src=" http://code.jquery.com/jquery-1.10.2.js" ></script>
<script type="text/javascript">

    $('#capture-data').submit(function (event) {
        if (!event)
            var event = window.event;
            event.preventDefault();
        try {
            var validation = new Validation();
            validation.check('name');
            validation.check('email');
            validation.check('phone');

            var data = '{"name": "' + validation.name + '", "email": "' + validation.email +
                '", "phone": "' + validation.phone + '"}';

            $.post('/path/to/server-url',
                $(this).serialize(),
                function () {
                    alert("The server said 'OK mate!'")
                });

        } catch (exception) {
            alert('There was some issue, please check browser console');
            console.log(exception);
        }

    });
</script>
</html>
```

This refactoring might make you remember Chapters 9 and 10, when you wrote a plug-in. You did the same thing that you are doing here. The difference lies only in the purpose to be fulfilled. Previously, your objective was to write clean code; here, your objective is to learn how to make some code testable by identifying the unit parts of the code. Resuming our discussion, the validation.js file containing the JavaScript code would look like

```
function Validation() {
this.name = !$('input[name="name"]').val() ? '' : $('input[name="name"]').val();
this.email = !$('input[name="email"]').val() ? '': $('input[name="email"]').val();
this.phone = !$('input[name="phone"]').val() ? '': $('input[name="phone"]').val();
}

Validation.prototype.check = function (what) {
    switch (what) {
        case 'name':
            var validName = /^([a-z](\.)?(\ )?){3,}$/i;
            if (this.name.length > 0 && validName.test(this.name) === false) {
                throw "Invalid characters in name";
            }
            break;
```

```
    case 'email':
        var validEmail = /^([a-z0-9]\.?\_?)+\@[a-z0-9]+\.?[a-z]{2,3}\.?[a-z]{2,3}$/i;
        if (this.email.length > 0 && validEmail.test(this.email) === false) {
            throw "Email format not proper.";
        }
        break;
    case 'phone':
        var validPhone = /^\+?[0-9]{6,15}$/i;
        if (this.phone.length > 0 && validPhone.test(this.phone) === false) {
        throw "Phone number needs to be worked upon";
    }
    break;
    }
}
```

Writing Another Test Case on the Refactored Code

Now, if you want to write more test cases, since you have already separated the JavaScript code from the
HTML page, you will just have to write more code inside the test runner file. The code with another test case
(the other test case was written by you to check the valid name functionality) would look like

```
<!DOCTYPE HTML>
<html>
    <head>
        <link rel="stylesheet" href=" http://code.jquery.com/qunit/qunit-1.18.0.css" />
        <script type="text/javascript" src=" http://code.jquery.com/jquery-1.10.2.js" ></script>
        <script type="text/javascript" src=" http://code.jquery.com/qunit/qunit-1.18.0.js" >
        </script>
        <script type="text/javascript" src="validation.js" ></script>
        <script type="text/javascript" >
        QUnit.test("Checking Valid Name", function(assert){
            var validate = new Validation();
            validate.name = 'Practical jQuery ED1';
            assert.throws(
                function () {
                validate.check('name');
                },
                /Invalid characters in name/,
                "Input String Not Proper"
            );
        });

        QUnit.test("Checking Valid Phone", function(assert){
            var validate = new Validation();
            validate.phone = 'test123';
            assert.throws(
                function(){
                    validate.check('phone');
                },
```

```
                /Phone number needs to be worked upon/,
                "Input phone not proper"
            );
        });

        </script>
    </head>
    <body>
        <div id="qunit"></div>
        <div id="qunit-fixture"></div>
    </body>
</html>
```

You have come a long way to be able to test the code that we wrote using jQuery. We have always believed that more practice results in more expertise, and, therefore, we encourage you to find more such examples and try and write more and more test cases, so that you are able to write better quality code.

Summary

With this, we come to the end of this chapter and the book. In this chapter, you learned about the importance of testing to assure software quality. You learned about unit testing and came to know what a unit is in relation to testing. This chapter gave you information about QUnit, a framework written in JavaScript that is meant to automate the unit tests for the code written, not only in jQuery, but also in JavaScript in general. While learning how to write test cases, you also learned how to refactor some code, to make it testable.

Index

■ **L**

Get the eBook for only $5!

Why limit yourself?

Now you can take the weightless companion with you wherever you go and access your content on your PC, phone, tablet, or reader.

Since you've purchased this print book, we're happy to offer you the eBook in all 3 formats for just $5.

Convenient and fully searchable, the PDF version enables you to easily find and copy code—or perform examples by quickly toggling between instructions and applications. The MOBI format is ideal for your Kindle, while the ePUB can be utilized on a variety of mobile devices.

To learn more, go to www.apress.com/companion or contact support@apress.com.

Printed in the United States
By Bookmasters